# Egypt, the Arabs, and the World

# Egypt, the Arabs, and the World

Reflections at the Turn of
the Twenty-First Century

Hani Shukrallah

The American University in Cairo Press
Cairo  New York

First published in 2011 by
The American University in Cairo Press
113 Sharia Kasr el Aini, Cairo, Egypt
420 Fifth Avenue, New York, NY 10018
www.aucpress.com

Dar el Kutub No. 24573/11
ISBN 978 977 416 486 6

Dar el Kutub Cataloging-in-Publication Data

    Shukrallah, Hani
       Egypt, the Arabs, and the World: Reflections at the Turn of the Twenty-first Century/
    Hani Shukrallah. —Cairo: The American University in Cairo Press, 2011
       p.    cm.
       ISBN 978 977 416 486 6
       1. Egypt—Politics and Government
       I. Title
       320.62

1 2 3 4 5 6  14 13 12 11

Designed by Fatiha Bouzidi
Printed in Egypt

To the beloved memory of my parents, Ibrahim and Jeanette,
whose boundless, unconditional love has been the bedrock of my life

# Contents

# Acknowledgments

MOST OF THE ARTICLES INCLUDED in this volume were written for *Al-Ahram Weekly*, the English-language newspaper issued by Egypt's largest state-owned news organization, al-Ahram. I joined the paper in 1990, a few months after it was launched. Though state-owned, *Al-Ahram Weekly* enjoyed the unique fortune of having at its head an exceptional human being, Hosny Guindy. A truly decent man, his commitment to the highest ethical standards of the profession was especially remarkable for his having held on to it in the midst of the cesspool of corruption, sycophancy, and opportunism that the state-owned media in Egypt had swiftly sunk into.

That these articles were published at all is owed to Hosny's courage, professionalism, and profound belief in freedom of expression. Hosny sympathized with some of my ideas, disagreed with many, but was unswerving in his support for my right to express them through my column in *Al-Ahram Weekly*. He would read my latest piece before publication, on occasion come to me, a worried expression on his face, asking—hesitantly and in the mildest of tones—whether I did not feel that a certain passage, or even the whole piece, had not crossed certain red lines, and might, therefore, pose a threat to my career or, indeed, freedom.

Invariably, I would shrug off the presumed risk and as invariably he would accede to my wishes, while aware that if indeed the article in question provoked wrath from the powers that be, he himself would also pay a price. Upon his untimely and deeply mourned death I took over as editor of *Al-Ahram Weekly*. Within two years I was chucked out, upon the insistent demands of the State Security Service, which was further evidence of the cover and protection that Hosny's presence had provided me for years. My debt of gratitude for Hosny's friendship and support is without measure.

Each of my *Al-Ahram Weekly* columns was edited by one of two brilliant colleagues, Pascale Ghazaleh and Nigel Ryan. With remarkable gentleness and depth of understanding the rough edges would disappear, clumsy sentence structure was refined, and poor grammar was made good, all of which would take place with amazing swiftness. English is a second language, which I picked up in my adolescence, basically through practice and reading. Pascale and Nigel's editing of my articles was a kind of schooling, from which I learned much, though I still have no idea what a split infinitive is supposed to be.

It is traditional for a published writer to acknowledge his debt to his publishers, yet my debt to the wonderful team at the American University in Cairo (AUC) Press goes well beyond the commonplace. Neil Hewison, Randi Danforth, and Nadia Naqib had more faith in this project than I did, and if it weren't for their relentless encouragement and support this volume would have remained a suggestion.

Which brings me to AUC Press's extraordinary chief, Mark Linz, himself a Cairo institution. I know of no one who has done more to bring Egypt and the Arabs to the world in such a brief span of time than Mark Linz. And it was in a casual conversation with Mark that the idea of this collection originated.

I also owe a great many thanks to Jasmina Brankovic, who diligently and sensitively made a final edit of the full text of this book, heroically going beyond the call of duty to correct the dates of publication of a good deal of the *Al-Ahram Weekly* articles, which I had—inexplicably—managed to botch.

To my wife, Fatemah, and my children, Hossam, Farida, Malak, and Sarah, I owe my inspiration and my will to live.

Finally, I would like to note a debt of gratitude I've held for decades, and this to a man whose name I have long forgotten: my science teacher in Amun School, who, in second year preparatory (grade 8), introduced me and my classmates to Darwin's theory of evolution.

I have no idea whether that particular class was in the curriculum or at the teacher's own initiative, but I remember, as if it were yesterday, the intensity of my sense of shock and internal turmoil, which was to set in motion a lifelong quest for forbidden truths and questioning of received and conventional wisdom.

# Introduction

# The Flood, Finally

*The Egyptian people are like the Nile, nine months low water and three months, the flood.*
— Nabil El-Hilali, Egyptian revolutionary and lawyer

*We have been surprised before in history. We can be surprised again. Indeed, WE can do the surprising.*
— Howard Zinn, author of *A People's History of the United States*

MEA CULPA!

I'd been at home recovering from a heart attack, thankfully a relatively minor myocardial infarction that did little damage to the heart muscle. A day that was to become a landmark in Egyptian history had begun inauspiciously: yet another Facebook-, SMS-based call for protest demonstrations meant, on this particular occasion, to coincide with National Police Day, January 25.

Sitting before my laptop, I was following with frustration, bordering on anger, the dozens of ardent postings by young people, many of whom I'd become familiar with through following their activism over the past few years; some I knew as the sons and daughters of my friends, including my own son and two nieces, and a great many more who had been coming in droves onto this virtual space of cyber political activism, God knows from where.

1

I had seen it all before, tediously and mind-numbingly replicating itself over and over again, especially since that chimera of a "Cairo Spring," the bizarrely named "year of political mobility," in 2005. A couple of hundred young people, joined by a few dozen growingly rickety, yet ever hopeful, old veterans of political battles stretching back to the 1970s, and even as far back as the 1940s of the last century, besieged by several thousand shield and stick-wielding anti-riot police, hundreds of plain-clothed thugs, star-studded generals in uniform busily shouting into walkie-talkies, and the ever cynically grinning officers of the State Security Intelligence in civvies. And beyond them all, a bystanding population, looking on with, as one activist friend described it, neither censure nor sympathy, but rather "bewilderment."

Communications technology activism had been with us for several years by then, drawing tens of thousands of young people into almost daily political campaigns, ranging from the world-famous April 6 movement to that in support of former International Atomic Energy Agency (IAEA) director Mohamed El-Baradei, to the Khaled Said movement, protesting the murder at police hands of the Alexandrian youth who has since become one of the iconic figures of the Egyptian revolution. As far as the rest of us were aware, their instruments of mobilization, awareness raising, organization, and calls to action were almost wholly 'virtual,' made up of blogs, Facebook groups, Twitter and YouTube, cellphone text messaging, and smart phone applications.

Yet, there I'd been, just a few weeks before the revolution, sitting on a panel on the media and politics in Egypt, arguing that it was quite possible that the virtual political activism of Facebook and the rest may in fact be serving as an easy alternative to real political activism, whereby joining 'a cause' or 'a group' on Facebook costs you little more than the click of a button in the comfort of your own home.

Certainly, the protest call this time around had come in the wake of a most inspirational event, the Tunisian revolution. The obdurate political stagnation of the Arab world had suffered a significant and wholly unexpected blow, and Egypt's young activists were quick to take up the call. "If the Tunisians can do it, so can we" spread like wildfire across the nation's cyberspace, with hundreds posting the Tunisian flag as their Facebook photo.

Yet, I was not convinced. "Egypt is not Tunisia," a host of Egyptian officials rushed to proclaim, and, while fully aware of the absurdity of that particular refrain, I still could not believe that the Tunisian example, inspiring as it had been, was sufficiently potent to trigger a domino effect in the rest of the Arab world, let alone in Egypt, the biggest, and, indeed, most self-contained of the lot. Egypt, long proclaimed the heart of the Arab nation, may export revolution; it is, however, a very unlikely importer, or so I believed.

But January 25 rolled along, the hundreds became thousands, and then tens of thousands, in Cairo, in Alexandria, in Suez, in one city after another in the Delta; reports were coming from across the nation. Young people were engaged in fierce battles with our ever vicious security forces, their numbers growing, and the battles fiercer. Something wholly new was upon us. By late afternoon, I once again sat before my laptop, opened my own Facebook account, and in my status line wrote: "how sweet it is to have been proven wrong."

How did I get it so wrong? This was a day that presumably I had been looking forward to for the best part of my life; the articles collected in this volume should give ample testimony to this, at least insofar as the period stretching from the mid-1990s up to the preposterously rigged parliamentary elections of December 2010, or the horrific bombing of the Two Saints Church in Alexandria in the early hours of New Year's Day of 2011 is concerned. In fact, it went much further back than that, embracing all of my adult life, beginning with my involvement in the student movement of the late 1960s and early 1970s and including my removal from my post as editor of *Al-Ahram Weekly* in July 2005, courtesy of the State Security Intelligence service.

# Black Swans and Butterfly Effects

In my defense I would suggest that, in fact, no one got it right, whether among those of us who longed for that day or among those who dreaded it. Certainly, since January 25 there have been many who have rushed to claim foresight, but I would suggest further that, even if true, they were right wholly incidentally, and most likely for the wrong reasons. After all, if you'd been reiterating that "the revolution is at hand," for decades you're bound to be right if and when a revolution does in fact take place. It is doubtful that this could be accepted as proof of your political astuteness, however.

Not even the young people who triggered the Egyptian revolution, and I have since had occasion to talk with a fair number of their leaders, were even partially aware of the historic upheaval they were setting in motion.

They were, nevertheless, privy to something which I for one would only find out well into the revolution: the fact of their real rather than merely virtual existence, of their political and mobilizational savvy, and of the extent of planning and organization that actually went into both triggering the revolution and providing it with field leadership once it broke out.

These young men and women, I was to find out in due course, had been out of cyberspace for some time, and while adept at using the latest communications technology, they were no less familiar than my generation and a great many before it had been with the more traditional means of organizing a revolutionary movement: meetings in coffeehouses; creating networks of movements, organizations, and groups on the ground, nationally and locally; setting up headquarters and communications centers; engaging in education, debate, and discussion; devising tactics for confronting the anti-riot police, for street maneuvering around police blockades; and all the rest of the details that revolutionary organization entails.

And they were something wholly new. Most of them had limited if any links to the major political and ideological forces that had for decades prevailed in sluggish decay over the nation's stagnant and diminutive political landscape. And even for those among them who did, such as the youth movement of the Muslim Brotherhood, they had evolved a character and discourse all their own. This is not to say that the youth groups did not include the usual range of ideological orientations. There were smatterings of Marxists, social democrats, liberals, and Islamists, and a whole range of in-betweens, but unlike the older, more established representatives of these tendencies, they could work together on the ground, without the kind of bombast and empty spectacle so favored by their elders.

These, furthermore, were subsumed under a novel political/ideological discourse and value system that presumably had evolved and taken shape gradually and subtly over five years of cyberspace discussion and debate. And I admit the fact of such a discourse, and its ascension to become the preeminent discourse of the Egyptian revolution, has taken me as much by surprise as the revolution itself.

A new Egyptian nationalism was catapulted across the land from Tahrir Square, taking it literally by storm. Rooted in a most profound hatred of oppression and a passionate yearning for freedom, it was a discourse of human rights, democracy, and equality. It spoke of fairness and justice, and, above all, of dignity, not the empty braggadocio so typical of Arab machismo à la Saddam Hussein (which I had come to associate with non-alcoholic beer), but the innate dignity inscribed in our very humanity. "Raise your head up high, you're an Egyptian" was among the more popular chants of the revolution, testimony to a redefinition of Egyptian nationalism in terms of citizenship; national pride is a function not of jingoism and paranoia, but of free citizens able to stand up for their rights and bring down their oppressors.

It was this discourse that lay behind what we might call the 'Tahrir code.' Almost everyone who has observed the Egyptian revolution has commented on it: its unyielding pacifism paradoxically conjoined—Gandhi-like—with immeasurable courage and boundless self-sacrifice; the self-discipline and civility that saw hundreds of thousands packed like sardines into a few square kilometers, yet not a single incident of violence or brutality was observed, not a single attack on persons or property, no scuffles or fighting, but rather an astonishing politeness and camaraderie; the spirit of tolerance and brotherhood that saw the crescent embracing the cross on hundreds of banners and posters with Copts standing guard around Muslims performing their prayers, and Muslims hoisting the Bible along with the Qur'an, and which saw the women, young and old, veiled and unveiled, in blue jeans and flowing robes, taking part in occupations, in demonstrations, in confrontations with anti-riot police and bands of thugs, prominently present in the leadership of the youth movements and no less involved than their male comrades in the organization, planning, and communications. And, as almost everybody has remarked: no sexual harassment.

We might note also, as many have done, such remarkable details as the U.S. and British embassies, sitting pretty at the edge of Tahrir Square and having lost their normally extensive Egyptian police guard, nevertheless being left in peace, the hundreds of thousands gathered just alongside apparently not having given even a thought to an attack on what on 24 January would have been deemed among the topmost profitable targets of a mass demonstration in Cairo. Arab League secretary general and presidential hopeful Amr Moussa remarked as well on the fact that the synagogue on Adli Street, before which tens of thousands passed daily on their way to and from Tahrir, was untouched, again despite the disappearance of the usual heavy police guard.

That disappearance of the police across the country was equally staggering in its ramifications. Clearly part of a contingency plan aimed at creating a state of chaos in the country, police evaporated overnight, prison gates were opened and prisoners let out, and bands of thugs and criminals, run by State Security Intelligence and other police bodies, were let loose to attack homes, businesses, and people. The plan was to force the Egyptian people to turn against the revolution, and to demand a restoration of order. It failed miserably, for overnight Egyptians were transformed into citizens, taking charge of their own security, as 'popular committees' sprang up everywhere, in such upper-class Cairo districts as Zamalek and Maadi, no less than in the so-called 'popular quarters' of Mit 'Uqba and Bulaq al-Dakrur.

In Tahrir Square, the unbounded cynicism and criminality of the Mubarak regime was glaringly expressed in a concerted attempt to set fire to the Egyptian Museum, the greatest storehouse of ancient Egyptian artifacts anywhere. A filmmaker friend saw it on TV and immediately called a number of his friends asking them to head immediately to the square itself to protect the museum. On the square, the few thousand young people spending the night, including, I'm proud to say, my own son, Hossam, were engaged in a heroic battle both to maintain their occupation of the square, which the ruling party–run thugs and police were bent on evacuating, and also to protect their and humanity's glorious ancient heritage. With each wave of attacks, with Molotov cocktails and rifle fire, shouts and whistles would echo around the square, among them "Safeguard the museum," upon which hundreds of young people, braving bullets, rocks, and fire, would rush into the breach.

Where did it all come from? Up until January 25, 2011, there had not seemed to be a single indication of any of it. Certainly, an explosion of some sort could not be discounted altogether. But pundits were thinking in terms of bread riots, a hunger revolt, a Cairo fire (on the lines of the Cairo Fire of January 1952), or even an Islamist uprising. In all scenarios, these were violent revolts waged by angry mobs bent on mayhem, destruction, and vengeance.

I referred above to the new discourse which I presumed must have emerged and crystallized in cyberspace. This may well be true, and I believe there is ample evidence to support such a supposition. It is inadequate as an explanation, however. It was as if Egyptians, or at least a few million of their number, had been gradually internalizing a checklist of everything ugly and flawed in the Mubarak regime, and indeed in themselves as well, and ticking its exact opposite.

We had no civic spirit, we had lost our sense of community, and could not be citizens: we had no civility, we expressed little, if any, social solidarity, our sense of our Egyptian identity seemed a function of soccer matches with foreign teams, lasting for the duration of the match and its often barbaric aftermath, and exhibiting the kind of ugly jingoistic tribalism that we had witnessed against Algeria about a year before the revolution. Our urban streets had become misogynistic jungles in which no woman was safe from harassment. And with every passing year, we seemed to become more bigoted, more obsessed with religious trivia; our Muslim majority growingly more intolerant of the nation's Copts, while that Coptic minority increasingly ghettoized itself, clinging to the Church, and seemingly forfeiting its national identity.

Yet, it was so. Overnight, Egyptians recreated themselves; their revolution—as I wrote at the time—was born fully armed, just as Greek mythology had Athena burst out of Zeus's forehead. But this is what revolutions are all about. We tend to forget that the very definition of a revolution lies in putting into effect great transformations in a very short span of time.

Why now? I have been asked by foreign correspondents over and over during the past few months. My answer: I have no idea. Certainly, we could draw up almost endless lists of contributing factors: the cumulative effect of the many small street protests of the past five or six years; the youth movements evolving in and out of cyberspace; the rising labor unrest; the capacious arrogance of the Mubarak regime and the depth of the open contempt in which it held the Egyptian people; the flagrantly rigged elections of November–December 2010, which after over thirty years of an ostensibly pluralistic political system, were to create a parliament of which some 95 percent of seats were controlled by the ruling party; the torture and brutality meted out daily to the millions of poor and underprivileged, with a massive police apparatus behaving as a lawless militia ruling over a subject population; the murder at police hands of the young Alexandrian Khaled Said, and the movement that erupted in protest; the return to Egypt of IAEA former director and Nobel laureate Mohamed El-Baradei, and the associated campaign against the Mubarak dictatorship. Indeed, I would include the inspirational effects of the election of Barack Obama to the White House and, even more, of his "Yes We Can" campaign. And, of course, the immediate triggering inspiration of the Tunisian revolution, transmitted almost blow by blow to millions of Egyptian homes via satellite TV, providing the model and indeed many of the slogans that would be taken up from January 25 onward.

But while one can string all of the above, and lots more, together to explain the revolution after the fact, it is doubtful that doing so before

January 25 would have led to the incontrovertible conclusion that a revolution was at hand. Rather, in the case of Egypt, and for that matter the rest of the Arab regimes, the revolution, any kind of revolution, had been long overdue; the most glaring feature of these regimes having been their seemingly interminable longevity, ambling along, senile, decadent, and decaying but still able to survive.

I recall conversations over lunch or coffee with such friends as veteran British journalist David Hirst—to my mind one of the most able political commentators on Egypt and the Middle East—in which the big question, year in, year out, was why is nothing happening? "Something's gotta give," we'd agree, only to meet a year or two later and wonder why nothing had.

Revolutions are black swans, as Nassim Nicholas Taleb, the author of the now world-famous book by that name, so aptly theorized. Taleb could have been describing the Egyptian revolution, and indeed the whole wave of revolts that so suddenly swept through an Arab world that had come to be defined as "exceptional," by virtue of its obdurate stagnation on virtually every level of human development. Revolutionary events, Taleb convincingly argues, are "outliers." They lie outside regular expectations, because nothing in the past seems to point to their possibility; yet they have, in Taleb's terminology, "extreme impact," and finally, because the human mind balks at unpredictability, such events are explained retrospectively, through hindsight. Ironically perhaps, in view of the role cyberspace has played in the Egyptian revolution, Taleb deems the Internet one such unpredictable, extreme-impact revolutionary event.

Chaos theory also sets out to provide a methodology by which unpredictability and "extreme events" may be explained. Complex non-linear systems exist in a state of dynamic stability, but their very complexity (which in the language of social science we might translate into the interactions of a great number of determinants) is a source of instability, which potentially could lead to chaos, that is to the explosive breakup of the system and its transformation into a new system, hovering around a new "strange attractor." Also, under such conditions of complexity, small, subtle changes could lead to great consequences: the famous "butterfly effect."

As such, while we might find it difficult to convincingly suggest that the Egyptian revolution was a direct result of the Tunisian revolution, we would by no means be disparaging the magnificent rising of the Tunisian people if we view it as that final, decisive flutter of a butterfly's wings, which upon reaching Egypt became a raging storm.

I remember reading somewhere that Bertolt Brecht had remarked that the problem with predicting human behavior is not that it is not subject to determination, but rather that there are too many determinants, ergo: chaos, sudden and unpredictable "extreme events," such as, for instance, falling in love.

It was quite a few years ago, in fact, that I reached the conclusion that revolutions and popular uprisings cannot be counted on. Having started my adult life a revolutionary of sorts, I had neither fallen into cynicism—as some tired and repentant ex-revolutionaries tend to—nor lost faith in the possibility or indeed the desirability of revolution, though I had come to hold violence in considerable dread, convinced that it almost inevitably brutalizes those who resort to it, even for a just cause.

Not for want of trying; a reading of my own, and my generation's, experience beginning with the student and workers' uprisings of the late 1960s and early 1970s had provided ample evidence that such events are highly unpredictable and, even more significantly, are things that you cannot plan, instigate, nor yet launch. They just happen in their own good time or, for that matter, might well not happen for a very long time. What you can and should do, I had come to believe, is prepare the groundwork, through relentless criticism, daily political, social, and cultural struggles, and organization. Presumably such work could serve to combine with a great many other determinants, of all sorts and relative weights, to bring about that magical and long-anticipated event, and no less important, once that event does take place, you would be in a position to help steer it in the right direction.

I also came to be convinced that waiting for the next 'uprising,' or 'revolution,' dulls the mind, and acts to impede one's critical faculties, including mostly the ability to hold one's own ideas and practice to critical examination. I have known political and revolutionary movements that, while meeting with little or no accomplishments on the ground, have tenaciously held on to the same set of ideas for years on end, even decades, on the grounds that a 'revolutionary situation' is yet to develop.

Moreover, while I had not lost my youthful faith in the necessity of people rising up against their oppressors, nor of their innate capacity to do so, I was no longer convinced that this was inevitable—that progress and human emancipation were somehow already inscribed as a logic of history unfolding, heading inexorably toward an ultimate peak, be it Marx's utopian world of "from each according to his ability, to each according to his needs," or Fukuyama's pathetic vision of a WTO, IMF, and World Bank–run, environmentally degraded, and heartless capitalist world being the ultimate goal of human history.

I fell upon what I believe to be a decisive refutation of such a shrunken, flattened view of history in a most unlikely place: an essay by one of my favorite writers, the world-renowned American paleontologist, the late Stephen Jay Gould. The essay was expounding what is now the standard understanding shared by school children in many parts of the world, though perhaps not those whose parents and teachers agree with ex-U.S. president George W. Bush's contribution to the biological sciences that "the jury" was still out on evolution.

Sixty-five million years ago, give or take, a comet hit the earth, creating massive climatic changes that led to the extinction of the dinosaurs, which had dominated life on the planet for some 160 million years. To my knowledge, Gould was among the first scientists in the field to popularize this theory. But what I found no less interesting in his essay was the suggestion that by clearing the earth of dinosaurs, this accidental, extreme event had opened the space for mammals, till then tiny creatures living in holes in the ground, to evolve, eventually leading to Homo sapiens and human history.

Now just imagine that that particular comet had missed the earth; is it not quite possible that dinosaurs could have ruled the planet for a further 65 million years and more, thus no Homo sapiens, no human history, and no George W. Bush spouting nonsense on evolution?

There is no cynicism in this. The arguments pursued in this volume are informed by a perspective that holds that rational enquiry, the yearning for freedom, the desire for fairness, empathy, and social solidarity are inherent attributes of our humanity, no less so than our inherent capacity for language or, for that matter, laughter. Unlike language, however, we are also capable of cruelty, cowardice, bigotry, narrow-mindedness, and intolerance.

It is all a matter of choice, though not in the religious, narrow moral sense of an individual choosing between good and evil. Since we're speaking of social human history, we are looking at the political choices of whole peoples. We are yet to learn, for instance, whether humanity will choose to save the planet or pursue Fukuyama's beloved free market to the end of history in a very literal sense, since there can be no history without people to make and record it.

During one of my more disheartened moments I wrote, tongue-in-cheek, the following nightmare scenario on my Facebook page: The year is 2025, my son and three daughters are among the demonstrators gathered along Cairo's Mediterranean shore, protesting an nth term for Gamal Mubarak and his progeny's grooming for dynastic succession. For those readers who are not familiar with Egyptian geography, Cairo is some two hundred kilometers south of the Mediterranean shore. I'm here referring to the horrifying prediction that as a result of global warming and the melting of the ice cap, Egypt's Delta could be submerged by the rising sea water.

## Arab Autumn, Arab Spring

All of which brings me to the most compelling reason for my having so glaringly failed to anticipate not just the Egyptian revolution but the whole Arab spring, and this is that, in fact, we had been living what many Arab writers and commentators could legitimately describe as the worst period in modern Arab history.

The Arabs had seemed to enter the twenty-first century looking forward to the past. The compulsion to turn back the clock was overpowering; it was equaled only by the depth of their loathing of the present and abhorrence of the future.

Yet, the Arabs' time machine, predictably perhaps, proved faulty. Ultimately, and as the turbulent first decade of the new millennium was drawing to a close, the Arab world had not disembarked a mere hop and a jump back in time, at the heyday of Arab nationalism, despite the pervasive Nasser nostalgia; nor a little earlier, at the Arabs' 'liberal age.'

The Arabs' time-machine did not bring them back to the glory days of the Abbasids. Theirs was not to be the magnificent Baghdad of Harun al-Rashid, but the killing streets of its ruined and violated namesake, pronounced with an American twang as 'Baagdaad.'

Nor to be had was the idealized and mythologized golden age of the Rightly Guided caliphs, embodying as it did a yearning for unwavering faith, righteousness, and a measure of justice. The time of the Prophet, viewed as the peak of human history, is by its very nature unreachable and unattainable. Our time machine did not stop there either, nor could it.

The Arabs' time machine seemed to have taken them to a vastly different, if equally mythical, age of human history: the state of nature, according to Thomas Hobbes, a time in which life is "solitary, poor, nasty, brutish" if not necessarily "short," and where every man is enemy to every man.

Post-Saddam Iraq became the picture in the attic of the Arab world, the ugly reality hidden just beneath a surface landscape made up of equal parts hypocrisy and repression.

It was not, however, the "bangs" of bloodshed on the streets that appeared to constitute the salient feature of Arab states and societies at the turn of the new century, but rather the "whimpers" of an extremely protracted yet, for all that, sure and inexorable process of disintegration, of both states and societies—slowly and seemingly irrevocably tearing and coming apart at the seams.

It is this breakdown of society which seems to go hand-in-hand with, or even a little ahead of, the breakup of the state structure, Hobbes' vision of the "state of nature," that seemed to me to be of particular relevance to contemporary Arab reality, rooted as it is in the notion that society cannot exist without the state.

Each Arab state has its own story, it goes without saying, but there was no getting away from the incredible commonalities, doubly remarkable for the fact of the enormous differences in wealth, systems of government, and social and cultural institutions and traditions. Yet, everywhere we looked we saw state structures fracturing and societies in fragmentation.

One half of the picture had been summed up in the Arab Human Development reports, of international renown: economic failure, obdurate authoritarianism, massive social inequities, *rentier*-based societies, which seemed inherently incapable of entering the industrial age, let alone catching up with the technological revolution, yet unable, meanwhile, to maintain the agrarian-based economies of their past. Societies innovating nothing, producing next to nothing, but consuming massively, their rich vying in their voraciousness and insatiable appetites with the super-rich of the richest countries on earth; however, never forgetting to mutter prayers of thanks to God for having created the industrialized world for their consumer pleasure.

The other half of the picture was even grimmer, for it was made up of political, social, and cultural degeneration: state structures that have forfeited virtually each and every task of government save for repression, with aging authoritarian potentates, or their offspring, ruling by whim, ringed by sycophantic factions of businessmen/bureaucrats, constantly at covert, and occasionally overt, war with each other, each tenaciously holding on to their own chunk of state power-cum-business ventures, each in fierce competition for the patriarchal ear, and all of them treating the state and the economy as so many spoils to be plundered and re-plundered, divided and re-divided among them and their progeny in perpetuity.

Indeed, the most intriguing aspect of the international standing of Arab states and societies during the first decade of the twenty-first century did not lie in their possessing any kind of global or regional clout, be it economic or military, made up of hard or soft power, but in what we might call their *catastrophic potential*; that fearsome ticking time-bomb aspect, ever threatening a blowout so dreadful it would send waves of suicide bombers and all manner of Islamic fundamentalists, no less than economic and political immigrants, flying every which way, but most especially and most ominously across the Mediterranean into the very heart of Christendom.

Paradoxically, the Arabs' 'catastrophic potential' came also to be their most potent source of 'influence' on the international stage; it was both their most effective bargaining card with other international actors, and the principal stimulus for all sorts of foreign assistance, ranging all the way from tanks and F16s to providing rural schools with even more rickety desks, to the either incurably optimistic or utterly ingenuous provision of human rights education for police officers.

I had come to describe these times as the "Arab age of horrible choices." Look every which way and the choices put before you seemed to range from the horrible to the horrendous, the hideous to the horrific. Bush or Saddam; submission or death; Fatah or Hamas; Mubarak or the Muslim Brotherhood; oligarchic and military dictatorships or Islamist theocracies; American occupation in Iraq or the video butchers of Zarqawi and co.; capitulation to Israeli hooliganism and occupation or transforming Arab youth into suicidal human bombs.

Up until January 2011, these seemed to be the kind of choices on offer.

"It is not pleasant being Arab these days," wrote the late Lebanese journalist Samir Kassir, one of the most brilliant political commentators in the Arab world, shortly before he was assassinated in 2005.

# The Realm of the Impossible

Samir, who I was honored to call a friend, though our meetings were few and far between, was a prominent spokesperson and advocate for what was an increasingly beleaguered minority tendency in the Arab world. By no means deriving from the same ideological and political views, the members of this trend had in common their utter refusal to buy into the prevalent choices that, for nearly three decades, were being forced on Arabs everywhere.

For the most part, we met in conferences and seminars, our discussions often taking place during cigarette breaks, even as we guiltily confessed to having promised our wives, both journalists, to quit soon.

In Lebanon, Samir was unwilling to concede to the notion that a necessary corollary to supporting the Palestinian liberation struggle and resistance to Israeli occupation—causes to which he had devoted most of his life—was to accept the oppressive, often criminal, dominance of the Syrian military and intelligence services over Lebanon, or to forfeit the right of the Lebanese people to equality and democracy, or yet again, to bow to Hizbullah's doggedness in holding the rest of the Lebanese nation hostage to its sacred struggle against the Zionist enemy.

Mr. Assad and his hooligans did not appreciate Samir's critique. His car was booby-trapped to explode as he turned on the engine. He was killed in front of his home, while his children were looking on to bid him goodbye.

Refusal to buy into the ugly choices history had thrown the Arabs' way was the defining feature of this trend, whose representatives throughout the Arab world shared as well a firm belief that Arabs and Muslims had as much a claim on rationalism, humanism, and the yearning for freedom as any other national or cultural group in the world, east or west.

As the bulk of the material selected for this volume will demonstrate, such a commitment lay at the heart of my own project as a political commentator and columnist.

Certainly, I got it utterly wrong as far as anticipating the Arab spring is concerned, but I believe I can legitimately claim to have been vindicated by it. And so has Samir Kassir, who paid the ultimate price for holding on to such a commitment. And so, of course, has been that trend's most illustrious representative, the late Edward Said.

Nearly everybody has commented on it. The whole edifice of thought that had held that Arabs and Muslim were inherently antithetical to such 'western' values as freedom, democracy, rationalism, and modernity came crashing down in Tahrir Square, where young Egyptian women and men were chanting the word 'freedom' over and over, with such passion and intense longing. It was only when Barack Obama, speaking on the morn of Mubarak's ousting, quoted Martin Luther King Jr., saying, "there is something in the soul that cries out for freedom," that I could find the perfect expression of what I had come to consider the most poignant, as well as the most germane, of the revolution's slogans.

Ever since the late 1970s, especially in the wake of Iran's Islamic revolution, a new conventional wisdom came to take thinking on the Arabs, the Middle East, and Muslims as a whole by storm. It burst out of the orientalist coffers of both western and Arab/Islamic academia; it was zealously taken up by government officials, the media, and talking heads and pundits of all shapes and sizes, and integrated in one form or another into the political and ideological discourses of a whole host of political groups and movements. The atrocity of 9/11 brought this conventional wisdom to the level of incontrovertible, self-evident dogma.

The crux of the emergent, soon to be overwhelmingly dominant, wisdom was that the behavior of Arabs and Muslims, their political, economic, cultural, or social choices, their worldview, and their perspective of the non-Muslim world could be understood only, and often exclusively, in terms of Islam.

The strangest bedfellows subscribed to the theory, from European neo-Nazi, Paki-bashing skinheads to the criminal gangs of Osama bin Laden and Ayman al-Zawahiri, but including as well a huge 'center' made up of most Arab, Muslim, and western governments, western liberals and moderate Islamists, the bulk of western and Muslim scholarship during the past thirty years, indeed, practically everybody.

For Arabs such as myself and Samir Kassir, it was an act of extermination, a denial of our heritage, of our very existence. It was, much more significantly, a denial of the great literary, scholarly, and artistic production of Arabs over some two hundred years. A popular Egyptian Muslim preacher used to boast that the only book he had read during the previous twenty years had been the Qur'an. The conventional wisdom on Arabs and Muslims during the past thirty years privileged him over Naguib Mahfouz, Rifa'a al-Tahtawi, Mahmoud Darwish, Salah Jahin, and dozens of other Arab luminaries.

The formula, fervently embraced by an overwhelming section of western scholarship since the late seventies, was simple, as pat as it was false. All of the above were 'westernized elites,' their sway over Arab political and cultural life a product of western colonial domination. Their attempts to pursue western models of liberal democracy or socialism were bound to fail, since they lacked authenticity, and finally Arabs and Muslims were coming into their own, reviving their inherently Muslim identity. And, unlike the Judeo-Christian tradition, civilization, or whatever, which ostensibly is inherently rationalist and secular, religion was central to Muslim behavior in all areas, political, social, and so on.

A considerable amount of this western scholarship on Islam and Muslims actually celebrated the rediscovery of our allegedly inherent Muslim identity. Some argued that 'Islamic revival' was similar to Europe's Protestant reformation and that it would ultimately prepare the ground for the development of capitalism in the Arab world. I recall attending a lecture in which an American scholar, reveling in his postmodern mumbo jumbo, argued that the Islamist movement in Egypt and other Arab countries was the Arab equivalent of the west's feminist and gay liberation movements.

The predominant version of the theory, however, one which was to gain overwhelming prominence after 9/11, was that there was something in Muslim culture, as Mr. Fukuyama would put it, that was antithetical to modernism, democracy, and the free market economy. Muslims, Fukuyama worried, seemed inherently incapable of making the necessary journey to the end of history. This, more or less, was the doctrine of the Bush administration, whose neocons were apparently convinced that they could bomb the Muslims into realizing what was good for them.

It was all so much stuff and nonsense, and the Arab spring, late and unexpected as it has been, has dealt it what I believe will prove to have been a death blow. Sure, Islamists were part of the Arab revolution, but is it not noteworthy, indeed momentous, that not a single uprising from Tunisia to Yemen has been of an Islamic character? With Islam ostensibly lying at the very center of our ideological, political, and cultural makeup, is it not somewhat surprising that the Arab revolutions were fought with tremendous heroism and self-sacrifice for such allegedly 'western' concepts as freedom, democracy, and human rights?

A well-known, albeit bitterly cynical, Arab proverb holds that "there are three impossibles: the ghoul, the phoenix, and a loyal friend." The point of the proverb, of course, is to suggest that loyal friends are no less mythical than the ghoul and the phoenix. Whoever came up with that saying must have been a very lonely, embittered person; probably a poetically inclined potentate of some sort. I could well imagine that Mubarak and Ben Ali are repeating this proverb quite often, having been so viciously disowned by a great many of their formerly sycophantic hangers-on, such as the former Egyptian editor who, in a discussion between us, pointed to the official portrait of Mubarak hanging on the wall behind his desk and in astonishingly passionate tones almost shouted: "I love him, I love him."

I, on the other hand, have been very lucky in that my life, turbulent and hectic as it may have been, has provided me with an abundance of exceedingly loyal friends; in fact, more brothers and sisters than mere friends, their existence in my life a source of immeasurable assurance and warmth.

So that takes care of one of the three impossibles.

What of ghouls? Are they really that impossible? What of Mubarak, Qadhafi, Ben Ali, Ali Saleh, Bashar al-Assad, and the hosts of torturers, murderers, and crooks they let loose on their peoples for decades?

Ghouls do exist. If anything this is possibly the starkest conclusion to be drawn from Arab history over the past thirty years or more.

My last article before the Egyptian revolution was written at dawn on the first of January 2011. A few hours before I had learned of the bombing of the Two Saints Church in Alexandria, killing and severely injuring dozens of worshipers who had been marking the advent of the New Year through prayer. Borrowing from Emile Zola's famous tract, I titled the article: "J'accuse." In it, I held practically everyone to blame; to my mind, Egyptians, Arabs, and Muslims had reached rock bottom.

Yet, I concluded the article by asking and replying: "Is it really so difficult to conceive of ourselves as rational human beings with a minimum of backbone so as to act to determine our fate, the fate of our nation?

"That, indeed, is the only option we have before us, and we had better grasp it, before it's too late."

Twenty-four days later, the Egyptian revolution broke out. A German friend of mine, one of those brothers I spoke of above, wrote me citing these two sentences, seeing in them a sort of forecast of the revolution. They weren't. In fact, I had not expected to see a positive answer to my rhetorical question in my life-time, hoping that my children would see it.

As 2011 came around, Egypt and the Arab world seemed to have plumbed the very depths of decline and disintegration. Yet, on January 14 Tunisia's Ben Ali is overthrown, fleeing to Saudi Arabia; on February 11, Mubarak is ousted from power and later taken into custody, accused of ordering the murder of unarmed Egyptians and of corruption. Uprisings break out in Libya, Yemen, Bahrain, and Syria, demanding freedom, democracy, and human rights.

According to legend, the phoenix rises out of its ashes. It looks as if this too is not impossible.

On February 11, and as the few of us holding the fort in the Ahram Online offices watched then vice-president Omar Suleiman deliver the shortest and most celebrated television address in the history of the Mubarak regime, I sat before my computer, wrote a brief item entitled: "Mubarak resigns, Egypt celebrates," and told my colleagues that Ahram Online was now shut for the day; it was time for celebration. Together, we headed to Tahrir.

There, we joined hundreds of thousands of Egyptians, young and old, men and women, singing and dancing and chanting slogans, in what was doubtlessly the most joyful day any of us had seen in our lifetimes. In the midst of this, a thought struck me. Following my heart attack, which had occurred while I was in my Ahram office, I was taken by ambulance to hospital. My blood pressure was 50/30. I later asked a doctor friend what that meant; chuckling, he answered that my heart had nearly stopped. My thought was to marvel at my luck. I had nearly been cheated of living to see this day, a day I had been waiting for all of my life, and had, for all practical purposes, given up on.

Congratulations exchanged among members of my generation were invariably accompanied by the refrain, "We've lived to see the day." Many of us, however, had been cheated of seeing it, indeed too many. To their memory, and to the heroic martyrs of the Egyptian revolution, I dedicate this volume.

# CIVILIZATION IN CARICATURE

WHY IS ANCIENT GREECE 'WESTERN'?

The obvious question is almost never asked.

Not only is the clash of civilizations "a pernicious myth," as a *New York Times* editorial described it at the time of Barack Obama's message to the Muslim world from Cairo University, but so is the whole paradigm of a world history demarcated into separate 'civilizational' stages, or of a contemporary world split along separate, essentialist civilizational fault lines. To ascribe essentialist civilizational attributes to people is to flatten the human experience, to rob it of its incredible richness, and to deny and obfuscate the multitude of cultural streams that, throughout history, have been joining and rejoining, traversing the globe, to and fro, mixing, amalgamating, transforming, and being transformed, thus ultimately presenting each and every one of us with the multifarious and highly varied component elements of his/her identity.

The western/Muslim civilizational fault line is pure fabrication, yet a great many vested interests on both sides of the divide would make it a self-fulfilling prophesy. In this preposterously absurd and destructive struggle I stand a conscious objector, calling on others—both at home and abroad—to join me.

# Tooning Out Humanity

WE MIGHT WELL LAUGH AT the absurdity of a notion that would put Adolf Hitler and Ernest Hemingway on one side of a battle line and Osama bin Laden and Egyptian novelist and Nobel laureate Naguib Mahfouz on the other.

Yet, the bogus 'clash of civilizations'—ludicrous, recycled nineteenth-century orientalist racism though it may be—is becoming all too real. The two sides are getting more enamored of the fracas with every passing day. To try to convince them that this is a bogus altercation looks increasingly to be as futile as attempting to convince a bunch of drunken English football hooligans that, win or lose, a soccer match is nothing to come to blows over.

Make no mistake about it: the recent west-versus-the-Muslim-world contention over twelve ignorant and offensive cartoons is not about freedom of expression and its limitations. It is first and foremost about the bleak reality of a great many powerful forces, on both sides of the Atlantic, north and south of the Mediterranean, and all the way to the Indian Ocean, having a decided stake in perpetuating and escalating the so-called clash of civilizations, even if for a whole range of very different reasons. This is no conspiracy but rather an ugly convergence of equally repugnant interests.

How else could we explain the supposed confusion over demarcating between freedom of expression and racist hate speech, a distinction that one would have thought was by now well established in the 'western' democratic tradition?

Presumably, one need not be particularly 'culturally sensitive' to recognize barefaced racism and hate-mongering in a cartoon depicting the

Prophet, venerated by over a billion and a half human beings, sporting a turban with a fuse-lit bomb in its center. Or another in which the Prophet is standing at the gate of a Muslim paradise telling an endless line of suicide bombers that he's running out of virgins to offer them. None of this is a question of subjecting a particular religious dogma to ridicule (as "we in the western world" are supposedly in the habit of doing). It is blatantly and unashamedly a matter of expressing contempt and hatred for a group of people by virtue of the race, religion, and/or ethnicity they were born into—the very definition of racism.

Not surprisingly, perhaps, a commentator writing in an Israeli newspaper had no difficulty in recognizing the Danish cartoons for what they are. "Of late, a new breed of anti-Semitic caricature has begun to circulate through Europe, an indication, perhaps, of a new breed of anti-Semitism. But the Semites, in this case, are not Jews," wrote Bradley Burston in *Haaretz* on February 6, 2006. Burston goes on to describe the message of the Danish cartoons as racist and obscene, adding, "in that sense, it also profanes the right of freedom of speech, distorting it into the freedom to foster hatred."

There is, indeed, a great deal of irony in the liberal 'western' pretensions of ambivalence and ambiguity over the Danish cartoons, as experts pontificate about the 'tension' between free expression and cultural sensitivity. No such ambivalence or pretended naiveté is shown when abhorrence is rightly expressed of the anti-Semitic cartoons that continue to plague some of the press in Arab and Muslim countries. Compounding the irony is the fact that Arab and Muslim editors jealously defend their 'right' to publish anti-Semitic cartoons, Holocaust denial editorials, and other garbage of the "Protocols of the Elders of Zion" variety by shouting "freedom of expression."

Meanwhile, the protagonists seem to be reveling in this new battle-front of the 'clash of civilizations.' For one thing, compared with the larger, global 'clash' launched by Osama bin Laden and George W. Bush in 2001, the recently opened Euro-Muslim front is superbly economical—for both sides. No billions of dollars or thousands of lives need to be expended by the western world on this particular front, merely newsprint.

The Arabs and Muslims, for their part, can engage in a glorious jihad in defense of the faith and their religious and cultural identity without fear of regime change, elimination of states, or the destruction of whole nations and the killing of hundreds of thousands of their peoples in order to liberate them. All they need do is shout slogans, burn a few flags, make the ultimate sacrifice of eliminating Danish blue cheese from their diets, torch a couple of European embassies, and—what could be easier—launch the odd attack on Arab Christians and publish hate cartoons about Jews.

Triggered by cartoons, the latest episode of the clash of civilizations is the caricature of a caricature, one in which our fundamental humanity is diminished, the almost limitless richness and diversity of that vast world of the intellect and the imagination that we call culture is flattened and shadowed over, the profound commonality of our human condition rubbed out, until finally all that remains is the horrible and the grotesque: the 'liberal' west represented by a T-shirted female American soldier holding a prone and naked Arab on a leash, and the 'devout' Arab/Muslim world represented by a masked terrorist holding a knife to a hostage's neck under a banner reading "God is great."

Salon.com, February 14, 2006

# The Crusaders Are Coming?

"THE POPE HAS SLANDERED ISLAM by equating it with violence and irrationality. Let's bomb the Vatican." No one to my knowledge has actually said this, though they might as well have if one is to go by the climate of hysterical frenzy that has swept the Muslim world since Pope Benedict XVI delivered his now famous lecture at the University of Regensburg on September 12, 2006. In refuting the Pope's alleged slander, a great many among us seemed determined to prove it right. "It's war," declared the editor of one Egyptian newspaper in a front-page commentary, seething with sound and fury. The newspaper's headline, in bold bright red, screamed, "The Vatican beats the drums of a Crusading war." Beneath it, the editor wrote ominously: "The deadly poison that has been released by the Vatican Pope [sic] should not be allowed to pass. It is war and it should be met with war."

It has been a week of ranting and raving, with the print and broadcast media competing over which among them can strike the most hysterical, frenzied notes. Hosts of political and religious figures and talking heads of all sorts scrambled over one another in their rush to hurl abuse at the "ignorant," Nazi Pope, warning of the dire consequences of his statements to the whole world and to the west in particular. Most of us are all too happy to condemn, or at least distance ourselves from the crazed fanatical terrorists of the al-Qaʿida variety, but they remain our card in the hold, jack in the box, whatever. "You do such and such to us, and the crazies will get you," we seem to be warning repeatedly, even as we rant on our way to the mall to stock up on two-dozen packs of Coca-Cola cans and other 'authentic' Ramadan goodies, car stickers proclaiming our willingness to sacrifice our fathers and mothers in defense of the Prophet and our religious and cultural identity.

It was the Danish cartoons, part two, and, if anything, it was even more pathetic.

This time around, the ruling National Democratic Party (NDP) was holding its annual party conference, promising us "a second leap forward" (so swift the first leap must have been, we're all hard pressed to discover when it was supposed to have taken place) and basically assuring us that they're here to stay, third leap, fourth leap, ad infinitum, ad nauseam.

But who cares? The Crusaders are coming. Pike-wielding Swiss Guards in puffed sleeves and striped knickerbockers are at the gates of Jerusalem. Well, maybe not. That particular holy land has been captured already.

Has it occurred to anyone that a scholarly lecture (however tenuous its scholarship) should possibly be countered by another scholarly lecture, a paper, a polemical work? That ideas, however ridiculous or malevolent you believe them to be, are countered by other ideas—what is known as a debate?

Certainly, the Pope is not some obscure professor lecturing in some backwater university, and neither is he an American televangelist of the type that are heaping anti-Islamic invective before millions of viewers practically daily on American airwaves. Certainly, His Holiness should have shown more wisdom and, indeed, respect toward his own flock, let alone to the followers of the second-largest faith in the world, than to jump on the bandwagon of the clash of civilizations, only worthy of mediocre, power-serving academics of the Huntington type.

Yet, I totally fail to see how any of last week's Muslim hullabaloo has served any purpose. We got an insincere, half-hearted apology; yet the reference to Islam is still out there and, thanks to our dubious efforts, it has won more publicity than the Pope in all his eminence could have imagined. Or is it that he, in fact, counted on our by now highly predictable foolishness? Is there anything like a learning curve in this part of the world? Does experience count for anything? Has anyone even paused to examine the farce of the Danish cartoons, which we managed to make available to tens of millions, instead of the odd forty thousand readers of an obscure Danish newspaper?

And has it yet dawned on any of our political, religious, and intellectual leaders how demeaning and insulting it is—for Islam, Muslims, and each and every one of us—to keep protesting that our religion is not a religion of terror and violence?

But jump on the 'clash' bandwagon Pope Benedict XVI did. His reference to Islam is gratuitous and wholly incidental to the argument he set out to make in his lecture—a jab delivered *en passant* and not very cleverly at that. The thrust of the Pope's lecture, for those who bothered to look up the text, was his call for rapprochement between religious faith and reason—quite possibly a commendable exercise. His basis for such a rapprochement is to redefine rational enquiry in broader terms than the empirically verifiable, as is prescribed in the natural sciences. This, he suggests, is to be found in philosophy, specifically Greek philosophy, about which he makes the rather dubious claim that it was intertwined from the very start with the Christian spirit and, indeed, with the Biblical tradition as a whole, including the Old Testament.

The validity of the Pope's argument is beside the point. It is all a question of reading. Where the Pope blunders incredibly is in his fleeting attempt to contrast the allegedly inherent rationality of Christianity to the equally inherent mysticism of Islam. This is little more than orientalist nonsense of the crudest kind. It is particularly glaring when the subject at hand is the Christian world's rediscovery of its presumably Hellenistic roots. Has the Pope, in all his scholarly wisdom, not heard of Ibn Rushd, known in the Latin world as Averroes? Is he perhaps not aware of what any undergraduate student of the history of philosophy knows, which is that Greek philosophy had been wholly lost to Christian Europe for centuries when its 'rediscovery' in the twelfth and thirteenth centuries occurred via translation from Arabic? Indeed, is it possible to deliver what is supposed to be a scholarly lecture on the relationship between Christian theology and Greek philosophy without a single reference to Averroes and Ibn Sina, or Avicenna?

Tellingly, it was not the slur about their alleged irrationality that so infuriated the elite of today's Muslim world, but the quoted reference to violence. Incidental and gratuitous, the reference is plainly silly. For a Roman Catholic Pope, whose predecessor recently apologized to the Jews for the Holocaust and centuries of pogroms and persecution, to try and suggest, however artfully, the inherently pacific nature of Christianity as opposed to the inherently violent nature of Islam is simply ridiculous.

Or need we remind His Holiness of the inquisition, the St. Bartholomew's Day massacre (on the occasion of which another of his long line of predecessors, Pope Gregory XIII, declared a public day of thanksgiving and had the guns of the Castel Sant'Angelo sound a joyous salute), or the way Christianity was genocidally introduced to the native peoples of South America, or of the Crusades?

The mutual taunting could go on forever. For Christian no less than for Muslim history, it is really a question of "let him who is without sin among you be the first to throw a stone" (John 8:7).

Ideas are countered by ideas. Instead of yet another show of irrational frenzy, we would have been much better served by demanding the right of reply, insisting perhaps that our response be published in all Catholic newspapers and magazines (God knows, there are a great many of those). And I know just the person to author it: Prof. Nasr Hamed Abu Zeid, one of the most brilliant Islamic scholars living today and a masterful expert on the rationalist tradition in Islam. We might, however, keep between us the fact that an Egyptian court ruled him an apostate and ordered him divorced from his wife, thereby hounding him and his wife out of the country for fear of their lives.

*The Daily Star Egypt*, September 25, 2006

# Into the Heart of Darkness

IT WAS LITTLE MORE THAN nineteenth-century racist drivel dressed up in late twentieth-century identity politics garb, and this by an erstwhile British spy in his dotage. Having received his schooling at London's School of Oriental and African Studies (SOAS) in the 1930s, at a time when the famed school was specifically designed as a training ground for future servants of empire in the 'Orient,' Bernard Lewis, arch-Zionist, old-school orientalist, and quack scholar, came to the United States in the 1970s, where he was eventually, and perhaps predictably, received as a prophet.

Having switched allegiance to the Pentagon—hardly a difficult transition—the old man hailed by the American corporate media as "the doyen of Middle East Studies" gave the military-industrial complex the one thing it desperately needed in a post-Soviet world: an enemy.

"This is no less than a clash of civilizations—the perhaps irrational but surely historical reaction of an ancient rival against our Judeo-Christian heritage, our secular present, and the worldwide expansion of both," Lewis wrote in the *Atlantic Monthly* in 1990. Samuel Huntington, a more mediocre scholar but no less fervent believer in the role of the intellectual as apologist for empire, took up the obnoxious thesis and, with the help of an ecstatic media, began its integration into American pop culture. Respected scholars—that is, people who have respect for their various disciplines and see their role as something other than providing ideological cover for the pernicious designs of a corporate-led power structure—soon made short work of the thesis. It was not that difficult.

Yet, in 2004, year three of the 'war on terror,' the 'clash' thesis, now firmly established as the official 'party line' of the neocon administration of George W. Bush, and the ideological foundation of its hold on power at home and abroad, appeared to become a self-fulfilling prophesy.

"Why do they hate us?" Bush asked rhetorically in an address to a joint session of Congress held in the wake of the 9/11 atrocity. "They hate what we see right here in this chamber—a democratically elected government. Their leaders are self-appointed. They hate our freedoms; our freedom of religion, our freedom of speech, our freedom to vote and assemble and disagree with each other," he went on, in answer to his own question. Clearly, "they" in this kind of context could not mean just a few hundred wild-eyed, Central Intelligence Agency–trained fanatics grouped together as al-Qa'ida. Bush had declared a global and perpetual war, the enemy clearly identified as western civilization's "ancient rival," supposed to be brimming over with an irrational hatred for "our Judeo-Christian heritage and secular present."

Significantly, however, Bush's Third World War in defense of 'western civilization,' along with its allegedly inherent rationalism, humanism, and liberalism (notwithstanding three centuries of colonial plunder, slavery, genocide, the Fascist and Nazi scourges, two devastating world wars, and two nuclear bombings), was predicated upon the American president's personal rapport with none other than God Himself. And its most solid base of support was the Fundamentalist Christian Right, in alliance with Likudnik Zionism.

This was just the tip of the iceberg. Ariel Sharon, "the butcher," whom his own people had two decades before declared a war criminal, was confirmed as a role model, a shining representative of western civiliza- tion, and a hero of the war against the ancient enemy. (Ironically, right up until the moment they took on the mantle of colonial domination them- selves, the Jews were as much an ancient enemy of western civilization as the Muslims, if not more so. But then, it was Arafat who looked like a Jew. Sharon, on the other hand, looks like a Serb.)

Which mementos of brutality and heartlessness should we clutch to our hearts as we go forward into 2005? The revelation by Britain's fore- most medical journal that over a hundred thousand faceless Iraqis were killed in the process of their 'modernization?' Or the torture carried out at Abu Ghraib and Guantanamo Bay (ideologically grounded, as we were to find out, in an orientalist tract suggesting that sexual molestation was the gravest insult an Arab or Muslim could suffer)? Or should we rather privilege the videotaped butchering of Nepalese workers to shouts of "God is great"? The massacre of children in Beslan? The slaughter of Spanish commuters in the Madrid subway? What kind of images of bloodshed and destruction, of sheer horror, stand out in our minds as we look back on the past year? The torn bodies of children in Rafah and Falluja? The hooded and cuffed father in Abu Ghraib, his frightened little boy lying prone and helpless in his lap? Or the weeping face of Margaret Hassan, before she was put to the knife?

And what of our supposedly inherent capacity for empathy? When we see a Palestinian family standing desolate and numbed before their bulldozed home, do we think of our own homes, of the memories and cherished possessions—a picture album, a sweater, a book—which, at only a moment's notice, could be buried under a pile of rubble? Do we think of what it might mean to be rendered homeless, often for the second or third time?

Or do we think of the greater picture of a world that has seemingly gone mad? A world that had to pass through the countless horrors of colonialism, world war, and genocide to be able to encode into law, in the aftermath of the Second World War, a relatively decent sense of our common humanity. Yet, it only took George W. Bush and his neocon cabal three years to bring the whole edifice down and confer instead the legitimacy of unmitigated power on invasion and occupation, illegal and 'preventive' war, torture, and the interminable detention of persons without charge, trial, or the merest semblance of due process.

In 2004, the clash of civilizations thesis looked to have become a self-fulfilling prophesy. Yet, within this bleak picture, there was hidden a significant twist. For this is not the war of a civilized west against a barbaric east. Rather, this conflict pits a barbaric and immensely powerful west against an equally barbaric, eminently powerless, and ultimately suicidal east.

*Al-Ahram Weekly*, December 30, 2004

# Capital Strikes Back

BERLUSCONI APOLOGIZED; BUSH FORSWORE a Crusade (even in "the broad sense of the word," as U.S. administration spokespersons were at aims to explain); the war in defense of "western civilization" was toned down to a war in defense of freedom for everybody; and "infinite justice" became "enduring freedom." Sensible Muslim leaders applauded expressions of western sensitivity to Muslim sensitivities, and such were the prerequisites of political expedience that western political leaders began to sound like Azharite sheikhs, preaching to all and sundry the true meaning of Islam.

It's not working. Bombs, after all, will be bombs. They kill and devastate; people die; families are shattered; homes are destroyed; lives and livelihoods, just as sure as limbs and bodies, are broken beyond repair—all of which is brutally, heartlessly concrete ("the proof of the pudding").

And let's not fool each other or ourselves. Nobody really believes the sudden sensitization, in New York and London or in Islamabad and Cairo. Muslim rage is all the rage in the western media. Meanwhile, every two-bit academic who has, with career-minded farsightedness and often (overt and/or covert) governmental connections, plagiarized other two-bit career-minded, etc., academics to write a PhD thesis, monograph, or book on Islam has become an 'expert' in high demand.

It is a clear case of "white man speak with forked tongue," sad to say. The leaders speak in easily decipherable code, at once swearing themselves blue in the face that the west is not at war with Islam—"Islam is a religion of peace," etc.—while continuing to use the 'trigger words' that incite the very feelings of cultural, religious, and racial superiority, bigotry, and hatred they claim to refute.

Huntington, all but consigned to well-deserved oblivion during the past few years, has been revived with a vengeance. Commentators vie to expound their particular take on the essential attributes of Islamic civilization, culture, and contemporary world, and the clash of civilizations is back in fashion. Royalties are rolling in. Even Francis Fukuyama, a rival and equally prosaic prophet of post-Cold War capitalist triumphalism (and U.S. policymaking circles), has jumped on the bandwagon of anti-Islamic rhetoric. His "end of history" thesis (all world societies have no option but to adopt western democracy and market-based economy, proven to be the summit of human progress) has not been proven wrong, Fukuyama asserts in a 2001 article in the *Wall Street Journal*. He goes on to concede, however, that "there does seem to be something about Islam, or at least the fundamentalist versions of Islam that have been dominant in recent years, that makes Muslim societies particularly resistant to modernity."

For a fairly short piece, Fukuyama's is a veritable mine of precious gems. "Of all contemporary cultural systems, the Islamic world has the fewest democracies," he informs his readers. In fact, he goes on to clarify, only one Islamic country qualifies (as a democracy): Turkey. This assertion (apparently so self-evident, it is made in parentheses) is so fantastic as to lead one to the conclusion that Dr. Fukuyama must base his writing on one of two assumptions: either his readers are utter ignoramuses or they are fully complicit in an entirely cynical and arbitrary definition of democracy. A democracy is simply what we say is a democracy, and let the Devil take care of the rest (including thousands of killed, tortured, and imprisoned Kurds, banned political movements and parties, gagged journalists and writers, and a state and society made hostage to the generals' goodwill).

Fukuyama's fundamental dilemma, however, lies elsewhere. Other non-western people may be having problems in their progression toward the western ideal (and, hence, history's peak), but "there are no insuperable cultural barriers to prevent them from getting there." It does seem, however, that such barriers may exist in the case of Muslims, suggests a troubled Fukuyama. After all, "Islam . . . is the only cultural system that seems regularly to produce people like Osama bin Laden or the Taliban who reject modernity lock, stock, and barrel."

The well-connected Washington ideologue approves of western leaders' change of tone. Their assertions "that those sympathetic with the terrorists are a 'tiny minority' of Muslims [are] important . . . to prevent all Muslims from becoming targets of hatred." And, we might add, to draw friendly Islamic states into the 'war against terrorism' alliance while maintaining as far as possible their fragile political stability. Fukuyama readily admits, however, that such assertions are merely expedient. The real issue, he tells us, is that "if the [Muslim] rejectionists are more than a lunatic fringe, then Huntington is right that we are in for a protracted conflict made dangerous by virtue of their technological empowerment."

But what if this is the real issue? The struggle, after all, is not between "equal cultures fighting among one another like the great powers of nineteenth-century Europe." The west, and in particular America, Fukuyama is confident, will ultimately prevail.

Fukuyama meets Huntington courtesy of Bin Laden—a synthesis of nonsense has been achieved.

There is tremendous irony in all of this. The expedient and transparent hypocrisy visible in western leaders' change of tone provides inadequate tactical cover for the bigger (strategic) lie of the confrontation between the west and Islam, but in lying twice they actually point to the truth.

The secret buried beneath all the garbage, both tactical and strategic, can be found in the shifting fortunes of Huntington and Fukuyama themselves. Their initial renown was a product of the winds of change that swept across Eastern Europe a little over a decade ago. Against the drumbeats of western capitalist triumphalism, the U.S.-led Gulf War slipped into the collapse of the Soviet Union. The Cold War was over.

That did not last. In less than ten years, the tunes of global capital's victory march had dimmed to a distant murmur. Democracy was no longer a malleable propaganda instrument to be manipulated cynically by the U.S. and its western allies. Rather, it had become the battle cry of a growing resistance movement against capitalist globalization. World Bank and International Monetary Fund officials were scavenging for capitalism's human face; spin had all but replaced politics; the World Trade Organization was in the process of replacing parliaments; America had an elected president who had lost the election; and the global economy was slowly but surely sinking into recession. Fukuyama and Huntington were silent.

Now they're back.

At its heart, the 'clash of civilizations' (or merely the west versus Islam) is no more than the fantastically fetishized expression of global capital's battle against genuine (rather than Turkish-style) democracy, everywhere. Things, as everybody knows, are rarely ever what they seem.

*Al-Ahram Weekly*, October 21, 2001

# Vacuous Identities

IF THE CENTURIES SINCE THE ENLIGHTENMENT show anything it is that people are as committed to their right to espouse ignorance, narrow-mindedness, and crass stupidity as to their right to reason, knowledge, and emancipation, personal and social. The French government's "secularist" drive against "conspicuous religious symbols" in public schools and the civil service is foolish and smacks more of racism than of reason. Let us not fool ourselves. This is not about big crosses and small kippahs. France's and, for that matter, Europe's real problem is with the burgeoning Muslim minority in their midst: six million strong in France alone. The real issue at the heart of the racket is the *hijab*.

It would be facile, however, to fall back on the now-entrenched Arab/ Muslim response to denounce Islamophobia. Given that the right to stupidity and ignorance extends as much to Muslims as to any other group, religious or otherwise, I might as well point out that there is something wholly absurd about shrill Arab and Muslim cries in defense of basic civil and personal rights. The inherent illogicality is comparable to American pronouncements that the U.S. is safeguarding democracy and freedom throughout the world. Both sets of claims are identical in their arbitrariness.

You can argue power or you can argue moral and legal precepts but to argue both, from both sides of your mouth and at the same time, is to become ridiculous. Arabs and Muslims vehemently claim in Europe the very civil and democratic rights they firmly believe should be trampled at home. In Europe Muslims have a fundamental right to proselytize everywhere and anywhere they please—boasting all the while of being

35

the fastest-growing religion in the world—but let any other religious group try to do the same in any of the many 'houses' of Islam and all hell would break loose.

Amid screams of conspiracy, foreign penetration, and endless red lines being crossed coming from the mouths of the very publicists who are now so valiantly and heatedly defending civil and personal rights in France, the culprits will be subjected to the barbaric forms of punishment that are supposed to be inherent to our cultural and religious identity.

But this is to speak only of the most glaring contradictions. It ignores the fact that the valiant defenders of civil rights in France have also been drawing red lines beyond which Muslims are not permitted to discuss Islam. For are they not the very same people who hounded Nasr Hamed Abu Zeid,* one of the most brilliant Islamic scholars of his generation, into exile in Holland? Are they not same people who went into paroxysms of fury when a French tutor at the American University in Cairo placed French scholar Maxime Rodinson's book *Muhammad* on his students' recommended, not required, reading list? And are these zealous defenders of civil and personal rights not the very same people who demanded Professor Saad Eddin Ibrahim be hanged in a public square for having dared to open the subject of anti-Coptic discrimination in Egypt?

The glorious armies of Islam may well once have approached the gates of Paris. Recently, they sort of vanished at the gates of Baghdad. And this is what is most absurd about our hypocritical civil rights discourse. Bush and his gang can afford to trample on civil and political rights while crying democracy; they have the armies and the corporations and the corporate media to back it up. What do we have?

The only coherent opinion made in the midst of all the hubbub has been that of the much-maligned imam of al-Azhar, Sheikh Mohamed Tantawi. A realist par excellence, Tantawi at least presented us with a consistently authoritarian argument. In effect, the sheikh's argument is that since we can, and indeed should, trample civil and political rights

---

* The late Professor Nasr Hamed Abu Zeid, a brilliant Egyptian scholar, whose work focused on reviving the rationalist tradition in Islamic thought, was proclaimed an infidel by Egyptian Islamists, who took him to court, charging him with apostasy, and demanding that he be forcibly divorced from his wife on the grounds that a Muslim woman cannot be married to an apostate. The court ruled in the plaintiff's favor, forcing Abu Zeid and his wife to leave the country for fear of their lives.

in Muslim countries (the *hijab*, he insists, is obligatory under Islam), Christians, secularists, or whoever should be able to do the same in their own countries, at least until we conquer them, God willing.

There is a much more significant aspect to the debate, however. Adonis, among the most celebrated of Arab poets alive today, wrote recently, asking, "Why do fundamentalist Muslims who have emigrated to the west see in the openness of their new home nothing more than an opportunity to proclaim their narrow-mindedness and isolation? Why do they choose to 'emigrate' once more from their point of their arrival?"

Pertinent questions. The answers, however, lie in the realm of neither culture nor religion but in politics. Identity politics is testimony to the impoverishment and degradation of politics in the age of globalized capital. It is the great con of a postmodern world.

Yet, the fact remains that while narrow-mindedness, ignorance, and stupidity can be critiqued, they cannot be banned.

*Al-Ahram Weekly*, January 8, 2004

# This Is the Way the World Ends

IS GLOBAL CAPITALISM IN MORE dire straits than anyone thought, or is it doing what it's doing simply because it can? Warmongering, national hysteria, jingoism, rampant racism, assaults on civil liberties—historically, these have accompanied intractable systemic crises and are, indeed, the system's way of dealing with major threats, if not to its existence then to the minimum requirements for its reproduction under fairly stable conditions.

But where is the threat? What has become of the market-driven global village, the praises of which were being sung with such abandon barely a year before the 9/11 attacks during former United Nations Secretary General Kofi Annan's millennium extravaganza just a few blocks away from the ill-fated Twin Towers?

The Soviet Union and its 'evil empire' had collapsed, not by virtue of war or nuclear holocaust but courtesy of an implosion so pathetic as to evoke revulsion rather than sympathy in the hearts of all but the blindest of its one-time supporters.

Well before, the 'phantom of communism' had ceased haunting Europe (it was always a mere shadow in North America), having stimulated as well as transmutated into social democracy's welfare state, ironically the very hallmark of capitalism's 'golden age.' The Reagan/Thatcher era put the lid on the welfare state; trade unionism was all but destroyed; Labour became New Labour; and social democrats, when in power, had no compunction about advocating and implementing the deregulation policies their conservative adversaries had already put in place.

If anything, the fate of the communist/socialist 'threat' in the Third World (which Mao had designated the "center of world revolution") was even more ironic. Third World communism's greatest triumph, in Vietnam in 1975, was also its swan song. The dreaded 'domino effect' was sunk in the marshes of Cambodia's killing fields, and barely a decade was to pass before the most populous 'communist' country in the world was setting itself up as international capitalism's most promising growth market.

The wave of Third World liberation movements, which had produced a host of populist/corporatist socialisms (producing also the Non-Aligned Movement, Afro-Asian Solidarity, and a certain UN clout), were to be found, repentant and hat in hand, queuing up before the doors of the International Monetary Fund, the World Bank, and, of course, the White House. Once-triumphant liberation movements (as in defunct Zaire) were making deals with multinational corporations even before they had finished 'liberating' their capital cities. And an old 'dependista' theorist like Enrique Fernando Cardoso could become president in Brazil in order to push forward the free market and greater integration into the world economy, while old Stalinists could return to power in this or that Eastern European country to do pretty much the same thing.

A single product is on offer for the whole world; only the size and the packaging vary.

What's left? Al-Qaeda, rogue states, the Muslim world and its alleged deeply rooted cultural/civilizational antipathy to modernism? No world power in history has ever had to contend with such a sorry group of enemies.

Admittedly, the scale of the 9/11 attacks, by virtue of their shockingly graphic symbolism as much as the devastating number of civilian casualties, sent Americans crying for vengeance. But what do we really have here? An organization of a few hundred or even a few thousand underground militants, long-nurtured by the Central Intelligence Agency and the Pakistani intelligence service but now hounded by the intelligence services of the whole world, including such repentant "rogues" as Sudan's Omar al-Bashir and Yemen's Ali Abdullah Saleh. The Egyptian Jihad organization, which seems to have been the ideological and organizational backbone of al-Qa'ida, was effectively crushed inside Egypt, thanks largely to the country's insouciant attitude toward due process and basic civil and political rights, that is, the very same attitude that is being embraced today in defense of western 'democratic values.'

And what if a group of the world's least industrialized and most author-itarian, corrupt, and inept regimes take up or reject modernism, whatever that means? The whole question is farcical, particularly given that Islamic fundamentalists had for decades been fostered and supported by the 'modernist' west as a bulwark against communism and secularist national-ism. A state that is spending $379 billion a year on its military is supposed to be afraid of war and sanctions–devastated Iraq and/or any of the rest of the sundry group of states designated as "evil" by an intellectually chal-lenged American president and his warmongering aides?

If anything, it is the absence of any real threat to world capitalism and the overpowering hegemony of its imperial center that seem to be the most distinctive feature of today's world, in contrast to that of two decades ago.

Yet, undeniably there is anger, seething, unbearable, and growing in intensity as the avenues available for its expression shrink. Dominant sys-tems are supposed to survive by virtue of more than mere coercion. There is supposed to be some sort of compact between the dominant and the domi-nated: rules of the game; a certain room for maneuver by the oppressed; a rationale by which they may, however grudgingly and rebelliously, accept their lot. Indeed, it is the disintegration of such compacts that, throughout history, has lent impetus to the transformation of the daily acts of resis-tance and subversion by the oppressed, turning them into revolutions.

What we see today is naked power, unmitigated by compacts or any semblance of reason, shameless in the flaunting of its stupidity and sheer madness. But there are no revolutions, no real rebellions, only ever-grow-ing, ever-futile anger. And, of course, such things as a fluke but devastating attack on the Twin Towers, a monstrous Eid-eve butchering of a journalist, Muslims killing Copts in an Egyptian village, Hindus massacring Muslims in Ahmedabad, Muslims massacring Hindus on a train—the world of (very) late capitalism, aptly ruled over by Dubya Bush.

*Al-Ahram Weekly*, March 7, 2002

# A Cultural Thing

ARAB AND MUSLIM PROTESTATIONS THAT we're really "nice guys," that only a few of us are bloodthirsty terrorists, that real Islam is a religion of tolerance, etc., are truly pathetic. We concede the most flagrant racism against us and, rather than confront it as the ugly and ignorant aberration all racism is, we whine and entreat that it is all a terrible misunderstanding.

Beneath the heaps of learned nonsense, the western debate about Muslims' propensity toward violence, authoritarianism, the oppression of women, and so forth is nothing but nineteenth-century European racism, trussed up in ribbons and frills, especially when PC, feminist, left/ liberal 'intellectuals' pitch in with their own hotly self-righteous platitudes. George W. Bush, the liberator of Afghan women.

What I find particularly absurd about the whole discussion (on 'our' side as well as 'theirs') is that no religious text I know of is free (at least on the surface) of the 'propensities' that are so liberally and self-confidently attributed to Islam and Muslims. Let he, one might say, who is without embarrassing religious texts cast the first stone. Take the story of Abraham/Ibrahim (the legendary ancestor of both Arabs and Jews). One may interpret it in any way one likes, but the attempted slaughter of a child, let alone one's own, does not strike a pretty picture in any 'culture' I've heard of. The three great monotheistic religions share many such stories.

In any case, all is not lost, it now appears. 'Our' culture and 'theirs' seem to have found a common ground, albeit one that reflects the development gap: torture.

Several years ago, the head of a U.S.-based human rights organization, in Cairo to lobby against torture in jails and police stations here, told me of a meeting he had with the ambassador to Egypt of an important European country. Having listened to the human rights mission's report on torture in Egypt, the ambassador, my friend recounted incredulously, had an interesting take on the whole matter. Unlike Americans and Europeans, His Excellency opined, Egyptians are used to being physically abused in police stations and prisons—it's a cultural thing, you might say.

I've recounted this story many times since then. It seemed, to my mind, to exemplify both the absolute garbage that all the endless talk (learned or otherwise) of cultural essence actually boils down to, and—more interesting still—the amazing complicity between 'us' and 'them' in defining what 'we' are supposed to be like. Essential cultural attributes are invariably used to justify the most hateful forms of oppression and criminal behavior, for which globalized humanity, in its great and wonderful cultural and ethnic diversity, continues to have a definite predilection.

Nazi propaganda chief Joseph Goebbels famously said that whenever he heard the word 'culture,' he reached for his gun. Today, culture (as in 'our' culture, 'their' culture) evokes a very different meaning, one with which the Nazi boss would have been more than comfortable, so easy is it to interchange it with another word that was especially close to his heart: race. So different, indeed, that when I hear the word 'culture' today, I immediately look out for the gun, tightly clutched by the person saying it.

The 'war on terror,' that 'monumental battle' in defense of western civilization, culture and values, democracy and perpetual freedom, has alas successfully bridged the civilizational divide. Sure, torture Guantanamo Bay–style has all the slick gloss that the imperial master of the world is capable of: red sci-fi suits and masks, a remote base in Cuba, and total sensory deprivation, instead of the more primitive beatings and hangings. It is doubly horrible for it.

And the arguments in justification of Guantanamo Bay are so utterly familiar. The prisoners on the base are 'thugs' unworthy of prisoner-of-war status. There has been no due process; they have not been formally charged, tried, or convicted; they have been denied the benefit of legal counsel and all the other basic rights upheld by international legal and human rights standards for any kind of prisoner—all this is unimportant. "What about the rights of the innocent civilians they murdered?" We've heard it all before, just one of the benefits of 'our' culture and civilization.

Hitherto, however, our moral development as human beings had achieved a certain limited success. Torture had become a four-letter word. Torturers abounded, but they had to do their dirty business in secret, issuing heated denials even as they advanced a host of arguments in its justification. Now, it is being done flagrantly, in public. Indeed, thanks to the information revolution and the global supremacy of the torturers, we are audience to the most public torture in human history.

In a horrifying dialectic, the war of civilizations has been realized as a descent into barbarism.

*Al-Ahram Weekly*, January 24, 2002

# West Is as West Does

"A WAR HAS BEEN DECLARED upon western societies. It is mistaken to view the events of 11 September solely as a war on America. It was an act of war in America, on the West," writes Anne McElvoy in the *Independent*. This statement/theme, or variations on it, is being shouted from the rooftops by politicians, media people, scholars and commentators, liberals and conservatives, right-wingers and social democrats, out-and-out racists, and Bible-thumping televangelists and pro-lifers no less vehemently than by strictly PC feminists, gay rights activists, and militant vegetarians. Thoroughly interchangeable with the west have been two old but robustly born-again self-designations: "the civilized world" and "the free world."

So not only did Bin Laden allegedly bring down the 'Soviet Empire,' he has now also achieved what that empire in all its nuclear might was unable to do in many decades: he has recreated the 'west' as a coherent, cohesive monolith in which left-wing liberals such as Ms. McElvoy can bask in the identity, values, and civilization they share not only with Tony Blair and Gerhard Schroeder but also with George W. Bush, Silvio Berlusconi, and—why not? They're 'western' too—the manifold White supremacists, Paki-bashers, and neo-Nazi skinheads who, indeed, have been prophetic in their warnings of the dire threat the non-western world poses to the west. Credited with so much power, it is little wonder that the Saudi millionaire's interviews read as the ravings of a megalomaniac.

So attached is Ms. McElvoy to her "war against the west" thesis that she makes a clumsy and transparent attempt at bluffing her way to proving it. The target, the World Trade Center, is apparently sufficient proof to

McElvoy that the terrorists' evil design was directed not at the U.S. alone but at the west as a whole. Why? Because it held people from many different nationalities, she writes, in complete seriousness. She skims over the obvious corollary to her argument, which is that these "different nationalities" were all "western." I don't have access to a civilizational breakdown of the thousands of men and women who were heartlessly murdered in the World Trade Center, but I would be very interested to find out how Ms. McElvoy would have gone about making such a distribution. For instance, we know that some one hundred British nationals were killed in the attack. How many of them, one has to wonder, were of South Asian origin (including turbaned/bearded Sikhs and clean-shaven Muslims)? Are they to be categorized as western or non-western? Is a third-generation Briton of Indian origin western or non-western?

And what of African-Americans? White Anglo-Saxons may (however improbably) trace their 'western origins' back to the ancient Greeks, who actually belonged to a Mediterranean civilizational bloc, which was even then in close and constant contact with other civilizational blocs in East Africa and South and East Asia.

If she thinks about it, Ms. McElvoy will discover that, despite their contribution to 'western' American culture, the 'western' roots of African-Americans may plausibly be traced back merely to the 1960s and 1970s of the last century—a dubious privilege they won, paradoxically, by reclaiming their African heritage.

And take the Jews. Notwithstanding Marx, Freud, and Einstein (the very hallmarks of modern western civilization), 'western societies' slaughtered six million Jews before affording them the privilege of being constructed as 'western,' and then only in conjunction with the creation of the state of Israel, through which Jewish colonists in Palestine proved that a Jew could be as 'western' as the next man. He, too, could plunder, dispossess, and subjugate a dehumanized 'non-western' population.

Define 'western.' It does not describe race, God forbid, though there are still a great many people in 'western societies'—not least in Mr. Berlusconi's government—who would argue otherwise. Clearly, it can no longer be defined in Cold War terms, as western democracies versus the 'totalitarianism' of the (eastern) Soviet system. Ah, but what of western culture and, even more significantly, western values? This, surely, is fine and dandy, especially if one refrains from such faux pas as the Italian prime minister's confidence in "the superiority of our civilization" over the Muslim one.

But here is the rub: western values, it is widely accepted by almost everybody (including both Berlusconi and Bin Laden), entail such things as democracy and human rights, the emancipation and equality of women, secularism, reason, and tolerance.

Do they now? Perhaps Messrs. Bush, Blair, Chirac, and Schroeder (who resolutely and hysterically refused to proffer an apology for slavery and colonialism) would explain to the less fortunate non-westerners among us where these western values were during the plunder of Africa and the enslavement of millions of its people.

And what of the overthrow of the elected governments of Mohammed Mossadegh in Iran, Sukarno in Indonesia, and Salvador Allende in Chile, to name but a few of the more grisly examples? What of the vicious dictatorships the 'west' put in place, bolstered and supported there and throughout the 'non-western' world?

Where were western values when millions of people in the non-western world were killed and tortured by butchers and villains sponsored by western governments, such as Iran's Reza Shah Pahlavi, Indonesia's Suharto, or Zaire's Mobutu Sese Seko? And what of the napalming and murder of two million Vietnamese, or the bitter irony of western support for Pol Pot's bloodthirsty brand of communism?

And what of Francism, fascism, and Nazism? Why are they not products of 'western civilization,' as well? Does Ms. McElvoy know that the Muslim Brothers (the fountainhead to which today's militant Islamists can trace their beginnings) started their political life in the late 1920s as "brown shirts," that they drew inspiration and ideological sustenance from that particular brand of western civilization?

"Berlusconi and Civilisation Do Not Mix," was the title of a devastating leading article published by the *Guardian* on September 28, 2001. Mr. Berlusconi, said the leader, "is living proof that there is nothing inherently superior about western civilisation." It went on to describe the Italian prime minister as a megalomaniac "who has compared himself with Justinian, Napoleon, and Jesus," a politician who was twice convicted of corruption and who has brought post-fascist and racist parties into his coalitions.

All in all, the Italian premier has proven a grave embarrassment from whom various western leaders have hastened to disassociate themselves. But one has to wonder whether he was merely saying what many others, including such liberal-minded people as McElvoy, are too ashamed (consciously or unconsciously) to express openly. Because if such things as democracy, rationalism, human rights, and women's equality are to be hailed as exclusively and/or essentially western values, it is only natural for those who uphold them to consider western civilization to be superior to other civilizations that do not.

It so happens, however, that we—in the non-western world—have a life-and- death stake in the struggle for democracy and human rights. Bin Laden and his cohorts are not a function of an inherent hatred of democracy by 'Islamic civilization,' but of its increasing obliteration at the hands of 'western'-driven capitalist globalization.

*Al-Ahram Weekly*, October 4, 2001

# Inherently Secular

ONE PAT THEORY THAT ENJOYS almost universal acceptance attributes the 'triumph' of secularism in the Christian west, as opposed to its 'failure' in the Muslim east, to Jesus's saying, "Render unto Caesar the things which are Caesar's and unto God the things which are God's" (Matthew 22:21). This is contrasted with the Islamic tradition, in which, it is said, much more attention is given to worldly concerns, as state and religion have been fused from the time of the Prophet. Here we have one prominent example of the dominant western discourse on Islam and the dominant Islamic discourse on the west happily converging. It is by no means the only one.

As Edward Said has pointed out, the construction of non-western 'others' was and remains a fundamental element in the construction of the west itself. The exercise assumes different and changing forms—more elaborate, more in keeping with the times, more fashionable—and definitely not all openly hostile or demonizing.

In his preface to Gilles Kepel's *Muslim Extremism in Egypt: The Prophet and Pharaoh*, renowned orientalist and arch-Zionist Bernard Lewis is concerned from the start with drawing lines of demarcation. "To the modern western observer, the political role of Islam in the world today appears to be something of an anomaly," he writes. For the western observer, Lewis notes, Islamic political behavior in the modern world seems "anachronistic and indeed absurd," but "it is neither anachronistic nor absurd in relation to Islam." He explains learnedly that "the difference must rather be traced back to the very beginnings of these various religions and to an intimate and essential relationship between religion and politics, creed

48

and power, which has no parallel in any major religion besides Islam." Lewis then gives us the commonplace "render unto Caesar" argument.

An Egyptian Islamist could not have put it better.

The fundamental notion here is that Christianity is inherently secular, while Islam is inherently antithetical to secularism—a notion that both the dominant western discourse on Islam and the dominant Islamic discourse on the west employ.

Universally accepted theories are somewhat daunting, though this has never been sufficient evidence of their correctness. Take, for instance, the one that held the earth is flat, or the ones that suggest International Monetary Fund/World Bank prescriptions lead to prosperity or that the Oslo Accords will lead to Palestinian self-determination.

And the western secularism theory suffers from such an obviously colossal flaw that its universality becomes all the more staggering, its ideological nature all the more stark: basically what we are being told is that it took over 1,800 years for the allegedly inherent secularism of Christianity to be realized. A fantastic leap of logic is required to gloss over the best part of two millennia, during which God was supposed to have reigned supreme throughout the Christian world, in order to explain a development that took place in their twilight, and this by reference to a single New Testament quote.

Such monumental sleights of hand abound in the construction of western identity and its necessary opposites. They do violence to both history and logic. The fact that they survive unchallenged is supreme evidence both of the mythical nature of the identities constructed by them and of the almost desperate need to maintain these mythical identities in the here and now.

In this particular case, a much stronger argument could be made in support of an Islamic, rather than a Christian, basis for secularism. Instead of a single quote, we have, as Sheikh Ali Abdel Razeq's *al-Islam wa usul al-hukm* amply demonstrated some seventy-five years ago, dozens. Rather, I believe that the early fusion of state and religion and Islam's greater concern with worldly affairs could be used to argue that Islam, much more than Christianity, is malleable to secularist interpretation.

For that matter, secularism in Europe did not originate in opposition to the domination of the Pope and the Church but in confrontation with the absolutist monarchies of the eighteenth century, under which state and religion had become fused in ways not at all unlike those that characterized the great Muslim states predating them.

In fact, the only real logic here is of teleology: because the west ultimately became secularist, secularism was already inscribed in its origins, and so this goes for individualism, rationalism, democracy, etc.—all the so-called attributes of western civilization.

*Al-Ahram Weekly*, July 27, 1995

# Greek Gifts

SOME TWENTY YEARS AGO, WHILE visiting someone for the first time, I found myself sitting before a huge map. Obviously an Arab map from the Middle Ages, it took me a little while to recognize what it represented. Recognition, when it did come, was a shock. Europe was below and Africa and the Middle East on top. Egypt was looking down the Mediterranean and a less sharply defined Italian boot was sticking up into the sea. My initial reaction was that the cartographer got it wrong. It came almost as a revelation to realize that our globe is as right whichever way you hang it.

It was with a similar sense of—to use a word very much in vogue these days—apostasy that several years ago I asked myself the question, "Why is ancient Greece western?" Just like for the question of why we are south and Europe is north, the answer lies simply in presentation. Both 'truths' are presented as self-evident, not because there is great evidence to support them but simply because 'everybody says so.'

Similar to the alleged origins of western secularism in "render unto Caesar," the western nature of ancient Greece is an ideological construct dependent on a version of history that deems a thousand years a mere blip, interrupting a simple progression from western infancy to western adulthood. Never mind that the heritage of ancient Greece was completely lost to Christian Europe for centuries and that Muslim Arabs conserved it. Muslim Arabs are conveniently dismissed as mere postmen of history, as they only transmitted the heritage to its presumably rightful owners.

The only logical foundation for the European/western claim on ancient Greece is that modern Greece lies on the modern continent of

Europe, a Europe that in ancient times did not exist, either culturally, geographically, or civilizationally. Another foundation is that Greece remained Christian. The first is little more than an accident of geography, just as the second is an accident of history. Greece, like Albania just next to it, could easily have been transformed into a Muslim country.

Of course, the reality is that ancient Greece was a Mediterranean country in a Mediterranean world.

But here again we see the sleights of hand so common in the construction of western identity. Modern geographical Europe is made to reappear as cultural/ideological Europe. Later, the west as well as the Christian and ancient Greek traditions, which have very little in common, can slip one into the other as essentially inscribed attributes of European or western man.

But the whole trick is exposed by the banishment of ancient Greece from the Arab and Muslim heritage. To sever so decisively a direct and obvious line of descent and replace it with what is so starkly a mythical claim required tremendous ideological violence. Such violence in thought could only have been possible through equally tremendous physical violence, no less than the conquest and subjugation of the world.

When I came across Martin Bernal's *Black Athena: The Afroasiatic Roots of Classical Civilisation*, I discovered that yet another cut had been made to ensure a totally 'clean' western appropriation of ancient Greece. Bernal identifies two models of Greek history, one he calls the "ancient model," upheld by the ancient Greeks themselves, which views ancient Greece as "Levantine, on the periphery of the Egyptian and Semitic cultural area." The other is the "Aryan or European model," produced in the eighteenth and nineteenth centuries.

In his introduction, Bernal writes:

> If I am right in urging the overthrow of the Aryan model and its replacement by the Revised Ancient one, it will be necessary not only to rethink the fundamental bases of 'Western Civilisation' but also to recognise the penetration of racism and 'continental chauvinism' into all our historiography, or philosophy of writing history. The ancient Model had no major 'internal' deficiencies or weaknesses in explanatory power. It was overthrown from external reasons. For 18th and 19th century Romantics and racists it was simply intolerable for Greece, which was seen not merely as the epitome of Europe but also as its pure childhood to have been the result of the mixture of native Europeans and colonizing Africans and Semitics.

Had the western claim on ancient Greece been merely something in the nature of nouveaux riches claiming noble descent, it would have been fairly harmless, whatever violence it did to logic and actual history. However, the construction of western identity has not been just an exercise in image building; its fundamental rationale lay in exclusion, in defining the westerners as something 'others' are not.

*Al-Ahram Weekly*, August 30, 1995

# Islamism:
# A Western Ideology

THE TITLE OF THIS ARTICLE IS, I admit, deliberately provocative. But let me make it clear at the outset, my intention is not to imply a conspiracy theory, that Islamism is a tool of western hegemonic designs, or some such nonsense.

Notwithstanding such episodes as the CIA–Afghan *mujahidin* connection, or the mysterious U.S. visa for Sheikh Omar Abdel Rahman, the love affair between dominant western discourse on Islam and dominant Islamic discourse on the west is much more complex than can be explained by the cynical dirty tricks of the game of nations.

In a previous article, I quoted the west's supreme self-styled expert on Islam, Bernard Lewis, as pronouncing: "The very idea of such a grouping ["the Islamic group of states," by which he apparently refers to the Organisation of the Islamic Conference, the OIC], based on religion, in the modern world, has been seen by some outsiders as anachronistic and indeed absurd. It is neither anachronistic nor absurd in relation to Islam."

Now let us word this a little differently. The very idea of stabbing an eighty-two-year-old novelist for an allegedly blasphemous novel has been seen by some outsiders as anachronistic and indeed absurd. It is neither anachronistic nor absurd in relation to Islam. The very idea of divorcing a university professor from his wife on the grounds of his apostasy has been . . . . The very idea of banning Youssef Chahine's *al-Muhager* has been . . . . The very idea of subjecting a doctor to the lash has been . . . . One could go on and on spouting similar statements designed to bring a warm glow to many a western heart and elicit vehement nods of approval from many an Islamist head.

And there is very little comfort in a 'moderate' Islamist telling us, for example, that while 'in relation to Islam' it is right to kill a man for apostasy, it is the state that should do the killing. The statement could be made in countless ways, depending on the speaker's view on what is fundamentally Islamic, but the idea implicit in it remains the same: western people behave and make judgments in accordance with 'rational criteria' that do not apply 'in relation to Islam.'

Pat theories abound and their very presence is in itself sufficient ground to view them with suspicion. Scholars, journalists, politicians, and laymen reiterate the same formulas ad nauseam, and, more striking, they do so from both sides of the supposedly deep gulf separating the Christian secular west from the Muslim east.

Iran's Islamic Revolution ushered in what we may call a meta-theory on modern Islamism that enjoys almost universal acceptance. It goes something like this: following unspecified centuries of deep slumber, the Muslim world was awakened by the storm of European conquest. In Egypt, that awakening shock was ostensibly provided by Napoleon Bonaparte's three-year-long misadventure. We were then hurled into the hands of secularist westernized elites, which embarked on various projects of modernization inspired by and styled upon various western models. Numerous reasons are then given for the failure or stumbling of these projects, be they socialist or capitalist, liberal or authoritarian, but throughout a fundamentally Islamic population remains as it should remain: fundamentally Islamic. Finally, the modern Islamist movement is explained as a sort of return to authenticity, as the rebellion of a fundamentally Islamic population against the alien cultural domination expressed in the rule of westernized secularist elites.

The axiomatic nature of this basic model is, I hope, easily discernible, despite the many variations under which it is presented, despite its almost complete disregard for the facts of modern history. Take, for instance, the fact that millions more Egyptians rose up in support of the Wafd Party in one period of our history and of Gamal Abdel Nasser at another than have as yet shown support for the Muslim Brothers or the Jihad.

Take also the fact that it is the self-same so-called westernized elite that has instituted the revival of Islamic fundamentalism in the country. The social/cultural base of the Muslim Brothers has little or no difference to that of the ruling National Democratic Party or the Wafd, and that of the Gama'a al-Islamiya and Jihad has little or no difference to that of the communists or Nasserists.

Take furthermore that the major bastions of the Muslim Brothers in the country are the professional syndicates and, most prominently, the doctors' and engineers' syndicates—the very professions in which a western education and western professional model are pervasive. As far as I know, there are no disciples of Hassan Fathy among the abundance of Islamist engineers in the country.

But, facts aside. These may be irrelevant 'in relation to Islam.' The biggest con in this model is the claim that we were ever ruled by secularists or ever had a secularist society.

*Al-Ahram Weekly*, August 17, 1995

# OUR CULTURE, OURSELVES

I GREW UP IN AN EGYPT where cultural identity was not an issue. Gamal Abdel Nasser, the heroic leader of pan-Arab nationalism and anti-imperialism, was nicknamed Jimmy by his fellow Free Officers. Egyptian cinema, from the 1920s onward, played a crucial part in molding the psyche of the nation, yet it was Hollywood's baby. What makes an 'authentic' Egyptian identity? Umm Kulthum, Abdel Nasser, *A Thousand and One Nights*, the "Sira Hilaliya," television soap operas, the mulids, Naguib Mahfouz, and Tawfiq al-Hakim, and Yahya Hakki? And where does Mahfouz begin and Balzac end? And can all this and more be reduced to the Qur'an and the tradition of the Prophet, let alone that these, too, are subject to hundreds of highly divergent, continually shifting readings? There is no such thing as an 'authentic' cultural identity; identity is an ever-evolving, ever-changing, ever-mutating composite with no beginning and no end, and it is intimately tied to competing political strategies and choices.

# A Stroll through the Mall

IT WAS DURING A ONE-DAY conference on overseas reporting, held at the University of California's Graduate School of Journalism, that I learned of yet another element of what purports to be my cultural identity. It was an excellent conference, held by an outstanding journalism school, where I had the privilege and pleasure of teaching a course on contemporary Arab political thought to a group of exceedingly bright students earlier this year. But nothing is perfect. A veteran and clearly well-intentioned American journalist was advising the young would-be foreign correspondents on some of the requisites of cultural sensitivity if and when their future careers took them to the Arab/Muslim Middle East: "Everyone you interview will insist on offering you coffee or tea. You must accept; to refuse is considered a grave insult."

I have come across a great many attributes of Arab/Muslim cultural identity over the years. They became especially profuse after 9/11 transformed every Tom, Dick, and Harry (who remain unable to locate "Ay-rak" on the map) into experts on Islam and Muslims. But this one was new to me. The image of caffeine-hyped, antacid-guzzling American journalists with queasy stomachs rushing from one interview to the next obliged me to take pity on those among the young men and women in the audience who might eventually find their way to our part of the world.

I explained that my own experience with interview-seeking foreign correspondents that refuse my offer of coffee or tea is actually relief. Not out of stinginess, I hope, but out of an often futile hope that they will keep it short so that I can get on with my own work.

But if our cultural identity does not lie in taking grave insult at our offers of coffee or tea being refused, or in our failure to understand the "western concept of satire," as an American cartoonist tried to explain to me in the course of a debate on the Danish cartoon fracas, wherein does it lie?

The mall on the outskirts of ever Greater Cairo is not really called the Super Animated Mall, but this name will serve for the purposes of this essay—in avoidance of unintentional libel, no less than inadvertent hidden advertising. The real name is in English, naturally. English has become the lingua franca of sorts for commercial activity in Egypt since President Anwar Sadat launched his Open Door policy in the mid-1970s, restoring Coca-Cola to the masses (the advertising jingle used to boast, "it has returned to us") and providing us with our first hamburger chain (though the dejected British Wimpy has long since given way to its considerably more vigorous American counterparts). When your corner hole-in-the-wall grocer renames his barely surviving family enterprise 'subermarket,' it is difficult to find fault with a super mall for opting for an English name.

The owner of the Super Animated Mall is widely known to be a Muslim Brotherhood entrepreneur (at an investment of LE100 million, possibly middle- rather than top-rung), which might explain its evident popularity with a conspicuously shrouded or hirsute and disproportionately rotund clientele. Spread over a hundred thousand square meters, the architecture of the two-story edifice is vaguely evocative of that of a mosque. This subtle architectural statement is further underlined by the similarly designed, if in miniature, mosque located at one end of the sprawling and perpetually brim-full parking lot attached to the mall.

A giant shopping cart holding an equally gigantic mock package of a famous 'international' detergent stands heroically in front of the mall, presumably providing esthetic flair combined with rather aggressive commercial promotion.

Now, there are malls and there are malls, as we've been learning over the past ten years or so. They come in all shapes and sizes; the generic term seems to cover a whole variety of activities. There are the slick highrise malls—all with multiplexes, brand-name boutiques, department stores, and massive food halls—that have been springing up in the Nasr City suburb, as well as along the northern stretch of the Nile Corniche, the latter hiding from view the endless expanses of slum areas lying behind them. We even had a mall housed in a World Trade Center, including twin (smallish) towers. It went into swift and unexplained decline soon after the destruction of its world-famous namesake, though as far as I know there is no connection between the two events.

The Super Animated Mall, on the other side of the Nile, is of a different sort. Essentially, it is a large supermarket, or what we're being told is a new concept in supermarkets called the 'hypermarket.' These sell everything from giant flat-screen televisions to frozen French fries. Beside this, there are some twenty shops, including two cell phone firms, one marketing a network and the other a cell phone brand. Inevitably, there are a couple of the new Starbucks-style cafés that have been taking the capital city by storm over the past five years (Starbucks itself is yet to make an appearance in Egypt, allegedly for political reasons; the chain apparently prides itself on its extremist pro-Israeli zeal). Then, of course, and as inevitably, there are the usual American fast food chain outlets, the MacDonald's and Hardees, etc.

The Islamist orientation of our particular mall seems to be expressed basically in the fact that on Fridays it will not open its doors for business until after Friday prayers. There is also, if you want, the French-named boutique offering an amazing variety of headscarves for the moderately and fashionably veiled woman. I very much doubt that the French name is intended as a political statement on the banning of the veil in French schools, however. The hypermarket's PA system also blares calls to prayer and the occasional Qur'anic recitation, interspersed by announcements of bargain offers, advertising jingles, and popular songs.

And if you have any doubts as to the robustness of the Egyptian middle class, go to the mall. Almost at any time of day or night, the place is packed with thousands of shoppers. Whole extended families, including dads and moms, rickety grandpas and grandmas, possibly even aunts and uncles, and swarms of little children, from newborn infants to wayward school-age brats, all seem to wonder aimlessly, expressions of open-mouthed awe and sensual gratification on their faces. And there is not a shopping list in sight.

Journalists work highly irregular hours, and I've often found myself dropping into the Super Animated Mall around midnight or after to pick up some item on my way home, only to be amazed at the throngs of extended family shoppers, carts loaded with the latest 'offers' their children guzzling Cokes and munching on pizza slices—and this on a school night.

It took me some time to discover that going to the mall was not a purposeful practical activity but rather a celebration, a cultural pursuit, indeed the paramount cultural pursuit of a great section of our middle class—that and fast food. Not surprisingly, perhaps, fast food home delivery is possibly the most (or is it the only?) efficient commercial activity in the country: order a Big Mac anywhere in the city and half an hour later you'll have a young man (very likely, an out-of-work law school graduate) knocking on your door.

As a metaphor for contemporary Egyptian society, you can read what you like into the Super Animated Mall. For some, it might be reassuring. Egypt under the Muslim Brotherhood will look pretty much the same as it has under Mubarak for the past quarter of a century, only the shops will be closed until after Friday prayers.

Liberal dogmatists who count on the middle class as agents of reform might need to think again. They're too busy shopping to stage an Orange Revolution.

For my own part, I see spiritual impoverishment, the loss of community, and the nonexistence of citizenship. I don't see cultural invasion, but cultural degradation. And yet, we continue to screech about our ever-threatened 'cultural identity.'

*The Daily Star Egypt*, October 10, 2006

# A Terror of Hamburgers

Being a journalist myself, I am fully aware that I make a poor interview subject. I have an irritating habit of thinking while speaking, I hem and haw a lot, and I have never seemed to develop the knack of speaking in bites. All in all, I'm just not very quotable. All of which is a foreign journalist's scourge.

The dissatisfaction, in my experience, has been mutual. A journalist likes to conduct interviews, not give them, and with my weekly column, I often feel that my interviewer would have been best served by taking an appropriate quote from it, thereby saving us both a lot of bother. Moreover, on the few occasions when my interviewer has courteously sent me a copy of the published story, my two-line contribution more often than not appears stunted, abrupt, and banal.

Foreign correspondents and I, therefore, have tended to avoid each other on the whole. But since the free and civilized world's declaration of war on evil, it was statistically inevitable that at least a few of the droves of foreign correspondents and television crews descending on Egypt these days would find their way to my cell, home, or office phone. The referral is almost always through a third person, and almost never a response to my writing. Who has time to read, with deadlines to meet?

So while I have no idea who it was that referred the crew from a big U.S. TV network to me and my cell phone, the poor jetlagged journalist who called was destined, in a few short minutes, to discover that she'd been sorely misdirected.

"We would like to interview you on camera."

"Okay, but not today," I replied with resignation (it was my day off and I had yet to recover from our last issue). That was okay with her, too.

The purpose of the interview, I was told, was to ascertain my feelings regarding the proliferation of American culture in Egypt. Aha, I thought to myself, we are to dig at the roots of Islamist terrorism, speak of cultural invasion, and pontificate about the threat to our cultural, religious, and national identity. This, after all, is why we produce the Ayman al-Zawahiris and Mohamed Attas of the world. In the best traditions of objective journalism, we are about to explain the "seas of people in which the terrorist fish swim."

But then I happen to believe that this whole cultural invasion/cultural identity ruckus is so much stuff and nonsense. I didn't put it that way; the woman was exceedingly polite and friendly, and I felt I had to be as well. It more or less came out in our 10–15 minute phone conversation, however. I like blue jeans, hamburgers (although I'm fully aware that they're bad for you), and Woody Allen films. I consider speaking a second language a privilege rather than a curse, and am envious of those who fluently gab away in three and four (sadly, my attempts at French and Spanish have been hopelessly inadequate). I honestly don't know what 'authentic' Egyptian, Arab, or Islamic culture is supposed to be. Nevertheless, I don't for a moment think of myself as alienated from my society or hopelessly westernized.

I also happen to believe that cultural identity is a dynamic composite creature that is constantly being recreated, and that, like everything else, it is subject to political choice. The diverse cultural components that make up my psyche sit, by and large, very happily together (my self-torment being of an existential rather than a cultural variety), and I'm constantly amazed at how fundamentally similar we all are. There is bad—that is, dehumanizing—culture and there is good culture that brings out the best in us, that helps liberate us, I tried to explain to my prospective interviewer.

She found what I said "very interesting," complimented me by telling me that I seemed "very moderate"—which is probably the worst insult anybody can direct at me—and went on to explain, rather awkwardly, that she'd have to check with her editor. "Umm, we're actually doing background right now . . . ."

Thankfully for both of us, I haven't heard from her since.

*Al-Ahram Weekly*, September 27, 2001

# Friends, Frasier, Flotsam

THE FREE ONE, IN THE feminine form, as in 'the free woman'—though in this case the allusion is to the satellite channel (which is feminine in Arabic)—is the most recent initiative dreamed up by the neocon administration in Washington to trick the American public out of its tax dollars and, much more significantly, intellects, as it fails to con, let alone convince, any of its supposed audience.

It is truly pathetic that the Free One, and its various sisters, Sawa (music radio) and *Hi* magazine, are the best our imperial masters can muster to win our hearts, minds, and consent to be ruled from the White House. Needless to say, we have no control at all over which group of ruffians runs the global show.

Irrespective of the actual intellectual abilities of "the lip," as the leader of the civilized world reportedly nicknamed himself while in high school, we tend to assume that the American system of government is considerably more complex and sophisticated than to be reduced to dependency on the IQ of whichever member of whichever first family is residing in the White House.

Ideology and worldview certainly come into play, if only because ideological blinkers have a way of making otherwise intelligent people appear stupid. But ideology always carries with it the question of how much its proponents actually believe rather than manipulate it as a fundamental instrument of hegemony, or in Orwellian terms, of mind control.

The millions of American tax dollars now being squandered on the Free One and her sisters, the aim being to sell the highly lucrative business of a perpetual "war on terror" to a susceptible, if increasingly dissatisfied, American public, would suggest the latter is in operation.

Ideology, believed in or cynically manipulated, is, after all, the only thing the Free One and her sisters are about. Now they are in the process of starting up another 'free' television channel in Farsi, allegedly to support the reformist trend in Iran.

All this child's play is premised on an equally childish view of the Arab and Muslim world that presumes we 'hate America' because we are mired in a backward culture of hate, one that the Arab media, in alliance with religious fundamentalism, continually reproduces and expands.

The solution, therefore, is simple: Americanize Arabs and Muslims. Show them just how good we are; how superior our civilization, cultural values, and products are to theirs. The world, after all, is a marketplace. All that needs to be done is to break down the barriers to free market activity, smash through or bypass Chinese walls of all sorts, and the shoddy goods of backward culture and civilization will give way before the superior, better packaged, and better marketed products of western, particularly American, culture and civilization.

Not that the neocons have any intention of obliterating Arab and Muslim culture and civilization. A nice mix of imported and indigenous prejudice, ignorance, and feeble-mindedness has always been the ideal formula for keeping the restless masses in line.

I don't buy any of it. Al-Hurra, Sawa, and *Hi* have not been giving me sleepless nights, just yawns of boredom. The ludicrousness of the American cultural invasion (or, if you will, aggressive marketing drive) is equaled only by the ludicrousness of the Arabs' and Muslims' paranoid conviction that a cultural invasion is actually afoot. The whole ideological edifice behind the two mirror-image sets of notions is simply false.

It's not culture, stupid, it's politics.

Seen an Arabic video clip lately? The fact of the matter is that Arab and Muslim societies are already westernized/Americanized in profound ways. Indeed, the past few years—the same years that witnessed a record number of American flag burnings on Arab streets—have seen an amazingly swift Americanization of the Arab world.

In Cairo, *Friends*-inspired Central Perk-style coffeehouses have been proliferating like mushrooms, literally sprouting out of the ground. The American sitcom itself is probably as popular in Arab middle class households as it is in the U.S. And when exactly did Valentine's Day become an

Egyptian national holiday, let alone a Palestinian and pan-Arab one? And what of the dozens of multiplexes that have mushroomed in Cairo and provincial cities in the past few years, showing not only the latest American films but also the new brand of *shababi* (youth) romantic-comedy Egyptian films that have become all the rage over the past couple of years?

And what of the Internet, the ceaseless online chatting and text messaging of our youth, and the satellite dishes that have transformed the skyscapes of Arab cities, and not a few villages, during the past decade?

Westernization in Egypt is at least as old as Napoleon's campaign (1798–1801), while Americanization has been with us for well over a hundred years. Pick any one of the hundreds of Egyptian films produced since the 1920s until today, from the nonsensically awful to the masterpieces of Youssef Chahine, and you'll see Hollywood's shadow looming large.

And what of music, song, dance, theater, and literature? Simply put, not just western culture but also a distinctly American culture are as integral to modern culture in Egypt as they are to the rest of the Arab world.

And just like the American people, we get heaps of garbage and quite a few gems. The other day, al-Hura was showing an excellent documentary feature on the evolution of life on the planet. Earlier on the same day I was reading an article in the *Sunday Times* about Georgia banning the teaching of the theory of evolution in its schools, an article that quoted the U.S. president as having given his learned opinion that "the jury was still out" on evolution.

But besides the odd good documentary, most likely bought from the BBC, al-Hura is astonishingly shabby, as shabby, indeed, as Egyptian television, even if its remarkably inept presenters and anchors have slightly better dress sense than their Egyptian counterparts.

So while I switch the channel, looking for the latest episode of *Frasier*, American readers of this column might want to call their Congressperson and ask for a tax refund.

*Al-Ahram Weekly*, February 26, 2004

# Phantoms of Liberty

A 1969 POEM, A LONG-DEAD poet, and the transcendental space called the World Wide Web. Such an ethereal realm, one would have thought, is out of reach for even the most control-obsessed state bodies. But it isn't.

Last June, Shohdy Surur, *Al-Ahram Weekly*'s extraordinarily talented webmaster was handed a one-year prison sentence, allegedly for publishing—on the web—a poem by his late father, the celebrated 1960s poet and playwright, Naguib Surur. The court found that certain phrases in the poem, known as the "Ummiyyat" (a modified form of the original, vulgar title), were in violation of public morality. Shohdy was released on LE200 bail pending his appeal, which came up for judicial review this week.

The 1969 poem, Surur's reading of which was recorded on tape, was never printed in Egypt, though it eventually appeared in book form in the then-hub of Arab free expression, Beirut. But well before the World Wide Web was a twinkle in Pentagon-attached scientists' eyes, the "Ummiyyat" was making the rounds of the Egyptian leftist intelligentsia and members of the left-led student movement in the form of tapes and handcopied manuscripts. Written in colloquial Egyptian Arabic and using sexual imagery in its most vulgar street form, the poem is a fierce critique of the Nasserist regime and indeed of the left-wing intelligentsia that regime so successfully coopted and from whose ranks Surur himself came. The "Ummiyyat" was the poet's bitter response to the June 1967 defeat, a cry of rage at a regime that had thoroughly (and often with extreme ruthlessness) impounded civil liberties in the name of "the national battle," only to lose that battle resoundingly within the space of a few hours.

The ever-impending war for the liberation of Palestine proved to have been a phantasm whose sole purpose was to keep the 'home front' in line, even as the military rulers of the country were too busy mismanaging, and plundering, the state sector, overseeing sports clubs, and dabbling in the worlds of art and culture. This latter interest was a source of particular chagrin to Surur.

The rage was by no means specific to Surur. It was out there on the street, palpable and indeed—as is the habit in streets the world over—expressed, more often than not, in the most vulgar terms.

Street language, along with a whole range of other aspects of lived culture, including, most notably, sex, has long been the arena of a cat-and-mouse game between artists and the state. Unlike the decadent, licentious west, we pride ourselves on our moral uprightness. This is not to say that the vulgar sexual imagery used by Surur in the "Ummiyyat" is in any way remote; it's out there on the street, at places of work, and, prominently as well as ironically, at police stations, shouted in insult or whispered in the latest joke. You can't escape it. The point, however, is not to acknowledge its existence. This might lead to the wicked suggestion that our cultural superiority to the west is essentially based on hypocrisy.

All of this begs the real question about the case against Shohdy: Why is there a case at all, let alone an appalling one-year prison term? The poet has been dead for a quarter of a century. He was never prosecuted for the poem though it was readily available in print outside the country and, less publicly, within it. Indeed, Naguib Surur has been posthumously honored by the highest cultural bodies of the state, and his plays are regularly produced by state-run theaters. The service provider for the website on which the "Ummiyyat" is posted is in the U.S.; the site, up until the security bodies decided to make it a cause célèbre, had few visitors (after all, it is one of millions); and it is actually next to impossible to prove that it was Shohdy who posted the poem in the first place. Why, then, this war on ghosts?

Two answers come to mind, both of which are telling. The first concerns attempts to control the web by control-obsessed state bodies. This is a dilemma, as unlike some other Arab states that close the tap at the source, Egypt prides itself on its free web access, which is viewed as an essential aspect of economic liberalization, attracting foreign investment, and all the rest of the catching-the-globalization-train imperatives.

But the web is uncontrollable. And what with Internet cafés sprouting all over the country, you don't need to own a computer to access millions of savory and unsavory sites, anything from the Israeli Foreign Ministry to a whole range of militant Islamist groupings to sites similar to the one that the adolescent daughter of a friend of mine shockingly fell upon when she misspelled "hotmail."

Now, what do state bodies that feel responsible for setting the parameters of our ideological and political leanings, religious persuasions, and moral values do? Whatever new high-tech departments these bodies have set up to oversee the web, their mandate seems to be defined by the crime being committed in the Arabic language and/or having an apprehendable culprit.

Then there is the state's attitude toward cultural production and what it deems morality. In a society where politics has all but disappeared, the only thing that seems to remain is a hypocrisy-grounded politics of morality (defined essentially as sexual control), which in its own turn acts to perpetuate the demise of politics. Our region may be on the brink of disaster, our economy is in shambles, we've never been as maligned and humiliated, but, hey, we remain as chaste as the driven snow. The late Naguib Surur, his voice echoing from the grave, begged to differ, rather graphically.

*Al-Ahram Weekly*, August 29, 2002

# A Very Good Likeness

HOW DOES ONE "TARNISH EGYPT'S IMAGE ABROAD"? The curiousness of the statement is belied by its preponderance in our political and intellectual life (there are even laws punishing would-be tarnishers). But even those among us who are most conscious of our national image must admit that it is very curious indeed. For the statement to make any kind of sense we need to assume that 'Egypt' is some sort of giant secret society that communicates in a secret and impenetrable language of its own. Presumably—since we boast day and night of the unprecedented nature of the freedom of expression we've come to enjoy in past decades—we can complain of poverty, corruption, authoritarianism, whatever, but only so long as we keep it *entre nous*, in the family. How do we do this? In sign language? By whispering, so that those 'abroad' won't hear? Only in Arabic? The language can be translated, after all, and not solely by errant Egyptians.

By all rights this should be an urgent question. Citizens should be able to walk the streets secure in the knowledge that they haven't inadvertently tarnished the national image by, say, whipping a donkey or throwing the newspaper wrapping of a *fuul* sandwich onto the pavement; that the act has not been witnessed or, even worse, captured on film by some appalled wanderer from abroad. Indeed, if you talk to many of the image conscious members of the country's elite, the mere sight of many of our citizens is a blot on the consecrated image. Of course, *entre nous*, we're all fully aware of the fact that 'abroad' in this context does not signify India or Zambia but is unanimously understood among us to mean the western world, with the U.S. at its throbbing heart. This is where image-tarnishing

71

is supposed to translate into decline in international and regional status, foreign investment, aid and trade, etc. But does it really? Naturally, the state bureaucracy seems to think so, despite overwhelming evidence to the contrary. Image defense invariably translates into the worst forms of 'image tarnishing.'

The sheer irrationality of the obsession with Egypt's image abroad serves here merely to illustrate a number of interesting aspects of our relationship with the 'west.' Bureaucratic minds work in mysterious and often unfathomable ways, but the fact that the state bureaucracy habitually resorts to such a clearly bizarre notion is surely an indication that the notion enjoys 'hegemonic value.' It must strike some responsive chord among the intellectual elite, and, through it, the people, domestically if not 'abroad.'

It does. In many ways, the prevalent sense of our relationship with the 'west' remains as naive and unrefined as that revealed by al-Gabarti as he tried to take in (with an often wicked sense of irony that we've meanwhile managed to lose) the 'shock' of the Napoleonic conquest over two hundred years ago: the profound sense of inadequacy; awe mixed with envy, fear, and antagonism; and the pathetic comfort derived from the notion that while 'they' can defeat and subjugate us, over and over again, we possess superior 'values,' which, jealously and most hypocritically guarded, make us winners all the same. It is thus that the Iraqi regime can celebrate the anniversary of its victory in the Gulf War (vicious dictatorships are, for some reason, among the supreme expressions of the superiority of our values).

And then we have Muhammad Ali and Ismail, missions and modernization, the drive to catch up, to face up to the challenge of the west, al-Afghani and Muhammad Abduh.

I don't know exactly when the contemporary usage of *hadara* (civilization, and especially urban civilization) evolved. It shouldn't be difficult to find out. But we've become obsessed with it, employing it in an evermore innovative and peculiar syntax. The traffic police exhort us to 'civilized' (that is, European) behavior on the streets. Echoing the official line, your taxi driver, even as he rushes madly through a traffic light, will tell you in no uncertain terms that our traffic problems are caused by the uncivilized behavior of everybody else. *Suluk hadari* (civilized behavior) and *sura hadariya* (presenting a civilized image) are especially important at tourist sites (at some resorts, the police ensures such a 'civilized image' by regularly rounding up 'uncivilized,' read, poor-looking, sorts, which in terms of protecting our 'image abroad' is as self-defeating as arresting Saad Eddin Ibrahim). Anything from a USAID-funded new sewage system to a behind-the-scenes Saddam-Hussein-sponsored attempt to wed revived Islamism to declining pan-Arab nationalism may be described as a *mashru' hadari* (translated inevitably, if clumsily, as 'a civilizational project').

Our image abroad is one side of the picture, the dangers of abroad coming in and wreaking havoc are the other. In both cases we're supposed to be a monolithic, undifferentiated mass. Indeed, it is by presenting a single visage, however hypocritical, to an equally undifferentiated west that we guard against that west coming between us, subverting our cherished values—our last line of defense, since in everything else that counts we've conceded defeat and submission.

We're all kings of our castles, even if, when we go out to work, we grovel at the boss's boots.

*Al-Ahram Weekly*, July 12, 2001

# Fear of Penetration

ONCE UPON A TIME THERE was a school in Maadi. The boys were young gentlemen and the girls were little ladies. But doom was hovering outside the school walls. Our haven of middle class propriety, where the older boys and girls would develop innocently romantic crushes to the tunes of Abdel Halim Hafez, was to be no more. It would be penetrated from without.

As far as I can remember, the destructive incursion comes in the form of three adolescent boys. One—the son of an upstart, up-and-coming businessman whose career began either in Wikalat al-Balah (the scrap metal trade) or Batniya (hashish) but who won a newfound respectability with the Open Door policy—brings drugs and vulgarity to the school. The second boy is a Jew of unknown origin who brings homosexuality (which we have recently discovered is otherwise known as "habitual debauchery with men")* and AIDS to our little piece of earthly paradise. The third assailant is at the gates, so to speak. The son of a *bawwab* or cigarette vendor or some other lowly profession, he stands outside the school inflamed with class hatred for his betters and sexual desire for the unreachable fair-skinned maidens that are their progeny. Sporting the inevitable beard and

---

*    This piece was written in the aftermath of what was known as "the Queen boat case," in which the police, for the usual reasons of distraction and outbidding the Islamists, entrapped and arrested a large number of gay Egyptian men, who were communicating via the Internet. Since there is no law in Egypt criminalizing homosexuality, the men were charged under the law on prostitution, which penalizes "habitual debauchery," in this case "with men."

short white *gallabiya*, the fearsome terrorist-in-the-making winds up raping one of the schoolgirls.

This is pretty much the storyline of the worst Egyptian film I ever saw and, I would hazard, that was ever made. I chanced upon it on television one idle and sleepless night several years ago and stuck to it to the end, held by that strange and masochistic fascination that on other occasions will have me watching CNN's 'Middle East experts' pontificating on the roots of Israeli–Palestinian violence or, for that matter, an Egyptian official digressing on the state of the economy.

My recollection of the film, I admit, is rather hazy. And even for the purposes of this column, I would not expose myself to that kind of punishment twice, so I hope the readers will forgive me if I got some of the details of the story wrong. I do recall, however, that it had a happy ending of sorts. The police, with the help of a patriotic and upright headmistress (or was it headmaster?), clean up the school. The invaders are repelled. As virtue triumphs once again, we are treated to a monstrously sordid scene involving the arrest of one of the schoolboys. Having been seduced by the drugs peddled by the son of the socially mobile Open Door magnate and by the presumably irresistible attraction of the gay Jew, the boy descends to the bottom of an abyss—an example to those who would let down their guard before penetrators of any sort. He contracts AIDS. The audience is supposed to applaud as a boy, condemned to long suffering and an untimely death by what was then an incurably fatal disease, is dragged from his home by a dozen policemen.

The film, as I later learned from industry insider friends, was a flop at the box office. There is also nothing particularly interesting in the fact that it was made by a female director. This merely confirms what Mrs. Thatcher has already made patently clear to the whole world: notwithstanding their alleged Venusian descent, women can be as remorselessly fascistic as the next man. Slipshod, ugly, and a commercial failure to boot: where was the fascination?

The mindset, naturally. I had been exposed, in a highly condensed and especially repugnant form, to a perspective on our contemporary reality that went well beyond bad cinema.

Some years ago, a respectable opposition newspaper carried on its front page what purported to be a news item of great importance to the public. Israel, it had been discovered, was in the process of smuggling into Egypt tons of doctored chewing gum, which, we were told in all seriousness, triggered feelings of intense sexual arousal in young female chewers. The objective behind the pernicious Zionist plan, the newspaper told us, was to undermine the virtue of young Egyptian women, thereby undermining Egyptian manhood, the family, and society as whole, making us easy prey to eventual Israeli invasion. Sure, some newspapers specialize in this kind of rubbish, but how, one has to ask, could the presumably well-educated editors of a major opposition newspaper print this absurd nonsense? Suspending disbelief is clearly not confined to moviegoers.

In a similar vein, we've been regaled with the ever-resurfacing story of AIDS-exporting Israelis or other foreigners who lure our young people into 'habitual debauchery' of various sorts, with the express purpose of destroying their, and the nation's, immunity systems.

Fear of 'foreign penetration' is not confined to sensationalist rubbish, however. Observe, for instance, much of the anti-normalization discourse prevalent today. Why, I have often asked, are Egyptian intellectuals content to reduce what could be developed into a fairly effective popular boycott movement to the largely passive posture of not themselves meeting with Israelis? Why, indeed, do we take such pride in merely refraining from meeting the odd Israeli who shows up in Cairo, or whom we might come across in an international forum outside the country? Where is the heroism in it? I fail to see from what Israelis (intellectuals or otherwise) derive this apparently irresistible pull, resistance to which is the source of such high self-regard. It is again a question of virtue rather than politics. The Israelis, apparently, are hell-bent upon 'penetrating' the Egyptian intelligentsia.

Ultimately, we need to remind ourselves that moral courage, dignity, fortitude, and other traditional attributes of manhood are essentially functions of the *mind*.

*Al-Ahram Weekly*, July 26, 2001

# Variations on a Theme

"Show us your tattoo," order the heavily made-up, impeccably chic female television presenter and her soberly suited, well-coiffed, smug male counterpart. The young prisoner, head shaven by, I strongly suspect, an agency other than his own or, for that matter, the Devil's, docilely complies, taking off his shirt and presenting a tattooed upper arm to his TV interrogators and their camera. Her face pinched in appropriate disapproval, the chic presenter admonishes, "Don't you know that you are violating God's ordinances by disfiguring His creation in this way?"

The young man, who could have pointed out to his inquisitor that there are those in Egypt and outside it who would consider her make-up and dress a much more serious violation of what God has ordained, did not do so, however. While obviously baffled by the charge of "Devil worshiping"—his two TV inquisitors seemed barely able to refrain from putting him to tests of water and fire to prove his innocence—he was more than willing to concede having sinned on this and practically every other count.

Self-styled arbiters of God's laws as interpreted by Egyptian officialdom, and more specifically Egyptian state television, the two inquisitors were thrown into total confusion when the young prisoner insisted that not just 'heavy metal,' which the Egyptian media and security bodies have uncovered as a fiendish plot to corrupt our youth and send them 'head-banging' into the arms of Satan, but *all* music is sinful.

In fact, the repentant youth said, anything that diverts a person from invoking the name of God is sinful. "Who told you this?" the two TV authorities said in unison. "The sheikhs," answered the young man after some hesitation. Torn between their initial response of firmly denying 'such nonsense'—after all, their mega-organization has been damned in countless Friday sermons over the past twenty years as a principal source of sinfulness, licentiousness, and immorality—and, I suspect, the dawning recognition that 'the sheikhs' in question may have been the very same sheikhs whom the Interior Ministry had brought in to lecture the kids in prison, the two presenters presented a comic sight.

Indeed, one of the main features of the crisis of ideological hegemony during the past two decades has been the inability of the state to demarcate between 'official' and 'unofficial' religious discourse.

Official or 'state' sheikhs, with the full paraphernalia of prime-time television and radio programs, newspaper columns, Friday sermons to tens of thousands at prominent mosques, lectures to 'deviant' Islamists in prison, widely distributed tapes, etc., have been turning with a fair degree of regularity into 'unofficial' sheikhs, stripped of the trappings of officialdom and, on occasion, consigned themselves to prison. One such 'state' sheikh had been renowned for his anti-Coptic harangues, until *Rose al-Youssef* weekly magazine published extracts from his taped sermons. Eventually, this official sheikh turned unofficial and was banned from TV and later from the large Cairo mosque where he used to deliver Friday sermons to huge crowds.

The star sheikh and others like him, many of whom are neither stars nor sheikhs but are all similarly fat with the cream of this and other lands, have for years been setting the stage for the kind of brutal and senseless massacres that the desperate, fanatical, and destitute Islamist militants of Upper Egypt have been committing against equally destitute Copts over the past few years. According to Egyptian human rights groups, last week's massacre in Abu Qurqas brings the number of innocent Copts senselessly murdered by Islamists since 1992 to over a hundred.

This is not then an 'aberration' that can be shrugged off merely as the work of 'foreign' states and bodies, out to subvert 'Egypt's role.' The muted coverage by the bulk of the media of last week's massacre will not undo the fact that it took place. It merely gives the impression that, in the eyes of much of the media, Egyptian lives are cheap, while fostering the climate that gave rise to this and previous massacres. There is, indeed, something eminently absurd and short-sighted about a nation dealing with its fundamental problems with an eye on the foreign tourist market, on the next tourism season.

In this space last week I wrote that hypocrisy often takes the form of 'public secrets' and blood lust, which are the twin symptoms of a crisis of ideological hegemony. I had no idea that this argument would be illustrated so soon, and to such devastating effect.

*Al-Ahram Weekly*, February 20, 1997

# It Does Turn

THE EARTH IS ROUND, it is not the center of the universe, and 'it turns.' The grand mufti of Saudi Arabia, as late as the mid-1970s, issued a fatwa that in accordance with Islam the earth was flat, that the advocates of its roundness were western atheists and secularists who wanted to destroy Islam and other revealed religions, and that for a Muslim to adopt this idea was to fall prey to blasphemy and apostasy.

I must confess that I have not been following the ideas of the Saudi mufti on the earth's shape, or anything else for that matter, and they may have changed since the 1970s. He was back in the news more recently, however, when he issued a fatwa that it was not contrary to Islam for Muslims to visit Jerusalem while it is under Israeli occupation.

Now, fatwas, be they in the realm of science, politics, or anything else, are by definition based on the Qur'an and the Prophet's sayings, Hadith. A fatwa is supposed to determine the position of Islam, and hence of God, on a certain subject. And fatwas may cover anything. We are told by the self-appointed spokesmen for Islam, and hence for God, that unlike the alleged origins of secularism in the Christian west lying in "render unto Caesar," Islam is *din wa dunya*, religion and everyday life. This, notwithstanding the highly familiar ring, in Christian/western terms, of religious rulings on the earth's position in the universe.

As it happens, I find myself in disagreement with the two above-mentioned rulings of the Saudi mufti, not on religious but, respectively, on scientific and political grounds, in both cases determined by what I believe to be the application of reason and experience.

The new *hisba* law, passed by parliament nearly two weeks ago in an apparent bid to halt the wave of so-called *hisba* cases against writers, journalists, and artists, establishes in its explanatory note that "every Muslim has the right to alert a judge, informing him that an encroachment has taken place against the right of God Almighty, or against those rights in which His right prevails, and to testify before him as to the occurrence of this encroachment, in order to take opportunity measures to correct it, once it is proven."

So, in what has become standard style, the government set out to foil the Islamists' hoisting of a particular banner by legitimizing it, subject to government controls. In this case, we are supposed to be thankful that petro-Islamists such as a certain Cairo University professor or a certain uniquely turbaned Maadi sheikh cannot take their accusations of blasphemy and apostasy directly to court. They first have to submit them to the state prosecution authorities, which decide to press charges or not.

The real question, however, is wherein does God's right lie? A citizen's right to appeal to the judiciary is demarcated by the law of the land. For instance, Egyptian law prohibits torture, so presumably a citizen has the right to initiate legal proceedings against persons who commit this transgression. Indeed, insofar as religious values guide people, and their parliamentary representatives, in drawing up legislation, such a law is well and truly in the spirit of religion.

But what about the earth's shape? Religious texts, in Christianity as in Islam, may be and have been read to indicate that the earth is flat, stationary, and lies at the center of the universe. Would the advocacy of an alternative 'theory' such as that the earth is, more or less, round in shape, turns around the sun, revolves upon its own axis, and is a member of a tiny galaxy in a limitless and centerless universe be tantamount to an encroachment on God's right?

True, most sane prosecutors—and one must assume the sanity of the prosecution authorities—will not initiate proceedings to divorce a teacher from his wife for telling his class that the earth is round. This, despite the fact that no less a religious authority than the mufti of the home of the two holiest shrines in Islam deems it otherwise. But why are the 'rulings' of our own myriad of religious authorities, self-styled or official, on any subject in science, politics, culture, whatever, any less questionable than those of the Saudi mufti? And in the absence of laws defining it, what prosecutor or judge is entitled to tell the rest of us wherein lies God's right?

*Al-Ahram Weekly*, February 8, 1996

# Dear Old Golden Rule Days

YEAR ONE OF THE NEW millennium has begun and, as the end of a year evokes reflection on the past, the beginning of a new one behooves contemplation of what the future may hold. Having spent the morning of January 1, 2001, helping my nine-year-old son revise his first term Arabic curriculum, my thoughts on Egypt's future would have been grim indeed had it not been for my belief in the indomitable rebelliousness of the human spirit and intellect—a belief my own little boy has been corroborating raucously for the past nine years.

My sense of foreboding was not, however, triggered by the timing of the midterm exams, which had most parents of schoolchildren howling. What I find truly frightening is the content of the curriculum itself, and this at a time when we are told constantly of the great strides being taken in educational reform. Reports that efforts to upgrade the curriculum have been receiving American funding as well as expert intervention have, indeed, triggered dire warnings of an American conspiracy to subvert our culture and traditional values. Admittedly, I have not made a study of educational reform in this country and, in any case, cries of conspiracies to undermine our traditional values tend to leave me cold. Judging from the third-grade Arabic language curriculum, however, I can only conclude that either the reform process (with or without the benefit of American conspiracies) has yet to reach that particular rung of our educational ladder or, if it has, that the object of the reform (conspiratorial or not) is to make cretins of our children and docile imbeciles of our 'leaders of the future.'

As to values, my son's Arabic-language textbook (glaringly mistitled *Read and Think*) highlights these in each chapter under the heading, "What do we learn in this lesson?" Thus, we are supposed to have learned such things as "the love of Egypt," "the upholding of noble traditions and values," and so on. As far as I could tell, the one "traditional value" that the textbook seems to uphold most consistently, if implicitly, is hypocrisy.

I have often wondered, while trying to interest my son in some children's program on Egyptian television, whether the producers'/presenters' assumption that they are addressing mindless idiots is based on their own experience of childhood or of their having totally expunged that experience from their memories. The curriculum designers and textbook authors seem to belong to the same school of thought. They cannot actually imagine that such inordinately dull, badly written, awfully illustrated, and poorly designed material will convince, or rather indoctrinate (as the obvious intention is), the children it addresses. An Egyptian learns, practically at his mother's breast, that while it may be judicious to repeat such 'official lines' to those who expect them, one does not have to do so with even the slightest conviction. The inescapable conclusion, then, is that the designers'/authors' effort, like that of their TV counterparts, is actually aimed at their superiors, not the children.

The real danger, however, is not to our children's intelligence, as they thankfully manage to find other sources for their intellectual development than the school system. What is under threat is our culture and language. At a time when the Internet, satellite television, and 'language schools' are becoming more and more pervasive, and with a job market that makes an even superficial knowledge of English the dividing line between the employable and unemployable, the educational system has united with Egyptian television literally to drive our children away from their cultural and linguistic heritage. Perhaps we should keep this in mind when we wail "cultural invasion."

Interestingly, the hidden hand of USAID and its ilk can still be detected in the third-grade Arabic language curriculum, not through westernization but via the Education Ministry's version of that golden synthesis our intellectuals have been advocating for the past two decades between tradition and modernity. Why anyone should believe that three chapters devoted to the Ministry of Social Affairs' Productive Families Project should be of educational interest to anybody, let alone third-grade schoolchildren, is beyond my comprehension. The real lesson behind the lessons, however, is child labor, gradually introduced as household labor in the three "productive families" chapters, as well as in a chapter on Egypt's various "habitats," it is forced down the children's throats in the story of "Sharara and the Chain."

Sharara is an impoverished little boy who (rather peculiarly) steals a chain from an ironmonger's workshop. The chain is hot from the smelter and burns the boy's hand, and the boy is then caught by the workshop owner. The latter, out of the goodness of his heart, decides not to report Sharara to the police, dresses his burns, and advises him to seek a job at a workshop. Sharara, repentant, takes the advice and grows up to become the owner of a workshop, where we might expect him to employ other small children. The free market moral is duly validated by an appropriate saying of the Prophet, in the same way that Qur'anic verses and the Prophet's sayings were drawn upon during my own school days to validate Arab socialism.

It is not cultural invasion we need to fear, but the debasement of all culture.

*Al-Ahram Weekly*, January 4, 2001

# A Day at the Museum

THE EGYPTIAN MUSEUM CAME UP with a wonderful idea some years ago. It launched a summer art class for children on the museum's premises. The children would be taken on a tour of a particular wing of the museum, helped to appreciate the ancient Egyptian artifacts on exhibit, given a bit of the history of these artifacts, all of which they would then use in class (set up in a room in the museum's basement) as inspiration for a variety of art projects, including drawing, sculpting, and so on. The idea was brilliant in conception, even if somewhat disappointing in execution.

Finally, there was an initiative designed to connect Egyptian children to their magnificent ancient heritage in an interactive, stimulating manner that transcends the crudely propagandistic and dreary rote learning methods through which ancient Egypt (and pretty much everything else) is introduced to our children in the school system. As soon as I found out about the program, I enrolled my son, Hossam, then around ten years of age.

Constructed in 1900, the neoclassical building of the Egyptian Museum, which to this day houses the largest collection of ancient Egyptian antiquities anywhere, is situated in what urban development has transformed into the very heart of Cairo, the chaotic and ever-transmutating Tahrir Square.

Surrounded by two Hilton hotels, standing a short stretch away from the headquarters of the Arab League, besieged by sprawling roads and flyovers, and designed piecemeal to ease the endless flow of motorized vehicles, inhibit street demonstrations, and kill all but the most nimble pedestrians, Tahrir Square makes access to the museum a Herculean task, with all the dangers to life and limb associated with such. A bad situation was made worse by a wave of militant Islamist terrorism in the 1990s that, by targeting foreign tourism, helped transform five-star hotels throughout the country into virtual police barracks, and particularly by a 1997 attack that set the museum itself as a potentially high-order target, what with its being top-full of heathen idols from the ancient past as well as infidel tourists from the contemporary present.

Subtlety is not among the more identifiable traits of the Egyptian security bodies. Indeed, their domestic "war on terror" must have served as a template for George W. Bush's global effort launched a decade later.

Last week, an Egyptian citizen, Amgad Hussein, was stripped, tortured, and sexually abused at a police checkpoint while traveling with his family to South Sinai, the country's most up-and-coming foreign tourist destination and hence a newfound target for terrorist attacks. According to press reports, the State Security Investigations department had learned that al-Qa'ida terrorists (who we've been assured repeatedly do not exist in the country) were planning a bomb attack on tourist resorts in South Sinai using a laptop. Hussein had a laptop that was only a laptop in his possession.

In the minds of Egyptian officialdom, the Egyptian Museum and South Sinai are abstracted from their concrete forms: beach resorts and stuffy corridors full of mislabeled treasures translate into identical dollar signs. And these are to be protected at all costs.

The street before the Egyptian Museum is closed to all traffic save licensed tourist buses. Egyptian pedestrians are belligerently asked to state their business—and, more often than not, to produce identification—merely for venturing onto the street. Yet, undaunted and filled with enthusiasm on that memorable day five years ago, I nevertheless negotiated the harrowing process of finding parking, taking my boy by the hand, and hazarding the street crossings, climbing onto and off of the privatized, ever-mounting sidewalks that must have contributed to making Egypt's disabled the top champions of the Paralympics. With great steadfastness, I calmly negotiated also the humiliating exercise of an Egyptian citizen having to gain police permission to walk onto a public Egyptian street. Until, with now a thoroughly exhausted and dispirited child in tow, I arrived at the gate of the museum. "Where are you going?" the policeman standing at the gate blandly asked me. It was the last straw.

The realization suddenly hit me that Egyptians did not belong in the Egyptian Museum. This was not the great home of our ancient heritage but a bazaar for foreign tourists, merely a large and rambling stall of curios that foreigners, in their strange way, like to spend money on, which will eventually spin off and spill over into our pockets, each according to how much he can grab. An Egyptian going into the Egyptian Museum is either a crazed terrorist wanting to blow it sky-high or some depraved, sexually starved lout wanting to ogle and/or hit on miniskirted foreign women. Both of which are presumably alien to our five-thousand-year-old civilization, so jealously safeguarded by our ever-vigilant police force, for the sake of our 'image abroad' and even more foreign tourists.

*The Daily Star Egypt*, September 11, 2006

# Within These Walls

WILL ALL MEMBERS OF THE 'yellow press' please stand up? Having followed the 'yellow journalism' uproar of the past few weeks, much of which took place on the pages of newspapers and magazines both as reports and as commentary, I find myself at a loss to understand what the term is supposed to designate. Basically, we seem to be left with the single option of waiting for the presumed culprits to stand up and make a clean breast of it all.

True, one Cyprus-licensed newspaper, the weekly *al-Dustur*, has been shut down, and Adel Hammouda, the deputy editor of national weekly magazine *Rose al-Youssef*, was transferred from his post but welcomed as a staff writer at *al-Ahram*. Another Cyprus-licensed newspaper, the biweekly English-language *Cairo Times* had one of its issues banned; a number of newspapers and editors are reportedly under investigation by either the Supreme Press Council or the Press Syndicate; and three journalists are in prison, 'incidentally,' as the libel law under which they were sentenced predates the whole 'yellow journalism' outcry by decades. Meanwhile, the Press Syndicate has vowed to enforce its long-dormant code of ethics.

It is difficult to perceive any 'system' in all this, however, other than the creation of an overall climate of fear and intolerance of press freedom. The difficulty is compounded once these disparate 'measures' are contrasted with the recent outpouring of statements and commentaries on 'yellow journalism.' *Rose al-Youssef* has been exonerated from the stigma, and its writers have been at pains to exculpate not only their magazine but also the defunct *al-Dustur*, which is just as well since by all rights *al-Dustur* was, more or less, a broadsheet version of *Rose al-Youssef*. One of the earliest and fiercest denunciations of 'yellow journalism' was a full-page article written by the editor of *al-Usbu'*, which, at least to my mind, was a latter-day, if decidedly less liberal, version of *al-Dustur*. Unlike *al-Dustur*, however, *al-Usbu'* had the benefit of a rare Supreme Press Council license.

To make matters even more confusing, the chief editor of *Rose al-Youssef* has attributed the closure of *al-Dustur* and the transfer of Adel Hammouda to a plot to discredit information minister Safwat al-Sherif. To all this we might add the barrage of whispered allegations that a certain entrepreneur (whose identity varies widely in different versions of the story) planted the alleged statement that al-Gama'a al-Islamiya was warning three top Coptic businessmen to leave the country or be killed. It was the publication of this statement by *al-Dustur*, and later by *Rose al-Youssef*, that triggered the 'yellow journalism' outcry.

More and more, then, 'yellow journalism' appears as a phantom that is haunting us all but remains elusive and intangible. Can the whole fuss have been about a few, largely unknown Cyprus-licensed newspapers of almost negligible circulation, which, moreover, have not been banned?

Yet, incidentally or not, three journalists are in prison for libel offenses, with more to come if the number of cases currently in the courts is anything to go by. *Al-Dustur* may have been as white as the driven snow, but it has been closed down. Journalism is beset by a climate of fear from within and intolerance from without. These are all tangibles. As elusive as it seems to be, the phantom of 'yellow journalism' is exacting a heavy price.

It is also impossible to hold a serious and healthy debate on journalistic ethics under these conditions. As I wrote last week, thousands of Egyptian citizens—although not businessmen, officials, or the increasingly prevalent combination of the two—are libeled every year on the strength of police statements. This is but one of the many problems raised by a discussion of journalistic ethics, one which, moreover, has been neglected by the bulk of the discussion of 'yellow journalism.'

The fact remains, however, that for such a discussion to be at all fruitful, more than finger-pointing and protestations of innocence, it needs to be conducted in a non-coercive climate. Journalists cannot be asked to take a critical look at themselves in the shadow of a prison wall.

*Al-Ahram Weekly*, April 2, 1998

# Relatively Dead

THE CURRENT EGYPTIAN DEBATE ON the definition of death is interesting. The Egyptian Doctors' Syndicate, notwithstanding its strong Islamist penchant (dominated as it has been for over a decade by the Muslim Brotherhood), is advocating a definition based on 'clinical death,' that is, that a person is considered dead once his/her brain stops functioning even though the heart may be still beating with the benefit of life-support systems. As I understand it, such an 'enlightened' definition is absolutely necessary for virtually all organ transplant operations from 'dead' donors—heart, liver, and so on.

The al-Azhar Islamic Research Academy, the mufti of the republic, and the ruling National Democratic Party's parliamentary speaker, Fathi Sorour, as well as other prominent members of the country's officialdom have all come out in fierce condemnation. For them, the concept of 'clinical death' is a blatant violation of the rulings of Islamic law, and hence of our religious beliefs, traditions, and heritage. The speaker of parliament went so far as to pledge that a draft law defining death clinically would never be passed so long as he remained in parliament—over his dead body, so to speak.

In defending their position, the doctors cited the case of Saudi Arabia, where they claim the law upholds a 'clinical death' definition. One is probably safe in assuming that the Saudi mufti, who until the late 1970s was convinced that the earth was flat and that the 'theory' suggesting it was round ran counter to Islamic tenets, had sanctioned such a scientifically enlightened definition of death.

Of course, Egyptians have for many years been going to Europe, the U.S., and elsewhere for the kind of transplant surgery that presupposes the existence of legislation upholding a 'clinical death' definition. And since this is exorbitantly expensive surgery, only the very rich or those benefiting from a state subsidy can even contemplate resorting to it. Both the opponents of the 'clinical death' definition and its advocates are, no doubt, well aware of this. I would moreover venture to suggest that it would not even occur to the bulk of the opponents to refrain from recourse to such surgery abroad should the need, God forbid, arise.

For the Egyptian medical profession, the great sums spent abroad are a waste of money that could be better spent at home, providing even more prosperity to our five-star hospitals, top surgeons, and doctors, as well as a host of other medical staff, who will certainly stand to gain from the 'trickle-down effect' within the profession. Such a consideration, however, is not a high priority among the powerful opponents of the 'clinical death' definition, who, moreover, can feel safe in the knowledge that medical centers throughout the advanced world are an air ticket away should they or their loved ones need their services in this contentious area of medical intervention.

And since the great majority of the Egyptian people are, in any case, bystanders to the whole controversy, with the concept of access to organ transplant surgery being beyond their imagination, whether at home or abroad, the affair is interesting mostly insofar as it reveals, once again, the great malleability of 'religious heritage'—that, ultimately, it is intensely secular and contemporary considerations of wealth and power, and the exciting ways in which they tend to combine, that determine the various 'readings' of religious doctrine, law, and tradition.

*Al-Ahram Weekly*, June 12, 1997

# A More Human Man

Two MONTHS AGO MY FATHER, Ibrahim Shukrallah, went into a coma from which he did not awaken. Around midnight on September 28, having returned home after several weeks in hospital that same day, he finally gave up the struggle with death that lasted more than two and a half years.

For thirty-two months, one of the most dynamic and vital men I have ever known was forced into inactivity and silence. A stroke took away all movement from the left side of his body, but, most horrible of all, it took away his speech, and with it his ability to read and write. The doctors called it 'global aphasia,' but beyond the mumbo jumbo that seems to account for a great part of modern medicine, the term apparently denoted little, if anything at all, beyond what was easily observable.

He continued to recognize his family and friends; his face would light up when an old and dear friend came to see him. He laughed heartily at the antics of his grandchildren. But how much did his fits of crying, the countless hours of depressed silence, denote a realization of the extent of his captivity?

I would like to believe that people can sometimes exercise a measure of control over their ultimate meeting with death. And in the case of my father, I would like to believe that for two and a half years he held on, bore the enormous suffering as an act of love—for his wife, children, grandchildren. By the time he went into his final and unexplained coma he could bear no more, even for love—no one could.

He died on the night of September 28, 1995, the same date on which Gamal Abdel Nasser died twenty-five years before, and on which, in

1961, Egyptian–Syrian unity collapsed—"a day of failed dreams." This was also the day he come back home after a month and a half of hospitalization, a day that was exceptionally free of the reparatory cries that were a feature of his weeks in hospital, and which always brought doctors and nurses scurrying to his bedside with their well-intentioned but horrifyingly intrusive equipment and 'life-saving' interventions. He spent an especially calm day at home. Close to midnight, he fell into what initially seemed a deep sleep. Without crisis, without fighting for breath, he just stopped breathing.

His poetry has already given him a claim to posterity. How much of a claim is yet to be determined. In his lifetime, recognition came very late: a special issue of *al-Qahira* literary magazine on his poetry and other literary work came out after his stroke. And other recognition has been forthcoming since his death. His production was too sparse, his poetic vision possibly too revolutionary, and it remains to be seen how much of a stamp he will ultimately leave on Arabic poetry.

All this I leave to his fellow poets and critics to settle. Save for lay appreciation, my father's literary talents unfortunately passed this generation of his offspring completely by. My concern here is not with his current or future claims to renown but with qualities and values that were rare in his time, and are becoming virtually extinct in ours. In my forty-five years, I have known very few persons who were as alive as my father was; yet today's obsession with closed and exclusive cultural and ethnic identity makes of him a virtual chimera, disavows him more than actual death ever could.

He did live, however—a very tangible and a very full life. And the fact of his having lived is testimony to the pernicious fallacies of the bulk of today's conventional wisdom. A multiplicity of 'identities' and cultures sat comfortably within him, with never a sense of his having to conform to one at the expense of the others.

Born in 'respectable poverty' into an Alexandrine Coptic family on one of the lower rungs of the middle class ladder, he was very much the urban Egyptian, the *ibn al-balad* (son of the soil). He loved colloquial Egyptian and in 1956 wrote an article celebrating its, then recent, admission—mainly at Salah Jahin's hands—as a 'proper' language of poetry. His wit and sense of irony were equally a testimony to this aspect of his heritage.

Yet, a very strong sense of his Egyptianness did not conflict with a lifelong commitment to pan-Arabism and to the dream of Arab liberation and unity. It was the Palestinian cause—which he embraced with encyclopedic knowledge of Palestinian history and a passionate empathy with the Palestinian people—that was the focus of his pan-Arabism, however. And it was the Palestinian cause that provided the purpose and direction for his career in the Arab League.

One of the founders of the Arab League Secretariat, he was nevertheless not a little cynical about the organization and the regimes that comprise it. It was, however, a platform that could be used to defend and advocate the cause of the Palestinian people, and to this he devoted the best part of his life. Camp David came upon us, the Arab League split, one part in Tunis and an Egyptian skeleton in Cairo, and he left.

He never lectured or tried to indoctrinate his children. Save for a mutually embarrassing occasion on which he tried to explain to me the proverbial 'facts of life'—an explanation that, as is usually the case, came somewhat late—I do not recall him ever lecturing me or my brother and sister on any subject. Nevertheless, we were, and remain, a uniquely like-minded family.

One of his most amazing qualities was a phenomenal reading speed, and he used it to the full. He read interminably, and always seemed to sweep through books. At a time when it is becoming increasingly rare to find an Arab who speaks and writes classical Arabic well, his mastery of both Arabic and English seems doubly amazing. He wrote beautifully in the two languages and was an outstanding public speaker and orator in both. He hated ornamentation and pretense, however, and spoke classical Arabic with an Egyptian inflection, and the accentless English of the non-native speaker.

He took pride in his Coptic heritage, yet he studied Islam deeply and thoroughly, writing an extensive study on the Sufi tradition. As head of the Arab League mission to India, he often attended Indian Muslim functions, never hesitating to join his hosts in communal prayer. He was fiercely anti-imperialist, yet he loved the English language and literature with a rare passion. He was committed to the Palestinian cause, yet one of his first acts when he took over Arab League missions abroad was to show the door to the anti-Semitic and neo-Nazi hangers-on whom other Arab officials had considered allies.

Within him one could find the influences of Jesus and Muhammad, as of Marx and Freud. Images from *A Thousand and One Nights* and the "Sira Hilaliya" mingled in his imagination with those from the Hindu

Mahabharata and the *Canterbury Tales*. Shakespeare and Eliot found pride of place alongside al-Nafazawi and Taha Hussein.

A multiplicity of 'identities' and cultures sat comfortably within him, not fully synthesized perhaps, but for all that he was a better, a richer, a more human man.

*Al-Ahram Weekly*, October 19, 1995

# The Seeds of Magic

WERE A PASSION FOR LIFE a factor in determining longevity, then cinema director Radwan el-Kashef, a lifelong friend, would have outlived us all. He did not, and the attempt to recapture Radwan, to keep him alive in my mind's eye, is at once a comfort and torment. The image of his face—broad receding brow, Semitic nose, intelligent, slightly protruding eyes, their unlikely green ever-shining in laughter as in anger—brings warmth, but the mind balks at its own attempt at acceptance. Memories will not do.

What of the days, months, years to come? What of the many films that are yet to be made, the shared triumphs, and defeats, the many stories that are to be told and retold, the political discussions that, within our old circle of friends, often descended into riotous shouting matches, but ultimately enriched us? And what of the laughter? Radwan, the ultimate storyteller, gave to his many friends the gift of laughter, at themselves, at their lives and reality, at one another, and at himself. Radwan's quip of the moment would swiftly make the rounds of our circle of friends, to be told and retold. Not that he would shy from repeating it himself. Having hit upon a good "*effets*," as he called them, he would peer from beneath heavy eyelids, eyes gleaming wickedly. "A good one, eh?" he would ask, and go on to repeat it to as many of his many close friends as possible.

Thus it happened that the many events, petty or formative, happy or sad, that made up our daily lives would take on new meaning, assume an element of drama and hilarity once subjected to the Radwan *effet*. They would become stories.

In the recounting, a Radwan stroll along the Nile is easily transformed into drama, sometimes too incredible to believe: a naked man walking down Shubra Street in mid-afternoon without anyone so much as commenting on the fact; or a man walking along the Nile Corniche in Zamalek with an ostrich under his arm; or even more incredible, the stories of how a *Sa'idi* (man from Upper Egypt) traveling third class would have his relatives hurl him onto the train through a window, and how one man spent the train ride between Sohag and Asyut standing on his head, held in place by the squashed mass of human bodies. We would harangue him about his all-too-fertile imagination. His standard response: "You don't look; I do."

Whether he really did see a man carrying an ostrich in Zamalek or a fellow *Sa'idi* traveling on his head we'll never know, but Radwan did look, and listen. People, friends he had known all his life, strangers he would be unlikely to ever meet again, were a source of endless fascination. There was no hello at the other end of the line when you received a phone call from Radwan, rather "Eh, what's the news?" The question was never rhetorical.

But there will be no more phone calls from Radwan.

Memories offer little solace, yet they keep coming. The January 1972 student uprising had just shaken the country—the time for great changes had come (or so we thought). A small-bodied young man, all nose and heavy eyeglasses, even then slightly balding, makes his occasional appearance on campus. He is not yet in university, but is pulled there by the 'movement.' Radwan is from Manial al-Roda, a middle-to-lower middle class island in southern Cairo. The 'Manial group' vouch for him. For some reason he singles me out. It was a time of relentless political discussions, readings, debates, and, always, activism. Trying to make up his mind among the different tendencies within the self-styled 'radical left,' the intensely curious Radwan would, almost slyly, arrange it so that the main protagonists would debate their positions before him.

A few months and he's in Cairo University, a classmate of my sister, Hala, at the Faculty of Arts, a short stretch away from my own Faculty of Economics and Political Science—the twin 'hotbeds' of left-wing activism on the main campus. I can see it now: the Faculty of Arts 'press corridor,' covered with wall newspapers. Radwan's contribution is distinct in being wholly alien to the agit-prop format of that peculiar medium, which despite, or because of, its very rudimentary technology was for a time instigating a communications revolution of sorts in the country. Radwan, however, specializes in extremely long analytical pieces, written in small print, which, I would jokingly berate him, make me his sole reader.

Memories come through as images: small Radwan and even smaller Hala, standing defiantly in defense of the wall newspapers before two giants—muscular, martial arts-trained police agents posing as concerned students. The inevitable scuffle begins, Radwan's eyeglasses fly through the air, followed by Radwan himself; Hala, only partially protected by her gender, shouts at one of the police agents the unlikely warning that she will 'squash [him] like a bug'; the more athletic Samir leaps in with a well-aimed punch at the police agent's jaw; dozens of wall newspapers are torn to shreds.

And then, the moments of triumph: tens of thousands of students attending rallies, occupations, demonstrations on campus; demonstrators rushing out onto the streets; confrontations with the riot police; young people in their early twenties, determined to change the face of the country and the world. And, naturally, the arrests, the going into hiding, the 'safe houses'—furnished apartments or rooms, hired with false IDs—the remembrance of which would in years to come provide innumerable anecdotes and much hilarity.

And somehow, through it all, a whole life was being shared as intensely as it was being created. Again, memories translate into images. A day trip to al-Qanatir: sixteen-year-old Azza, who is to become Radwan's lifelong partner and the mother of his two children, makes her entrance into our lives. We jokingly berate Radwan for being a 'cradle robber.' Evenings spent at the very tip of Roda Island, in the garden of the Manasterly Palace, sipping cold Stella beer, gazing at the Nile and, always, talking. Snatched excursions to Alexandria, where the boys and girls surreptitiously defy convention by spending the night under one roof. Radwan's dimly lit parental home in Manial, family members lined up in a narrow corridor before an ancient black-and-white television that gives shadows instead of a picture and that Radwan will replace, years later, with his first earnings. The inevitable *tabikh* (rice, meat, and stewed vegetables) that is insistently offered to Radwan's friends even on the briefest of visits. The hilarious luncheon that saw two ducks Radwan brought all the way from his Upper Egyptian village cooked *à l'orange* by my mother, to Radwan's utter mortification.

Radwan and Azza's wedding party, boycotted by his family, is held in her family home, a small apartment in the same Roda building where his own family lives. We need a suit that will fit the bridegroom. We hit upon one belonging to my brother, Alaa, bought at a C&A sale in London a few years before for another wedding. The trousers and cuffs are shortened slightly. Azza, in her white wedding dress, looks like a fairy-tale princess.

Memories of Radwan invariably slip into recollections of Radwan's stories, the stories always generating a world of images. I visited Radwan's village of Kom Ishgaw, near Sohag, twice, once on the occasion of the death of his younger brother (some ten years ago) and then when we accompanied him on his final journey home last week. Both times I was struck by the instant recognition. Through innumerable stories of the *Sa'id*, Radwan had brought his home village alive in the imaginations of his friends, at once humdrum and mythical, everyday and legendary. Radwan, the left-wing activist and intellectual, the philosophy graduate, searched for essences and laws of motion, yet his vision of the world was intensely sensual, finding endless fascination in the details of people's lives and the many ways in which they shape and are shaped by their physical and spiritual environments. Radwan's curiosity about the sensual world had but one boundary: people.

This passion for detail Radwan would explain as an element of his *Sa'idi* or, to use his preferred designation, southern roots. Ask a *Sa'idi* the most mundane question, Radwan would remark, and you get a story. "It was a Wednesday," the story would begin, according to Radwan. Above all, however, Radwan's attachment to the *Sa'id* was intimately tied to his mother, and through her to the world of women. *Sa'idi* machismo notwithstanding, Radwan was unabashed about his preference for women's company and friendship. Notes we found in his papers upon his death contain the following passage: "The world of women, for me, is a world of symbols, concealment, and allusion. It is a world in which messages have a magical, deeply intimate character, implying a reality different to that which is lived. For me, the world of women is a storehouse of genuine feelings, expressed indirectly, magically."

He speaks of the stories of grandmothers, mothers, aunts, and women servants as epic poetry, laden with sorrow, but ultimately reconstructing reality, not as it is lived but as it is desired.

Radwan's two films about the *Sa'id*, the little-known but stunning *al-Janubiya* (The Southern Woman), his graduation project at the Cinema Institute, and the prize-winning *'Araq al-balah* (Date Wine), were firmly situated within just such a women's world: reality, mundane and magical, seen through women's eyes.

Yet, the *Sa'id* was just one part of Radwan. He was also a son of Manial al-Roda, urban to the core, streetwise, and possessed of remarkable *ibn al-balad* (son of the soil) wit. Two worlds sat on his shoulders, one of the past, another of the present; one magical, the other earthly; one female, the other male. Deeply attached to an almost legendary past, he was also a consummate modernist, militant in his secularism, and, to his very last day, unwavering in his dream of a more equitable, free, and just world. His different worlds may have existed as parallel universes between which he traveled swiftly and with great ease, or they may have been synthesized by his profound belief in an indomitable human spirit that, chained and bound, is nevertheless constantly craving freedom.

Whatever the case may have been, Radwan had many more stories to tell, films to make, loved ones in whose lives he alone could instill a unique quality of joy.

The need to recollect is checked by the need to explain. But what is it that could be explained: Radwan himself, our friendship, or the mysterious bond that made the two of us part of a curious extended family that took on natural parents and children as well as progressively new members, all of us from the most diverse backgrounds, but inseparably joined?

There may be no explanations that would suffice. After all, who can explain magic?

*Al-Ahram Weekly*, June 13, 2002

# EMPIRE AND ITS DEMONS

As the twentieth century was drawing to a close, its Henry Luce designation as an 'American century' seemed truer than ever. The Soviet Union's 'evil empire' imploded, America won the Cold War with hardly a shot being fired, and, for the first time in modern history, there was a single global hegemonic power, its supremacy challenged or contested by none—for the moment. But, having reached the pinnacle of its power, the American empire (launched in the Spanish–American War of 1898) seemed also destined for decline. Maintenance of America's global hegemony, or world leadership, came to be clearly identified by American strategists as the great challenge facing the U.S. in the twenty-first century. But empires need their demons. Without a threat there is little need for a hegemon, or, for that matter, a leader. America did not fabricate the Islamist or the terrorist threat, they just fell upon it as the answer to a prayer. And thus the great paradox of the twenty-first century was created: one of the weakest, most dysfunctional, and least developed regions of the world became the reputed source of its greatest threat. And as it is in the nature of the hegemonic power to exaggerate and build up the threat posed by its demonic 'other,' so it is in the interest of the volunteer demon to appear as threatening as possible. No conspiracies, just convergence.

# Urban Legends

THE "WAR ON TERROR" FULFILLED the promise of the Gulf War, to which the implosion of the Soviet Union, a few months later, was practically an afterthought. History, rather like God, moves in mysterious and often sardonic ways. And as the vagaries of history would have it, it fell to George Bush Junior to complete the job that a complex web of historical processes had thrown his father's way a decade before. Nearly in the Gulf, and conclusively in Afghanistan, America's imperial hegemony—counterbalanced, contested, and bitterly fought for a hundred years—was made absolute. The world after 9/11 is one in which history's first truly global empire stands, for the first time ever, totally supreme.

History can have its morbid jokes, and so a century of American imperial expansion is brought to a climax at the hands of a lackluster, mediocre president and his intellectually challenged son. Of course, the paradox of an extremely powerful political office that can be filled by practically any Tom, Dick, or Harry testifies to the complexity and sophistication of the American system of governance (after all, in other, less fortunate parts of the world, lackluster, mediocre, and intellectually challenged heads of state rule without benefit of an 'office' in any real sense).

The real joke, however, is the 'enemy'

An 'enemy,' it needs to be stressed, is an absolutely necessary ingredient in any and all imperial ventures, and especially in the case of the relatively young American empire, which took the path to world domination seemingly under protest and requiring always the noblest, most selfless of motives: making the world safe for democracy, all the way to 'infinite justice' and 'enduring freedom.' Indeed, one of the fundamental features of American imperialism has been the apparent reluctance with which the Land of the Free and Home of the Brave has been 'called upon' to don the mantle of 'world leadership.'

All of this could be why the majority of Americans are so utterly clueless with regard to the devastation their ever-growing empire has wrought upon the world during its hundred-year history; clueless, indeed, with regard to its very existence. "Why do they hate us?" "Because we're so good." And, naturally, because they're so evil.

But it was not 'huns from hell,' the 'yellow menace,' 'reds' under beds, or the 'evil empire' that justified America's ultimate domination of the whole 'global village.' That privilege fell to 'us,' aptly represented by such absurd figures as Saddam Hussein and Osama bin Laden. American global domination was born, molded, and massively expanded through two devastating world wars. It came to fruition in the farcical military excursions of Iraq and Afghanistan.

Which leads me to one of my favorite Egyptian folk parables. It goes something like this. A long time ago, most Egyptian townfolk lived in *hara*s, or alleys or quarters. The *hara*s had gates, which were shut at night. They also had *futuwwa*s. The *futuwwa* (tough guy, for want of a better word) provided protection for the *hara*'s community from robbers, other *futuwwa*s, and the like, and in return received protection money from the residents. Not surprisingly, being a tough guy, he also lorded it over them, which was often not to their liking, but they had to put up with him—it was a dangerous world then.

Two other aspects of life in the *hara* need to be explained before we continue our tale. *Hara*s invariably had *kharaba*s. A *kharaba* was a ruin, the site of an old house or bathhouse, whatever, which had fallen into disrepair, or merely a piece of wasteland that eventually became a sort of open rubbish dump, where discarded building materials, broken pieces of furniture, and similar items would find their way. *Kharaba*s, for some reason, were also the favorite haunt of *afrit*s, which, again for want of a better word, we'll call demons.

Now we can proceed with our tale. At the time our story begins, the *hara*'s residents were feeling quite content. There had been no attacks or incursions against the *hara* or its community for years. Naturally, people, probably at the urging of some troublemaker (something like today's anti-globalization activists), started wondering about the worth of their *futuwwa*. The tough guy, as is the wont of his sort, continued to lord it over the community and collect his protection money. Gradually, one and then another of the *hara*'s residents started to fall back on their payments, at first giving elaborate excuses but eventually giving none at all. Our *futuwwa*, naturally, was incensed.

One night, the *hara*'s residents were awakened by a terrible noise. Shouting and screeching, banging and clanking: an enormous battle seemed to be going on within the *hara*. And it all seemed to be coming from the darkness that shrouded the ruin. Frightened out of their wits (the *hara*'s residents were no warriors, after all, merely ordinary people, craftsmen, and tradesmen with wives and children), they stood outside their homes, shuddering in their night attire. With dawn, however, the noise diminished and finally disappeared altogether. The *futuwwa*, somewhat battered and disheveled, could be seen approaching from the direction of the *kharaba*. A demon had made an appearance there and he had been fighting it all night long, he informed them. From then on, nights were punctuated by similarly terrible noises. The *hara*'s residents no longer left their beds, however; they knew that the *futuwwa* was having it out with the *afrit*. They certainly paid the *futuwwa*'s protection money, though.

All of which begs the question: Why complain about the *futuwwa* when we are so willing to keep playing the role of the *afrit*?

*Al-Ahram Weekly*, January 10, 2002

# Director's Cut

I MIGHT AS WELL ADMIT to one of my shameful little secrets. I've enjoyed the Indiana Jones film series. And since I'm baring all, you might as well know: I doubt if I've missed a single James Bond movie (ever since way back when the still-dashing Sean Connery was doing it, up to the current hero, whose name I don't recall). But then, I tend to be highly tolerant of my various (human) failings—not to mention everyone else's.

The Indiana Jones film I have in mind was possibly one of the most blatantly racist films ever produced by Hollywood, which is saying a whole lot, especially when the object of racism, as in this film, happens to be Arab (make that Arabs, all of them). Most of the action is supposed to be taking place in 1930s Cairo, where, amazingly, the army of the Third Reich holds sway. Cartoon, you may say, but how many, I wonder, among the film's American audience, not least George W. himself, actually came out of the theaters fully convinced that Egypt was under Nazi German rule in the 1930s (our imperial masters' arrogance, after all, is equaled only by their enormous ignorance of the world they insist on 'leading,' by the nose)? I remember little of the film. There is a final grisly scene where Old Testament God meets Hollywood and kindly melts the skin and flesh off the German soldiers' bones.

One scene, however, has stayed firmly in my mind. Indiana Jones is being attacked by various turbaned and robed 'Arabs' in a Cairo souk, which is borrowed from a medieval Baghdad souk, as portrayed in a 1950s Hollywood version of a tale from *A Thousand and One Nights*. Indiana Jones (a younger and less haggard Harrison Ford) kicks and punches his way through half a dozen of these evil-looking baddies and, finally, the worst of them all appears on the scene. The earlier fighting has cleared the middle of the souk and it is in this space that the American hero and his villainous Middle Eastern–featured antagonist face off. Dressed all in black, including the inevitable turban, the hook-nosed 'Arab' wields a mean curved sword. He prances and preens, his sword twisting and swerving elegantly.

We've been cued. Our Hollywood-conditioned neurons rush through our brains: we anticipate one of those semi-climactic swashbuckling scenes, which used to take our breath away when we were kids but tend to bore us as we grow older. Here is where the hero comes this close to having his throat slit, but ultimately, surprisingly yet predictably, prevails. But here is where the filmmakers have their little joke on us. There will be no swashbuckling scene: Indiana Jones nonchalantly pulls his pistol out and shoots the villain dead.

I was watching the film along with an old friend (a film director, as it happened), and we fell about laughing. There was instant recognition; despite the racism and imperial arrogance, we could actually identify with the prancing and preening villain, whose absurd death ('martyrdom'?) seemed to encapsulate one of the salient features of the modern political history of the Arab world. Neurons leapfrogged over cultural boundaries and, in our minds, the racist imperial slur became a typical Egyptian joke (Egyptians are invariably the butt of their own most vicious jokes). The grand Arab battle for the liberation of Palestine was summed up: we prance and preen; the Israelis (the ultimate embodiment of half a millennium of western imperialist oppression and plunder), silently and coldly, shoot—and kill.

I can't remember exactly when or where we saw *Raiders of the Lost Ark* (it was released in 1981), but the scene was definitely being replayed in my mind in 1990–91, while Saddam Hussein was threatening to use his 'double-barreled' chemical warheads to bomb Israel into oblivion. Iraqi 'steadfastness' lasted only for as long as it took the U.S.-led coalition to finish "bombing Iraq back to the Middle Ages." It ended as soon as the ground war began. Thankfully, and pathetically, the chemical warheads never got off the ground.

"I wish to declare that if America used chemical or nuclear weapons against us, then we may retort with chemical and nuclear weapons. We have the weapons as a deterrent," Osama bin Laden told a Pakistani journalist the other day. Typically, the White House's first reaction was that it was taking Bin Laden's threat "seriously." Within the week, Kabul had fallen.

Major historical events are repeated twice, said Hegel. Marx, writing on the 1851 coup d'état of Louis Bonaparte, agreed, adding that the first time occurs as tragedy, the second as farce. In the Arab world, we've managed to best them both. For a people who have lived the full tragic cycle of Nasserism, which reached its zenith in the June 1967 debacle, it should have been impossible to fall for Saddam's 1990 farce. Yet, fall we did. Still, the wheel does not cease spinning: farce is repeated as greater farce, repeated as even greater farce. We began with the heroic figure of Gamal Abdel Nasser, the nationalization of the Suez Canal, Bandung, Afro-Asian solidarity, and the Non-Aligned Movement. Now we have Bin Laden, the Taliban, and the World Trade Center. How low can you go?

Leaders preen and prance. People, from Palestine to Afghanistan, continue to die.

"Where are you Salah al-Din? The nation awaits you." The huge banner hanging from the downtown headquarters of the Bar Association hits me in the face on my way to work every day. Is it not time that we stopped waiting for a savior? They're becoming more clownish and absurd with every passing day.

*Al-Ahram Weekly*, November 15, 2001

# The First Year of
# the Second Century

YEAR ONE OF THE 'new American century' seemed to end on a propitious note. Saddam Hussein, embodiment of history's first truly global empire's demonic 'other,' was captured and, in the best imperial tradition, put on public display. Haggard, dazed, and disheveled, he was the star of the televised medical examination that was made to substitute for the parade of manacled barbarian chieftains and booty that once drew the crowds.

And not just that. One surprise swiftly followed another. The 'barbarians,' it appeared, were everywhere on the run. On December 20, 2003, a week after the capture of Saddam, the flamboyant leader of the Libyan Jamahiriya, Muammar Qadhafi, made a clean breast of it all. Publicly confessing to having dabbled in weapons of mass destruction (WMDs), he announced his "voluntary" decision to dismantle all such weapons as may be found offensive by the masters of the universe, and to open his arsenal—and anything else that might take their fancy—to direct inspection and supervision. Significantly, perhaps, he revealed that he'd started negotiating this "voluntary" decision with the U.S. and Britain nine months ago, that is, just about the times the bombs started dropping on Baghdad.

George W. Bush may or may not be writing his 'war commentaries' these days, but I suspect that fireside reflections on the year's harvest are bringing a warm glow to his—or is it imperial?—cheeks this Christmas. International law, the United Nations, and basic morality be damned. Brute force works. As any mafia boss can tell you, crime pays.

Examine the balance sheet. In terms of international law, the Anglo-American invasion and occupation of Iraq in 2003 are as illegal as Saddam's invasion and occupation of Kuwait in 1990–91. Which means that the UN was obliged, by its charter, not just to condemn these actions but also to put a stop to them by resorting (in accordance with Chapter 7 of that charter) to sanctions and/or military intervention. Instead, less than a month after the fall of Baghdad, the UN Security Council was laying the mantle of legitimacy on both invasion and occupation through a May 22 resolution to lift the sanctions imposed on Iraq.

And speaking of sanctions, what about Iraq's WMDs? By the end of the year, as images of the bearded and vanquished Saddam were being plastered over the world's front pages and television screens, the fundamental justification for the war and the intricate, flagrant web of lies constructed to bolster it seemed all but forgotten. What's done cannot be undone. So let us debate when and how Iraqis are to regain 'sovereignty' and establish democratic government in their indefinitely occupied nation.

Contradictions between obeisance to imperial dictates, backed by open threats to use massive military force, and notions such as sovereignty and democracy are, it seems, dependent on the eye of the beholder. After all Israel—where nearly five million people exercise a brutal and murderous dominion over another people and where, moreover, one-fifth of the citizens of the Jewish state are effectively disenfranchised and systematically discriminated against Palestinian Arabs—is the foremost democracy in the region.

Needless to say, Muammar Qadhafi made a giant stride toward democratizing Libya when he "voluntarily" decided to scrap his WMDs and open his country to Anglo-American inspections. The Palestinian Authority, meanwhile, takes small steps toward democracy when it replaces its elected president with an unelected prime minister and sanctions his appointment by a legislative council that has long exceeded its mandate. And the fact that it enjoys no sovereignty over any kind of territory is not deemed a serious obstacle to political reform.

Glaring inconsistencies, backed by sufficient military hardware, have a remarkable ability to appear clothed in the most profound logic. And as 2003 draws to its pitiful close, it is the illusion of logic that prevails.

Not just Qadhafi's Libya but also other potential targets of the empire's perpetual "war on terror" were bending over backward to show goodwill. In October of this year, Syria displayed remarkable 'restraint' in response to the Israeli bombing of an abandoned refugee camp on the outskirts of Damascus, the first such attack in three decades. Iran, a member of the Bush-designated "axis of evil" and the bookmakers' favorite as target number three in the 'war on terror,' may have begun 2003 defiant. By the end of the year, however, it was sufficiently reasonable to sign a sweeping additional protocol to the Nuclear Non-Proliferation Treaty, giving inspectors freer access to Iranian nuclear facilities.

The fact that Israel is not suspected but *known* to possess a huge stockpile of nuclear, chemical, and biological weapons as well as highly advanced delivery systems is, of course, beside the point. Meanwhile, Ariel Sharon is talking unilateral separation, while dispossessing Palestinians of what is left of their land and livelihoods with his apartheid wall.

The first American century, America's "age of empire" (as Gore Vidal put it), began early, in February 1898, with the Spanish–American War and the invasions of Cuba and the Philippines. According to my reckoning, it ended a little late, as the bombs and missiles began to rain on Baghdad and Basra in March of this year, a culmination of one century of empire and the beginning of another.

All in all, the last days of 2003, the first year of the second century, appear to have confirmed the delirious imaginings of Washington's neocons and their dream project for the "new American century." Except at the heart of the logic lies a single flaw: arbitrary power, however massive, is only really effective at destroying things. It is hopeless at building. The thousand-year Reich, after all, barely managed a decade.

*Al-Ahram Weekly*, December 25, 2003

# "A Splendid Little War"

THE TWENTIETH CENTURY IS LIKELY to end belatedly, sometime in March–April 2003, with the establishment of American military rule in Iraq. A *short* twentieth century (as defined by British historian Eric Hobsbawm) had ended with the fall of the Berlin Wall in 1989. And while Hobsbawm's "age of extremes" opens with the First World War, our long century's beginning is less immediately devastating, if no less obvious: the 1898 Spanish–American War, the "splendid little war" that gave the U.S. dominion over Guam, Puerto Rico, and the Philippines. It launched the world, irrevocably, into the age of American empire. By the 1940s, an American (*Time* and *Life* publisher Henry Luce) could refer to the "American century." Half a century on, few around the world, friends or foes of U.S. global hegemony, would dispute his assertion.

And it is not without merit, I expect, to view the impending war in Iraq as a sort of seal on the first American century; a kind of culmination of the long, if by no means inevitable, historical process that placed Bush Junior and his gang of global marauders as the reviled but uncontested masters of the world.

The commonalties between the two events that began and culminated in the American century are remarkable: the flimsy pretext (the sinking of the Maine versus Saddam Hussein's weapons of mass destruction and links to al-Qa'ida); a powerful mass media (from Hearst's yellow press to satellite television) that has the ability to create a fictional reality well suited to American business interests; and the absurd, trigger-happy 'rough rider' mindset, its flagrant stupidity shored up by a mindless ('God's on our side') arrogance. And, of course, the penchant for "splendid little wars"—what, according to Noam Chomsky, the American military establishment currently calls "conflict with much weaker enemies."

Of course, neither Teddy Roosevelt nor William Randolph Hearst could have dreamed of the amazing sleights of hand that a century of empire and technological innovation has witnessed from U.S. rulers and their ever-compliant and complicit media. The now-you-see-it-now-you-don't bag of tricks is fabulous in its audacity: the "very weak enemy" is made to appear a horrifying threat to humanity that must be confronted at any price, conjuring images of Hitler, Stalin, and, much more relevant, Hollywood disaster movies. But with a shake of the wand the monster is to be turned back into a rabbit. War against this terrible enemy will be conducted at very little cost in lives, will require very little sacrifice, and will be over before you can say body bags. It will be "a splendid little war." The cost in human lives is naturally calculated in terms of "our boys"; enemy losses do not count since a cooperative corporate media has made it possible to blame them on the enemy.

It began with one little war and ends with another, both ugly, sordid, and blatantly contrived. The one set the American republic on the road to empire, the other is designed to proclaim the absolute, irrevocable, and uncontested global supremacy of that empire. But will the last century go down in history as simply the American century, or as the first of other American centuries? Have we seen the rise of the American empire, and can now look toward its fall, or are we merely at the start of a thousand-year American Reich?

One such answer was recently provided by Bill Emmott, the editor of the *Economist*, in a lengthy article published in the *Sunday Times* of January 12, 2003. Under the rhetorical title, "Will America Surrender?" Emmott offers an elegy for American imperialism in the last and, it would seem, this and all future centuries, revealing an embarrassing degree of sycophancy of which only certain British gentlemen seem capable. (The best explanation for that propensity that I can come up with may be summarized in a popular Egyptian saying, "the bald headed woman flaunts her niece's hair.")

The article, as it happens, is an extract from a book entitled *20:21 Vision: Twentieth-Century Lessons for the Twenty-First Century*. Having apparently studied the history of the last century, the *Economist* editor concludes that only two questions matter in this one: "One is whether capitalism will survive, thrive, and retain the current, unusual allegiance that it commands around the world. The other is whether America will continue to keep the peace, making the world safe for capitalism to spread, by retaining its clear preeminence as a political, military, economic and cultural power, by retaining the desire to exercise its power as a force for peace and progress."

Would that the answers were as simple as the questions, Emmott laments. Soon enough, however, we discover that the answers are not only simple but also simple minded. Emmott has no doubts that capitalism is the best of all worlds, and neither does he have any doubts that American 'preeminence' is the only way to save the world from utter chaos and collapse. Sure, there are some problems with capitalism (such as the fact that more than half the world lives on less than $2 a day), and with Pax Americana (Vietnam?), but these he dismisses as incidental to his basic and, as far as I am aware, unique premise: the first and second world wars were a result of the fact that the U.S. was yet to succeed Great Britain as the undisputed master of the world. Who needs a Hobsbawm and genuine, hard-earned scholarship when American-style journalists such as Mr. Emmott can turn out such facile history? But as Mr. Emmott's book was hitting the shelves at the beginning of February 2003, and as the author was, perhaps, coming to take his proper place beside such paragons of hilarious history as Huntington and Fukuyama, the scene was very different.

Ironically, both in Davos, where a thousand captains of global capital and their bureaucratic cronies had collected, and in Porto Alegre, where over a hundred thousand members of a whole range of social movements from around the world gathered, American 'preeminence' was under attack. The prospects of an American-governed capitalist world system were a source of gloom in Davos and profound opposition in Porto Alegre.

The long (American) century will soon be over. What's to come next? Will the coming war in Iraq herald the advent of a new, brutal, unchangeable, and incontestable imperial order or, alternatively, the beginning of the end of empire? I do not know. I very much doubt, however, that there can be a second American century, simply because (and here I'm borrowing from something Chomsky said in Porto Alegre last week) it is very doubtful that the human species can survive another century "under existing state capitalist institutions," ruled over and made safe from democracy by force of American arms.

*Al-Ahram Weekly*, February 6, 2003

# Conspiracy Theory

"WHERE IS SADDAM?" my taxi driver asked in belligerent tones a couple of days after the fall of Baghdad. Hesitantly, and rather shamefacedly (I'd been, I confess, among those expecting the battle of Baghdad), I began to advance a couple of the theories then doing the rounds, only to be interrupted almost immediately. The question, as it turned out, was of a rhetorical nature.

"He's in America."

The cab driver answered his own question in no uncertain terms. Indeed, he had it on good authority that not only Saddam but also Bin Laden was enjoying the good life in the good old US of A.

"They're both American agents, you know. They did all this to give the Americans the pretext to come and occupy the Arab world."

I did not try to dissuade my driver from this most original of conspiracy theories. (Well, not that original. Soon after 9/11, my barber informed me that Osama bin Laden and Ariel Sharon went to the same school; conclusive evidence, in his view, of the al-Qa'ida leader's Mossad connections.) Images of the two murderous megalomaniacs sharing a little suburban house in some remote American town were too delicious to dismiss for the sake of what would have inevitably been a futile discussion. My Hollywood-programmed brain, drawing on scenes of American gangsters enjoying Federal Bureau of Investigation hospitality under the Witness Protection Program, was producing a multitude of comic images: Saddam and Bin Laden walking a Great Dane round the block, buying halal meat at the corner kosher deli, or else haggling over whose turn it

115

was to do the dishes or record the next tape addressing the *umma*. What cover story, I wondered frivolously, would the Americans have provided the two housemates, one a stocky, grim elderly man, the other younger, slim, and handsome.

Nonsense, you might say; yet another proof of the Arabs' propensity for conspiracy theories. This latter assertion, I might point out, smacks of racism, even though it is reiterated by certain Arab, no less than American, pundits. Rather than accuse the 'Arab mind' (whatever that may be) of being enamored of conspiracy theories, the pundits would be much better served by looking into the effects of authoritarianism, a debased and sensationalist media, and the near total absence of political space in the political consciousness of the masses.

There is more to it. Someone once said (was it Woody Allen?) that paranoia is greatly heightened awareness. The joke is not without insight. While conspiracy theories of the sort above may be utter nonsense when judged on the facts, they are far more erudite if viewed as a reflection of the *truth*. After all, in both the natural and the social world, the appearance of things/phenomena is rarely, if ever, an accurate expression of their true nature. Take my barber's suggestion that Sharon and Bin Laden went to the same school. As a fact, it is patently absurd. As a metaphor underlining the similarities between the two thugs, it could not be more apt.

No less interesting is the taxi driver's Saddam/Bin Laden theory. Indeed, a fairly substantial section of the Egyptian 'street' (regardless of ideas on the whereabouts of the two miscreants) has in the past few weeks come to subscribe to the notion that both Bin Laden and Saddam are American agents. I have since christened this line of thinking the Bulaq al-Dakrur School, in reference to a sprawling—literally on the wrong side of the tracks—slum district in Giza, where one of the theory's most zealous proponents resides.

Factually, the Bulaq al-Dakrur School's conjectures are laughable. As metaphor, however, they reveal a whole host of truths. One need not subscribe to conspiracy theories of any sort to recognize that Saddam and Bin Laden have been heaven-sent insofar as the U.S.'s post-Soviet imperial ambitions are concerned. There is incontrovertible *factual* evidence that the neocons had been praying for a Pearl Harbor and clamoring for Iraqi blood and oil well before 9/11; indeed, well before Jeb Bush and the Supreme Court delivered the White House into their busy and eager hands. Bin Laden provided them with their Pearl Harbor (or is it

Reichstag fire?); Saddam, sitting on a sea of oil, became a uniquely abominable target of repugnance in addition to state-of-the-art missiles.

What I find most telling about this particular conspiracy theory, however, is the 'street's' profound rejection of the two sets of bloodthirsty tyrants, local and foreign, Muslim, Jew, and (born-again) Christian. Since they are equally loathed, they must be in cahoots.

What a great many pundits, on this side of the Atlantic as well as the other, fail to understand is that the Arab masses' profound sense of national humiliation at western imperialist hands is inevitably interwoven with their status as disenfranchised and abused citizens in their own countries. Their anger at one set of oppressors is pretty much of the same order as that directed at the other.

Now, let me suggest a conspiracy theory of my own: the neocons are a Trotskyite group whose ambition is to foment world revolution. Like most conspiracy theories, there is a factual grain at the core of this one. We know that a few of the neocon ideologues (notably the Washington Institute for Near East Policy's Patrick Clawson, he of *Navigating through Turbulence* fame) are reconstructed Trots. But are they? Reconstructed, that is. What if, having been disheartened by the steep decline in revolutionary fervor following the fall of Saigon in 1975, some especially militant Trots figured that the international working class movement needed to be nudged out of its complacency? What if they then set about infiltrating intelligence and administration-connected think tanks, as well as searching for a likely point of entry into the White House? Was Junior, a wealthy wastrel from a patrician and politically and corporately well-connected American family, heaven-sent, or one of several possibles? Was he, sometime during his lost years, recruited to the cause, or merely played for a fool as others exploited his well-known naiveté?

Look at the results. In less than two years in office the neocons have succeeded in splitting the western alliance as never before; Russia and China have been propelled out of their decade-long slavishness; and most significant of all, a new, uniquely internationalist anti-capitalist/ anti-imperialist movement has been galvanized into action, as evidenced in the February 15, 2003 anti-war demonstrations, the likes of which the world had not seen before.

And the Arab 'street' seems to have been awakened out of its long slumber. America's 'friends' in the Arab world have not been as discredited, shaken, and destabilized in over a quarter of a century.

The 'enduring,' permanent "war on terror" being pursued by the neo-cons with arrogant vigor, is it not evocative of grand old Lev Bronstein's "permanent revolution"? Is permanent imperialist war designed to act, in well-established Marxist idiom, as the midwife of permanent revolution?

It's all nonsense, of course, but fun all the same. There is a point to the frivolity, however. The American invasion and occupation of Iraq may indeed prove to have put the Arabs on the road to democracy, not by force of American example but in opposition to it. There are clear signs that the anger triggered by the new and unprecedented level of Arab national humiliation is increasingly taking an inward bent. A democratic awakening of the Arab masses may well be at hand; the invasion of Iraq will not launch a new American century but will prove to have been the seal on the first, and last, one.

*Al-Ahram Weekly*, May 15, 2003

# We Are All Iraqis Now

MY LITTLE NIECE RECEIVED a baptism of fire of sorts last Friday: her first police beating. Well, not so little perhaps; she's nearly eighteen and has just graduated from high school. Thankfully, the beating was not too harsh. Salma, along with her friends (none of whom had seemed to me very political before), had been out on the streets with tens of thousands of others, finally able to express a popular outrage so bitter and profound that the nation has almost visibly been choking on it for the past two years, since the outbreak of the Palestinian Intifada. To be absolutely precise, since the televised and brutal murder of twelve-year-old Muhammad al-Dura, as he was cowering behind his father's back.

A wave of demonstrations by university students had erupted then. Another, stronger wave erupted in April 2002, as Ariel Sharon sent his troops wreaking death and destruction throughout the Palestinian territories. Yet, by the time George W. Bush, Tony Blair, and their assorted aides were beating the drums of war against Iraq, the Egyptian 'street' seemed to have sunk back into its decades-long stupor. The anger and outrage were palpable, but in a country with no political parties worthy of the name, with no independent trade unions or social movements of any sort, there seemed no way for it to go, only to simmer and simmer. The ideal recipe for producing suicide bombers.

Then came February 15, 2003. More than thirty million people, from Los Angeles to Tokyo, were out on the streets protesting against the war in Iraq. One million people demonstrated in London, three million in Rome; it was a day the like of which the world had never seen. In the Arab world, there was almost silence. Even the governments were embarrassed. After all, in their desperate appeals to their White House patron and his overzealous adviser at 10 Downing Street to "go easy" on the Arabs, the Arab governments' major bargaining card (indeed, their only card) has been their feebleness.

"A military attack on Iraq would push the region into an abyss of chaos—instability and terror would rule the day," they protested repeatedly. Yet, so successful had they been in depoliticizing their citizens, so complete seemed the disenfranchisement of the Arab peoples, that the masters of the universe called the regimes' bluff. They held the Arab masses in the same contempt in which their rulers held them.

Robert Fisk, in the *Independent*, put it brutally: "One million people demonstrate in London, while the Arabs, faced with disaster, are like mice." Even before it appeared in translation in one of the opposition newspapers, Fisk's article was picked up on with almost masochistic relish. It was forwarded by email, in the original English and in various ad hoc translations, testimony perhaps to the profound effect the day had on popular consciousness in Egypt and in the rest of the Arab world. Not only was the perceived confrontation between Arabs and Muslims on the one hand and a monolithic west on the other proved absurd, but western Christians and atheists were defending an Arab cause much better than the Arabs themselves could hope to do.

On Thursday, day one of the invasion, thousands of protesters collected in Tahrir Square, in Cairo. "It's like Hyde Park," was the common refrain, expressed in exhilarated tones. The anti-riot police, while very much in evidence, stayed its hand, letting demonstrators be as they peacefully occupied the square until the evening, chanting slogans, making speeches, painting political graffiti on the ground, and staging street theater. On Friday, the beatings began, and continued. The government's message was loud and clear: "You've had your one day. No more."

The anger and outrage fester, yet alongside them a new mood, something very like euphoria, has also been growing, almost grudgingly ("dare we hope?"). The Iraqis, devastated by wars and crippling sanctions, have been offering what appears to be stiff resistance to the invading force of the most powerful and deadly military machine in history. "Where is this shock and awe?" people ask one another at newsstands, on public transport, and in coffeehouses, this last providing the majority of Egyptians with communal access to Al Jazeera and other satellite television news channels, which carry the latest news of the fighting in Umm Qasr, Nasiriya, and Basra. (Few seemed to have been tuning in to Egyptian television in the past week.) The buzz about it is incessant and inescapable—it is everywhere.

"Now they're talking about the Geneva Conventions, what about Guantanamo?" sneered the owner of my local newsstand. A friend, a veteran of the 1970s left-wing student movement, was similarly reminded of Guantanamo, if in more emphatic terms. Televised footage of obviously scared and bewildered American prisoners of war had left my friend upset. She whispered something to that effect, only to be upbraided by her teenage daughter, who instead was absolutely thrilled by evidence that the Iraqis had indeed taken a number of the invading soldiers prisoner.

"The Americans are talking like Arabs and the Arabs are talking like Americans," laughingly commented an elderly man, probably a retired civil servant, at an Alexandria coffeehouse. I'd been in the coastal city on business and had stopped for a spot of tea and Al Jazeera. His meaning was immediately clear to the other patrons, who laughed in appreciation. Egyptians are naturally skeptical about the statements of their own officials, and by extension those of other Arab states. But as the days of invasion rolled by, they became increasingly struck by the rhetorical tone and prevarication of the statements of coalition military and civil officials, in contrast to the almost calm detachment and precision of the statements of the Iraqis, particularly their information minister, Muhammad Saeed al-Sahhaf. Saddam had not been killed in the 'window of opportunity' bombing of Baghdad that opened the war. Neither did Umm Qasr fall on day one of the invasion, as coalition statements had claimed, but was still fighting valiantly into day six. "It's a very small town, you know?" "Do you realize that Umm Qasr is just across from the Kuwaiti border?" Such were the comments that people exchanged incessantly as the fighting in the port town kept going on, and on—the admiration mixed with wonder.

Perhaps the most enthusiastically greeted piece of news has been the shooting down of an American attack helicopter south of Baghdad. "Did you see the old man who downed the Apache helicopter?" I've been continually asked, the rhetorical question uttered always in tones of glowing pride. Very few, if any, are under any illusion that Iraq could win the war, though many will dutifully mumble "may God grant us victory" as they discuss the latest reports of Iraqi resistance. All are outraged and grief-stricken at the death and destruction being wreaked on the Iraqi people, and most people realize that much more lies ahead. Yet, none can help but feel a certain pride, a sense of dignity restored. We are not, after all, mice.

How far back does one trace the sense of humiliation and deeply injured dignity at western hands that have been such a formative element of Arab awareness and self-image for decades? Do we need to go as far back as the 1917 Balfour Declaration, or as recently as the 1948 war, the dispossession of the Palestinians, and the resounding and humiliating defeat of the combined armies of the Arab world? The 1948 war would be carved in common Arab memory as *al-nakba*, the catastrophe.

And then there was the Six-Day War, the resounding defeat of Egypt, Syria, and Jordan in June 1967 at Israel's hands, resulting in the occupation of Sinai, the Golan Heights, and all that remained of the historical land of Palestine. The sense of humiliation born out of June 1967 was perhaps the most shattering of all in proportion to the immense hopes of emancipation and restored national dignity that the wave of pan-Arab nationalism, led and symbolized by Nasser's leadership, had come to trigger. It was so profound that Lebanese philosopher and political writer George Tarabishi, some ten years ago, authored a large work in which he used psychoanalytical concepts to analyze the effects of the June war on the Arab psyche in terms of trauma leading to neurosis.

The humiliations have been piled one on top of the other ever since. The October War of 1973 offered a very temporary relief. Egyptian President Anwar Sadat, in one and the same breath, proclaimed Arab victory and, asserting that America had entered the battle alongside Israel and declaring, "I cannot fight America," accepted the UN call for a ceasefire. Egypt got back the Sinai, eventually.

The interplay of a resigned and defeatist realism and a deep and increasingly intense sense of humiliation has been a defining feature of Egyptian and Arab awareness ever since. Egyptians, for the most part, seemed resigned to it, their resignation interrupted by moments of rude awakening, such as the 1982 invasion of Lebanon, the first Intifada, and the 1991 Gulf War. Even then, with Egypt part of the U.S.-led coalition against Iraq, people on Egyptian streets were proudly discussing the latest news (soon enough proven to be myth) of this or that 'secret weapon' in Saddam's possession.

And then came the second Intifada, the collapse of the peace process, the ongoing destruction of Palestinian life, 9/11, and the "war on terror." It had all become too much to bear.

Injured dignity lies at the heart of all rebellions. Throughout history, human beings have revealed an enormous capacity to bear and cope with the harshest forms of oppression and exploitation. It is only when they perceive these as 'injustice'—when the implicit or explicit compact between oppressor and oppressed appears to have been shattered and violated by the oppressors, when the exercise of power appears lawless and arbitrary—that people rise up.

Yet, for the Arabs, as galling and bitter as the sense of injured dignity has been and continues to be, it has also been disabling, creating a situation and mindset in which their choices seemed to be limited to either suicidal vengeance or abject and bitter hopelessness. It remains to be seen whether the war in Iraq will put the Arab masses on a new trajectory, one in which they fight to win rather than just to die while maintaining some sense of their basic human dignity. But whatever the course of the war in the coming days or weeks, for the moment the Arab masses have two things going for them: they are not mice, and they are not alone.

*The Guardian*, March 27, 2003

# Nights at the Circus

OSAMA BIN LADEN AS MIDWIFE may cut a somewhat comic figure, but that, in fact, is the most apt way to describe his sordid contribution to a no less sordid post-9/11 world. The ugliness and inhumanity of the delivery portended the grotesque nature of the newborn: the world according to Dubya.

"A blow to the heart of imperialism," an Egyptian leftist gleefully opined soon after the attacks on New York and Washington a year ago. Rubbish. I don't know where the comrade got his Marxism from but I've yet to find a work on imperialism that has traced its ever-elusive 'heart' to the Twin Towers of New York's World Trade Center. But then rubbish seems to be the stuff of which much of Egyptian and other Arab intellectual and political production is made these days.

Over the past year, I've been as horrified and enraged as most people in our region and elsewhere by the madness that has swiftly come to hold the world in an iron grip. The viciousness, the cynical cruelty, the double-speak, the heartlessness of the masters of the universe and their countless minions found its supreme expression in Palestine. The world looked on as a whole people were being coldly and systematically destroyed, where every known moral or legal canon was being flaunted with the abandoned brutality and the pitiless precision of a Nazi occupation. War criminal Ariel Sharon is butchering the Palestinian people, albeit with a blunt American knife, while the civilized west, basking in the superiority of its democratic values, is ensuring that the sacrifice is tied and gagged and ready for the slaughter.

But the past year has also been one in which I've grown more and more disgusted with our own helplessness, with the way we seem to wallow in it, indeed, to hang on to it as a cherished identity, a political ideology, and a way of life. I am, I must confess, as sick and tired of the comrades as of the brethren (and all those in between); of the masses no less than of the intellectuals; of the opposition as much as of the governments. I'm sick and tired of the whining, the self-pity, and the debased, wife-batterer's machismo, all of which seem to constitute the bases of our self-definition as a miserable, dysfunctional Arab/Muslim family. But oh, how we cling together, morbidly joined in lamenting past glory and moaning over contemporary humiliation.

As it happens, comrade, the attack on the Twin Towers (in which some 3,500 'fellow workers' were killed) was not a blow against imperialism, neither to its heart nor, indeed, to any other part of its corpulent corporate corpus. Rather, it provided the golden opportunity, the necessary ideological cover, for a new form of global imperial domination to come into its own—a new imperial world system that is unprecedented in the degree of its centralization (a single imperial power) and the depth and breadth of its global reach, what with the tremendous advances in transport and communications; the collapse of the Soviet system and Third World industrialization and urbanization; and the virtual disappearance of subsistence economies (if you're outside the market, you're most likely dying of starvation, and even then you're probably receiving food aid). In addition, U.S. military technology is said to be at least a generation ahead of that of the most advanced western countries, and the U.S. is said to possess more military hardware than the rest of the world combined.

And so midwife it is, for Bin Laden and his sorry band of suicidal simpletons cannot take credit for helping conceive this new monster, they just helped with the delivery. The conception, in fact, was happening well before the Saudi billionaire was a twinkle in the Central Intelligence Agency's eyes. It was happening back in the early 1970s, as the working classes around the world were everywhere reaching the limits of their various 'interventions' in the capitalist state, through social democracy in the west, the Soviet system in the east, and different forms of populist authoritarian state systems in much of the Third World.

It was these interventions that gave us the 'golden age of capitalism,' the United Nations system, and Third World independence, capitalization, and industrialization. It all ended in crisis and collapse, so enter in Reaganism and Thatcherism, deregulation and neoliberalism, the World Bank, the International Monetary Fund, and then the World Trade

Organization, a repentant Third World begging for forgiveness, of debts as well as past rebelliousness, the 'winds of change' sweeping through Eastern Europe. It came to a head with the Gulf War (putting the U.S. at the head of the biggest military alliance since the Second World War, with another Arab clown on hand), followed shortly after by the final, shocking, if hardly lamented collapse of the Soviet Union. Interestingly, though, it would take another decade, a rigged poll in Florida, and Bin Laden's "blessed blow" to bring it all together.

On 9/11, Bin Laden helped deliver the world a new Rome that, parodying the mythological Minerva, was born fully grown. Hopefully, a year after the event, we will come to the realization that even if the new Rome, like the old, cannot survive without a circus, we should perhaps be a little more hesitant to volunteer so readily to be the object of the entertainment.

*Al-Ahram Weekly*, September 12, 2002

# Multiple Personality Disorder

AT BOEING'S HIGH-TECH FACTORY in St. Charles, Missouri, reports the *Washington Post*, three shifts are working twenty-four hours a day turning out smart bombs to replenish Air Force and Navy inventories, which ran "dangerously low" during the Afghan war.

Afghanistan has been merely "the first theater in the war against terror," President Bush does not tire of repeating, "This nation must seize the moment. If we blink, the rest of the world will blink as well." And while the American president's Asian tour seems to have shown him that two of the three members of the "axis of evil" are proving somewhat difficult as prospective bomb-and-peanut-butter-sandwich markets, Iraq continues to be easy pickings.

Capitalism is on a rampage, a bloody, shameless, and ever-'enduring' rampage, with no apparent end in sight. War, profits, and national (or is it civilizational, cultural, ethnic, racial, religious?) bigotry have not been so flagrantly intertwined since the Third Reich. The war in Afghanistan alone ("the first theater") is going to cost American taxpayers $30 billion before the end of 2002, according to Pentagon estimates. This is nearly double the emergency allocation of $17.4 billion zealously handed over to the generals and their business buddies by a revenge-thirsty Congress and American public in the aftermath of the 9/11 attacks. As of January 31, the Pentagon had spent or committed to contracts some $11.9 billion. This, interestingly, includes $61 million for humanitarian supplies (the ubiquitous peanut butter sandwiches?), $19 million for holding al-Qa'ida prisoners in Guantanamo Bay, and $100 million for a murky category called "additional security assistance and defense cooperation expenses" (otherwise known as bribes), but excludes the $1.1 billion necessary to replace the eighteen thousand bombs and missiles that have been used to date in the war.

Under the banner of the "war on terror," U.S. annual military spending has been hiked by a staggering $48 billion for fiscal 2002. The increase alone is larger than the military budget of any other country in the world, while, at $379 billion, the American military budget is (according to the Washington-based Council for a Livable World) six times larger than the third-largest military spender in the world, Russia. It is also larger than the combined military budgets of the next twenty-five countries on the list of military big spenders, and more than twenty-six times larger than the combined military budgets of the seven countries traditionally identified by the Pentagon as America's most likely adversaries (Cuba, Iran, Iraq, Libya, North Korea, Sudan, and Syria). The "axis of evil" collectively spends a paltry $21 billion.

Not one to blink first, the 'Enron administration,' thanks to the "war on terror," easily shrugged off its largest campaign contributor's scandalous collapse. The Carlyle Group, after all, is doing very well out of the war. The Wall Street firm, which has Bush Senior on its payroll, made $237 million in a single day in December through the sale of shares in United Defense Industries, the Army's fifth-largest contractor. The *Los Angeles Times* last month quoted Charles Lewis, director of the Center for Public Policy, as commenting, "It's the first time the president of the United States' father is on the payroll of one of the largest U.S. defense contractors." Lewis added, "Between [former Secretary of State James] Baker and [former Secretary of Defense and close friend of Donald Rumsfeld Frank C.] Carlucci, not to mention dear old dad, the relationship of the president with this particular company is as tight and close as, well, anyone can imagine."

But then, the Bush family and its various government buddies have many fingers in a whole range of corporate pies, not least in oil, which in fact had various ever-hopeful Arab analysts celebrating Junior's Third Worldish electoral win. And what with Gulf War II in the works, the time is more than ripe to open up Alaska's Arctic National Wildlife Refuge for oil drilling. It is, the president told Americans last Sunday, a matter of "national security." "America is already using more energy than our domestic resources can provide and unless we act to increase our energy independence, our reliance on foreign sources of energy will only increase,"

Bush said. Polar bears be damned, there is money to be made, even if the arguments used in its defense would put a Third World leader in the World Trade Organization/World Bank/International Monetary Fund dog house. 'Independence' in the age of the global village is a dirty word.

Profits, jingoism, racial and 'civilizational' supremacism, attacks on civil liberties, radical solutions to Third World immigration, sleaze—the "war on terror" is proving an answer to capital's wildest dreams. The war's overwhelming payoff is particularly amazing in view of its total absurdity. From the very start, it was obvious that, if anything, it was designed to promote Islamist radicalism rather than eradicate it, while its 'success story' (the ridiculously easy overthrow of the equally ridiculous Taliban regime) has been shown for the farce it was, with American forces shooting, arresting, and torturing Hamid Karzai's men while protesting, "It's impossible to say these people are on this side and these people are on the other side. People [in Afghanistan] are on multiple sides, and they switch sides," as Pentagon spokesperson Victoria Clarke had the gall to tell the ever-compliant American press following a particularly gruesome incident of this sort. Rear Adm. John Stufflebeem in the same briefing complained that it was hard to "pin down" the real identities of people in Afghanistan: "They've got multiple identity cards. They've got multiple passports. They've got multiple names and certainly multiple stories. And so you really find . . . how problematic this part of the world is."

Afghanistan's liberators, itching to liberate Iraq from Saddam Hussein and having dropped over eighteen thousand bombs and missiles on the country, have discovered they were fighting "a shadow war" against "shadowy people who don't want to be found." And, "[to say] that . . . conditions in Afghanistan are confusing is an understatement, you know." The sheer audacity of these and similar statements, their utter inanity, and the fact that a prosperous, highly educated people could unquestioningly swallow such utter rubbish while issuing heated avowals about protecting their "civilization" and "way of life," this is what is truly frightening about this phantasmagoric shadow war against shadowy terror.

Meanwhile, back at Boeing's high-tech factory in St. Charles, three shifts will go on working twenty-four hours a day. Next stop, Iraq.

*Al-Ahram Weekly*, February 28, 2002

# The Infinite Crossroads

"As WE GATHER TONIGHT, our nation is at war, our economy is in recession, and the civilized world faces unprecedented dangers. Yet, the state of our union has never been stronger," declared President George W. Bush in his first State of the Union address on January 29, 2002. Gathered in the House of Representatives chamber to listen to the address (as per tradition), the members of Congress, the cabinet, top military brass, and other dignitaries (including, this time around, benighted Afghanistan's Hamid Karzai) rose in a standing ovation. The ghost of energy giant Enron (the biggest single contributor to Junior's presidential campaign) may have been hovering somewhere in the chamber; it did so very discreetly, however. "War" and "unprecedented dangers" to "the civilized world" ensured its proper behavior, here as on the outside. From the millions of Americans watching the "at times, uplifting" (according to Reuters) presidential address on television, George W. was basking in an above-80-percent job approval rating—a record high for a first-year American president.

Enron and recession notwithstanding, "war," however ridiculous, and "unprecedented dangers," however absurd, are good for business. U.S. corporations get to gorge on the best part of $1.35 trillion in tax breaks. Democrats and organized labor may grumble, but hey, there are tens of thousands of Bin Laden's "ticking time bombs" around the world, not to mention "the axis of evil," fantastically made up of two archenemies, Iran and Iraq and remote and isolated North Korea. The U.S. president is renowned for his original way with words, and he has given "axis" a new meaning here, but "what we have found in Afghanistan confirms that, far from ending there, our war against terror is only beginning." And, "This campaign may not be finished on our watch—yet it must be and it will be waged on our watch." It may sound like unintelligible, if appropriately "uplifting," nonsense to many of us, but probably not to ears long accustomed to advertising jingles and Hollywood promos (of the "love means never having to say you're sorry" variety). In any case, the gist is clear enough: the war against terror is to be milked for all it's worth. After all, "the state of the union has never been stronger."

Now, to someone like me, all this is a scene out of an insane asylum. The war in Afghanistan, as far as I could see, was won decisively in a couple of weeks, and that only after the concept of war had been stretched to its extreme limits: on the ground, a sordid and backward little civil war between eternally warring warlords in one of the world's most economically, technologically, and culturally backward countries (where severed hands and feet are taken as war trophies); from the sky, the full might of the superpower to end all superpowers, wielding a war technology so advanced it is said to be at least a generation ahead of that of its industrially developed allies. In a world that, mere decades ago, was presumably threatened by nuclear annihilation, the leader of the sole superpower can speak of Bin Laden's allegedly "ticking time bombs" as an "unprecedented danger to the civilized world," and no one is laughing. They are, in fact, as much of a joke as Bin Laden's nuclear capability; yes, the one he threatened to deploy only days before the fall of Kabul. As for the "axis of evil" made up of bombed-and-sanctioned-back-to-the-Middle-Ages Iraq, famine-benighted North Korea, and *mullah*-devastated, western-friendship-seeking Iran—can any of this be serious? It is, and the fact that it is boggles the mind.

A few weeks ago, I had the opportunity to hear a high-ranking European diplomat explain that the war against terrorism was the European Union's top priority. Surrealist images from Louis Buñuel's film *That Obscure Object of Desire* flashed through my mind as the diplomat spoke: bombs were exploding in European capitals; machine gun-wielding terrorists were ambushing cars, mercilessly shooting their bourgeois occupants down. Where is the war? The Americans, at least, have the excuse of 9/11. What, other than blind servility, is Europe's?

All this brings to mind the so-called Karine A. affair. I can't remember exactly who spoke of it as "the ship of fools," but the designation struck me as totally apt. *Madness and Civilization*, Michel Foucault's first book, immediately came to mind. Finally, some sense could be made of the sheer insanity. A nuclear occupation power (the last colonial state in the world since the demise of apartheid in South Africa), armed to the teeth and led by a well-known war criminal, has kept a whole people disenfranchised, dispossessed, and subject to murderous repression for over thirty years, yet in this mad world, the occupying power can still be portrayed as a victim, while the victims are portrayed as aggressors.

Foucault describes "the ship of fools" as follows: "Confined on a ship, from which there is no escape, the madman is delivered to the river with its thousand arms, the sea with its thousand roads, to the great uncertainty external to everything. He is a prisoner in the midst of what is the freest, the openness of routes: bound fast at the infinite crossroads."

Subtitled *A History of Insanity in the Age of Reason*, Foucault's critique brilliantly outlines the historical process involved in delineating the absence of reason, that is, madness, as one of exclusion. I'm no disciple of Foucault's, and while the lines between reason and its opposite may be much more blurred, arbitrary, and coercive than was once believed, they do exist, even if only as parody. The dividing line is sharper than ever, but today only sheer power determines whose 'reason' prevails.

*Al-Ahram Weekly*, January 31, 2002

# Let's (All) Go Fly a Kite

DON'T HOLD YOUR COLLECTIVE BREATH, comrades. There'll be no Vietnam in Afghanistan. Kandahar is not Stalingrad and the Sierra Maestra hilltops have about as much to do with the widely advertised caves of Afghanistan as Havana does with Kabul. The two are as different as Fidel and Che from Mullah Omar and Osama bin Laden.

So this particular party is, for all practical purposes, over.

And we might as well admit it; it's been very neatly done. The much-dreaded ground war was finished almost before it began. It involved a mere spattering of American and British forces, basically directing aerial bombardment (allied soldiers, we've been told, have sustained "a few light injuries"). For what it's been worth, the "fighting" was mostly done by "friendly forces"—the self-same Afghan *mujahidin* who have been busy butchering each other, and tens of thousands of their people, for the past ten years.

Now, "the curtain has been lifted," announced U.S. Secretary of State Colin Powell in his much-hyped address at the McConnell Center for Political Leadership, in Louisville, Kentucky, on Monday. He drew his audience's and the world's attention to "the joyous pictures of liberated Afghans, of women throwing off their burqas, children happily flying kites." Less joyous images of the liberators' assorted lynchings are easily blocked out of the larger picture. After all, these are bearded, pajama-clad, burqa-bedecked Afghans and, even worse, Arab Afghans; they're not American soldiers in Somalia, or Israeli undercover agents out to create mayhem at a Palestinian funeral. Indeed, the war in Afghanistan has far outdone Iraq as a collateral damager's dream, what with the major networks waving the flag even more frantically than their governmental/ corporate masters, the Taliban keeping the media out of the country, and the Afghans having, in any case, killed each other with admirable consistency for as long as anyone can remember.

Certainly, the Taliban are not finished yet. But then, they're not supposed to be finished. Back in the caves or the madrasas, from this point on they are destined to play a very similar role to that which Saddam Hussein has been playing in Baghdad for the past ten years: keeping a low-grade conflict alive, and U.S. or allied forces in the region.

So let's not fool ourselves. This war was never about "eradicating terrorism," whether or not Bin Laden and a number of his al-Qa'ida generals are captured and/or killed. From the very start, anyone who is not blinded by official and media rubbish has recognized the war in Afghanistan for what it is: a matter of using one stone to kill a whole host of big, small, and medium-sized birds, none of which is "international terrorism." Assuaging the American public's rage over the 9/11 attacks has certainly been a major motivation, but so has asserting the U.S.' global hegemony and power. A terrorist is whoever we decide is a terrorist. The devil take definitions, and who needs evidence?

Overnight, Dubya became a war president, the powerful and estimable leader of the free and civilized world. Totally forgotten are the Third Worldish elections that brought him into office (chads? What chads?). Europe, which was smarting over Kyoto and various other slights by Washington, has been brought smartly into line, as has Russia (so much so that, this week, the American media declared themselves "charmed" by Putin, who is possibly second only to our very own Yasser Arafat on the world's most charmless political leader list). And, "oh, what a lovely war for profits," to borrow the title of a *New Statesman* article by its U.S. editor Andrew Stephen, who asks pointedly, "what patriotic American could say no" to the Economic Security and Recovery Act? This, Stephen explains, provides for $100 billion worth of tax breaks, three-quarters to major corporations, with only $14 billion going to poor and middle-income families.

The United States Armed Forces are sitting pretty (and, I would hazard, enduringly) on yet another petroleum-strategic region while, back at the military-industrial complex, they're most likely guzzling champagne by the crateload. After all, consumption for its own sake is every capitalist's dream, and what more can an arms manufacturer hope for than an enduring war without targets, and hence with unlimited targets?

All this in the middle of a frenzied revival of patriotism, jingoism, and racial hatred that would warm the heart of a Krupp von Bohln. Not since the Jews, it is safe to say, has modern western capitalism reveled in such a wonderfully unifying enemy as the Arabs and Muslims after 9/11. It might get embarrassing domestically, and awkward from a foreign policy perspective, but the rewards are beyond belief: emergency law in Britain; secret military trials in the U.S.; laws for citizens and laws for noncitizens; different standards for law enforcement according to citizens' ethnic and religious identity; a thousand people (both citizens and noncitizens) held in America without charge or trial for over two months; appeals to loosen legislation prohibiting torture; a free hand for the state to invade everyone's privacy through unrestrained surveillance; docile legislatures; imperial presidencies and autocratic premierships; a war-drum-beating media that openly and slavishly boasts its self-censorship—and this while waving the flag of "our democratic values."

The quagmire of Afghanistan has been smooth sailing and, all in all, the "war on terror"—boasted of as the most significant military operation since the Second World War—has been a tremendously successful enterprise. So successful, indeed, that it has achieved a hitherto elusive, and to me unfathomable, American scholarly invention, "the win-win situation." For, lo and behold, the "terrorists" have won, too. On the ground, it may have been nothing but a sordid little war—one set of cutthroats (in new American-supplied uniforms) replacing another, thanks to American carpet bombing—but it's billed as the Third World War, and it's being fought on a virtual terrain that has set 'our values' against 'theirs,' the civilized against the uncivilized, the good against the evil; ultimately, the west against Islam. Bin Laden, if they do catch him, will die with a beatific smile on his face.

On both sides of the battle lines in this war of civilizations, however, democracy is being put to the slaughter.

*Al-Ahram Weekly*, November 22, 2001

# Operation Enduring Madness

THIS APOCALYPTIC WAR OF CIVILIZATIONS is a monumental con. People are being killed, homes are being destroyed, lives are being shattered, but all of it is shadow boxing, none of it really matters as far as the protagonists are concerned. The real war is elsewhere.

This is the ultimate postmodern war. The actual theater of operations is the realm of symbols, and the target is people's minds, their innate capacity to reason and question. In every modern war, propaganda has been deployed in the service of military objectives. In this war, military operations are not even in the service of propaganda, they are the propaganda.

And in this sense it is a truly global war, "a sustained, comprehensive and relentless operation" to make blithering and bloodthirsty idiots of the greater part of humanity, at least that part covered by the three great monotheistic religions.

Latin America, I might qualify, is largely, and blissfully, immune to the polarization. Its bona fide claim to 'westism,' both geographically and in terms of cultural descent, is made dubious by its 'southern' identity as an object of imperial hegemony. Besides, it is, to borrow from a highly enjoyable American novel I'm currently reading, just too 'vivid.' There is no room for 'vividness' in the all-pervasive black, white, and gray of the good-versus-evil, God-versus-the Devil battlefront between the 'Judeo-Christian west' and 'the Islamic nation.'

The objective of war is victory, and both sides promise us that, with God's help, they will ultimately prevail. "We will fight them with everything material we have, and with all our faith in God we will be victorious,"

136

vowed al-Qa'ida spokesman Suleiman Abu Gheith. "We will not waver, we will not tire, we will not falter, and we will not fail. Peace and freedom will prevail," vowed George W. as he announced the attack on Afghanistan. "We will continue to act, with steadfast resolve, to see this struggle through to the end and to the victory that would mark the victory not of revenge but of justice over the evil of terrorism," pledged America's "staunch friend" and occasional public relations man, Tony Blair.

Yet, unless one totally surrenders one's mind to CNN and its 'expert' generals (rtrd.), the faintest hint of skepticism would reveal to the simplest-minded among us that the one clear objective of this war is its perpetuation ad infinitum, even if "infinite justice" has given way to "enduring freedom" (whose?).

The accent everywhere is on "sustained, comprehensive, and relentless," to quote Bush's opening volley again. More ominous still, in the same statement he promises, "Today we focus on Afghanistan, but the battle is broader. In this conflict, there is no neutral ground." Two days later, British Defense Secretary Geoff Hoon, in Moscow, assured the BBC that "the prime minister has made it clear we will root out international terrorism wherever it arises, so it could follow that once we have dealt with the situation in Afghanistan we could turn our attention elsewhere." Meanwhile, U.S. Air Force General Richard Myers has discovered that "his early assessments that the Taliban and al-Qa'ida had very little in the way of valuable material and infrastructure were being borne out." He goes on to make the utterly bizarre statement: "We're not running out of targets, Afghanistan is."

We have, Hoon tells us, "just started the very first part of the military campaign." No terrorist leaders have been killed or captured, as far as we know, but hurrah, "essentially," the U.S. and Britain believe they have "air supremacy over Afghanistan right now," as U.S. Defense Secretary Donald Rumsfeld has told us. The anti-terrorist allies are now able "to carry out strikes around the clock, as we wish," he points out. The world can sleep better now that twenty ancient Taliban MiG fighter planes are effectively out of operation.

And, according to CNN, senior U.S. officials are now "playing down the prospect of any major deployment of ground forces . . . after the initial air assaults." The earnest network quoted a Pentagon official as saying that "there will be a first wave, then an assessment and very possibly a pause before further action is taken."

Can any of this be serious? The U.S. and Britain, with their gigantic intelligence bodies, spy satellites, cutting-edge spook technology, tons of shared intelligence from allies throughout the world (even Sudan), and long experience in fighting as well as sponsoring, aiding, and abetting terrorism (not least Bin Laden's), must have known from the start what anybody with any sense seems to know: (1) there is very little valuable material and infrastructure in Afghanistan, and (2) you do not use Tomahawks, B-2s, nuclear submarines, and aircraft carriers to fight an underground movement with bases of support in almost every country in the world (including the U.S. and Britain), whose most bloody and devastating act of terrorism was enacted via the use of "knife-like instruments."

Al-Qa'ida training camps have been destroyed, but what are these? Rumsfeld tells us that "this is where they have their classrooms . . . firing ranges." What kind of "valuable infrastructure" is necessary for a classroom or a firing range? No spy satellites needed here: the answer is an open space and a few mats. A dilapidated two-room building is optional.

The truth is, neither side has any hope, or indeed serious intention, of defeating the other. Meanwhile, as "the allies" go on with their sustained and infinitely roving war against the enemies of "our values," and "the believers" search for new "storms of planes" to unleash against the infidel, the absurd monoliths of western civilization and the Islamic nation are solidified. More people die. Reason and our very humanity are trodden underfoot. A triumph, indeed, for our values.

*Al-Ahram Weekly*, October 11, 2001

# PALESTINE:
# PROCESSES OF DOMINION

THE RISE AND FALL OF the Israeli–Palestinian peace process was so much hullabaloo, clatter, and noise designed to cover up, obfuscate, and distract from the one fundamental fact about the 'conflict,' that of one people disposing and oppressing another. The collapse of Oslo and the outbreak of the second Intifada did not, however, open the way to Palestinian emancipation. Israel, under Ariel Sharon, resumed its "war of independence," declaring the subjugation and ongoing dispossession of the Palestinians an immutable condition for its very "existence," indeed for the existence of Jewish people everywhere. Meanwhile, the Palestinians' will to struggle on was being consistently subverted and undermined by the petty, indeed cynical, maneuverings of their divided 'leadership,' both Islamist and semi-secularist, 'radical' and 'moderate.'

# Back to Basics

THE SENSE OF 1948 REVISITED is overwhelming. Early in his premiership, Ariel Sharon told the Israeli daily *Haaretz* in a comprehensive interview that he was still fighting Israel's "war of independence." It was an interesting take on his war on the Intifada, even then, and it blatantly gave the lie to one of Israel's founding myths: that the so-called "war of independence" was an anticolonial struggle against the British mandate. The 1947–48 "war of independence" was always about "independence" from the original inhabitants of the land: the Palestinians.

The ethnic cleansing of over 70 percent of the land of historical Palestine was an absolute prerequisite for the founding and perpetuation of the "Jewish state." This is indisputable; the historical evidence (to which Israel's "New Historians" have contributed massively) is overwhelming. The fierce protestations of even the most dovish of Zionists regarding the Palestinians' right of return—"It would mean the destruction of Israel," they wail in protest—is simply the icing on the proof.

One of the more interesting aspects of the predominant Zionist myths is what we might call the 'waiving of rights' argument. The Palestinians and Arabs did not accept the 1948 United Nations partition plan, which gave a then-minority of newly arrived armed Jewish settlers the best part of their land, and for this alleged mistake they are to be punished in perpetuity. What is right or fair was thrown out the window. The Zionist armed forces could now grab over 70 percent of historical Palestine, drive its population out, take over their lands and homes, destroy thousands of their villages, and hold those who remain as a captive population, whose land and homes are forever easy pickings for "the organic growth" of their Jewish neighbors—and keep it all, forever. Any concept of justice and law is made to disappear. And it goes on, and on and on, with every new blood-drenched grab justified by the "Arab failure" to concede the previous one, every new massacre explained by the anger at the one that preceded it.

So pervasive has been this 'waiving of rights' argument that for many years many 'realistic' Arabs came to swallow it, hook, line, and sinker: "If only we had accepted the partition plan"; "If only we had recognized Israel after 1948"; "If only we had gone along with Sadat in 1978." And there are those among us who are waiting for Sharon's bloody carnage to come to a halt so they can leap up to berate us: "If only Arafat had accepted the shrunken and besieged bantustan so 'generously' offered by Barak and Clinton in Camp David II."

Stuff and nonsense. It is as it's always been: Israel's perpetual "war of independence." Whether it is fought by force of arms or over a nego-tiating table, by massacres or "historic handshakes," by Shimon Peres or Ariel Sharon, or by the two "nationally united," the aim is the same: a final solution to the Palestinian problem. It is simply a demographic problem: the mere existence of the Palestinians is "a threat to the existence of the 'Jewish state.'" Any final solution of a "demographic problem" is genocide. One step down the ladder you get "transfer," which by necessity involves some genocide, since people (especially Palestinians, whose attachment to what remains of their land has grown exponentially in proportion to their dispossession of ever greater parts of it) will not simply pack up and leave.

Then, of course, there is the binding and gagging. In a word, apartheid: to keep the Palestinians enslaved, locked up in their cantons and town-ships, overseen, preferably, by quislings of their own number, charged with keeping them in line. This is called "security guarantees." This was what Oslo was all about; it is what Camp David II was designed to carve in treaty-bound stone.

It all goes back to 1948. The 'original sin' of Israel's founding is a sin in perpetuity. It is not a question of Palestinians and Arabs recognizing the Jews' right to national existence in the region, but of Israeli Jews' recognition that Jewish nationhood cannot and will not be realized as a negation of the Palestinians' very existence as human beings with dignity and rights. Zionism, fully realized, is not merely racism, it's Nazism.

Meanwhile, the war goes on.

And amid the horror, we listen closely for a note of hope.

Earlier this week, my ten-year-old son, Hossam, sat at the computer, loaded PowerPoint, and wrote the following, in English:

JUSTICE

"There are many people that are hated and killed because of their color, religion, and country. For example, the Palestinians have been occupied 54 years, they've been hurt and left to bleed to death without any medical attention, killed and tortured. Also black people in America are accused of crimes they didn't commit just because of their color. Well . . . I think that stinks [a sad face]! BUT Palestinians & blacks standup to their oppressors and that's what matters."

*Al-Ahram Weekly*, April 18, 2002

# Almost Apocalypse

WHO SAID THAT APOCALYPSE IS the only alternative to the 'peace process'? True, the statement is entirely familiar: it has been an article of faith of the peace processing discourse for many years, even in the days of its 'heady' successes, when Nobel peace prizes seemed a dime a dozen. At each and every juncture of the process (its innumerable stalls, deadlocks, and crises, as well as its countless breakthroughs, eleventh-hour rescues, and great-moments-for-peace), we've been warned, in no uncertain terms, by the various parties and by hosts of governmental, academic, and media busybodies that it's either a deal (any kind of deal) or all hell will break loose: unbridled violence and terror will drown the region (even the world) in blood.

For years, the process has been marching to the deafening din of warning bells, in Washington, New York, and Moscow, in European capitals and Arab capitals, in Jerusalem and Gaza. From big, resounding cathedral-sized bells to tinkling little service bells, everyone seems to have a warning bell of some sort to sound. Even the odd, obscure North European monarch would take the trouble to slip, for a moment, out of the pages of *Hello* and onto CNN screens to ring his or her own little glockenspiel.

And they've all been sounding the same admonition: save the peace (process), keep it going at any cost, or it's the apocalypse.

The most powerful argument was yet to come, however. It seems, after all, to be borne out by developments on the ground. The 'ides of March' are upon us, the prophecy is being fulfilled: the peace process has broken down. And does it not look very much like the apocalypse now?

Why must it be so? One need only shut out the din of warning bells, big and small, to realize that there is absolutely no intrinsic rationale behind the all-pervasive proposition. Anticolonial struggles have gone on for several hundred years. Decades would pass without any deals being offered; decades would follow unacceptable deals. Nelson Mandela, even as he appeared destined to spend his remaining days in prison, rejected for several years a proposed deal stipulating that the ANC "renounce violence." The struggle continued. There was no apocalypse.

And why on earth must there be a process? The alternative to submission has always been continued struggle. Where's the riddle?

It is not all ideology, however. Or rather, ideology here serves as the grotesquely magnified and distorted expression of the adversaries' reality, to borrow the idiom of a certain well-known nineteenth-century German. It does so in two ways. The first is gimmicky; it is the great spin lying at the heart of the peace process since its inception. All the parties have had a profound interest in maintaining the semblance of movement toward a continually deferred final settlement. The goal is spurious here: movement, or the process, is all, and not because lack of movement means imminent catastrophe.

More important, however, is the second aspect to this ideological transfiguration, for the gimmick is actually grounded in the fundamental contradiction in the Zionist colonial enterprise since June 1967. What most people seem to forget is that Israel needs the peace process much more than do the Palestinians, let alone the rest of the Arabs. One is always tempted to say to the Israelis, "You want the land and the water—it's your ancestral home, the burial ground of your patriarchs and matriarchs, and all the rest of it? Okay, then, take it. But come on, really take it, annex it." There's the rub, though: the land is inhabited. In 1947–48, a world war had just ended, the Holocaust was headline news, not history, the 'post-' was yet to be affixed to colonialism, and there was no cable or satellite television. The big lie of Israel's founding is no longer possible. "Transfer," if it's to be done, will now be done on prime-time television. And, thank you very much, no one is about to leave so that the Arab armies of salvation can step in and save the day. There will be a Palestinian fighting, even with bare hands, for every square foot of land. Take the land with the people (you do need the cheap labor and the market, after all) and it's goodbye to the "Jewish state," already a dubious proposition, since 20 percent of its population (despite the free and blood-drenched hand 1947–48 made possible) is, after all, Palestinian Arab.

Apartheid is the solution, naturally. But it is rather passé. "Interim" arrangements whereby you maintain dominance over the land, the water, and the people while deferring as much as you can acknowledgment of that dominance is, then, a tailor-made way out of the dilemma.

Everyone else wants a piece of that action. The U.S. would like to see Israel get away with the venture while maintaining, as far as possible, the stability of its friends in the region—there's still plenty of oil down here. The friends, for their part, are desperate for American goodwill, aid, investments, armed protection (for an influential section at least), and, naturally, the stability of their regimes. The Palestinian leadership, especially since Tunis, had been a hovering bureaucratic spirit waiting for a state (any kind of state) to materialize, in every sense. All are concerned (to varying degrees) about opposition movements, in particular the "Islamist threat," for which the Israeli occupation is a constant source of ammunition, however misfired. The Europeans in particular, I have long suspected, are especially worried about the waves of secularist asylum-seekers Islamist takeovers across the Mediterranean might send slapping against their shores. Their societies are already too 'mongrel' to bear.

After a spin in the ideology of the peace processor, the failure to meet these needs takes on apocalyptic dimensions.

But what of the Apache helicopters, the F-16s, the ceaseless suicide bombings, the talk of regional war—does not all this substantiate the supposition that the apocalypse, if not already here, is around the corner? My answer, however, will have to wait until next week.

*Al-Ahram Weekly*, May 31, 2001

# Apocalypse Deferred

THE NOTION OF AN APOCALYPSE kept at bay underpinned the peace process from the start. How else could heroic dimensions be given to a process whose very logic is deferral, the self-conscious avoidance of dealing with any issue of substance? Heroic status was a function not of what was being achieved but of what was being precluded. The process had magical properties, similar to an incantation, the sheer repetition of which keeps the surrounding forces of darkness and chaos in chains.

Now they're unfettered, and they're coming in.

But wait, there's something not quite right here. What's taking place now is actually very different from the augured apocalypse we've all come to know and dread.

In the peace process gospel, the forces of light (euphemistically, the peacemakers) have been heroically engaged in warding off the forces of darkness, an amorphous mass defined basically by its irrational and fanatical hatred of peace and other good late-twentieth-century values such as globalization, liberalization, and security cooperation under the tutelage of the Central Intelligence Agency, but most potently symbolized by Islamist 'terrorism' of the Omar Abdel Rahman/Osama bin Laden variety. The fact that these two representatives of evil incarnate had engaged for years in intense 'security cooperation' with the CIA has been, naturally, glossed over.

In fact, no criticism could expose the farce that was the peace processing ideology as dramatically and thoroughly as its overnight collapse has done. It lies in a total shambles. Ariel Sharon, the "butcher" of Sabra and Shatila and the only Israeli general found by his own people to have committed war crimes, is Israel's leader, with (super-dove) Shimon Peres acting as his public relations man. Yasser Arafat, the Palestinian peace partner par excellence and the winner of half of a Nobel peace prize, has been reconstructed as an unreconstructed archterrorist. Egypt, the Arabs' ultimate good guy and peace pioneer, has been rediscovered as a wicked, ill-intentioned authoritarian regime and the site of rampant anti-Israeli and anti-American attitudes.

Sharon is fighting Israel's "war of independence" all over again. Peres is speaking of a battle for Israel's existence, describing the current situation as an existential dilemma the likes of which he's never seen before (and he's seen a lot). Uniquely, both Sharon and Arafat are now calling for a "'ceasefire," not a cessation of violence. Note the shift in idiom: we no longer have peace partners whose failure to "keep talking" results in "violence," which either party could blame on the other, but war adversaries talking truce.

More ominous still, references to the possibility of all-out regional war have become commonplace. President Hosni Mubarak, who has consistently dismissed as farcical the possibility of another Egyptian–Israeli war, is now forced to tell the Israelis that June 1967 will not be repeated (that is, if it comes to an Egyptian–Israeli war, Egypt will not be defeated as in 1967). The fact that Egyptian involvement in another war with Israel is no longer considered a fantastical proposition advocated by overheated student demonstrators is the most potent illustration of the utter collapse of the peace processing ideology.

This, then, is a very different apocalypse from the one the peace process prophesied. And rather than being a result of the failure of that process, it is the outcome of its completion. Deferral had provided the primary logic of the Palestinian–Israeli peace process since the Madrid talks (then Israeli Prime Minister Yitzhak Shamir later revealed that he had planned for the Madrid-launched peace talks to go on for decades). And the deferral was grounded, above all, in Israel's own desperate need for some form of 'separation,' which is equal to: (1) maintaining control over the land, water, and other resources; (2) disclaiming responsibility for the people who happen to inhabit the land; but (3) ensuring that they are bound and gagged (through security installations, settlements, byroads, security cooperation, and a Palestinian gendarme) so as not to threaten Israel's security.

Deferral provided the ideal means of bantustanizing occupied Palestinian land without acknowledging it. But all good things must come to an end. Final status talks, delayed and delayed, had to come nevertheless. In Camp David last year, they did.

And there is where it all came to head, for the process had another salient feature, which by last summer should have borne ample fruit. Settlements and land grabs of all sorts, which had their golden days precisely while the process was ongoing, were supposed to have defined both the basic territorial limits of Palestinian statehood and the extensive reach of Israeli security requirements. The Palestinian Liberation Organization's bureaucracy, transplanted from Beirut via Tunis, was supposed to have adapted to its subservient status, evolved appreciable vested interests in the status quo, and grown accustomed to acting as Israel's gendarme. Most important of all, however, the Palestinians in particular and the Arabs in general were supposed to have been taught enough lessons in "realism"—to use my favorite Benjamin Netanyahu quote—to accept apartheid in Palestine and Israeli supremacy in the region.

It did not work. The Palestinians, simply, were not ready, and a domino effect ensued that has surpassed the wildest imaginings of the most pessimistic of peace processors and the most optimistic of rejectionists.

But if the peace process apocalypse was a chimera, does not the 'existential' apocalypse of today appear much more real? There is a lot of ideology in it still, and no indication yet that any of the major protagonists has shifted strategy drastically. The Israelis still want an apartheid solution to the Palestinian question. The difference between Ehud Barak and Ariel Sharon is that the latter would like to extend, ad infinitum, the 'interim' coverup Oslo provided for years. As for the Palestinian leadership and its Arab allies, they continue to bank on a revival of peace talks (hopefully, with the Americans and Europeans leaning more heavily on the Israelis) leading to a somewhat more respectable final settlement than that offered at Camp David.

The mood on Arab streets is unprecedented, but one would be hard-pressed to find portents of revolution, Islamic or otherwise. No Arab state would start a war with Israel, and while not totally improbable, it is as yet difficult to imagine even a Sharon-led Israel starting one. It is equally difficult to conceive of Israel getting away with the reoccupation of the Palestinian territories and/or launching an ethnic cleansing operation on a 1947–48 scale.

Apocalyptic rhetoric continues to serve tactical interests, with each side hoping that its version of the coming apocalypse will intimidate the other, as well as various international sponsors, into making or imposing concessions within the same strategic framework.

All this appears extremely tenuous; however, with or without a ceasefire, a revival of the peace process is now next to impossible. How long can it go on before an apocalypse? Looking for signs and portents, soothsaying, or standing before this or that oracle are no help at all. The most absurd prophesy can be self-fulfilling if people believe in it sufficiently. Ultimately, people make their own history, and we need to make it with a view to winning, not to dying, however many of the enemy we take with us.

*Al-Ahram Weekly*, June 7, 2001

# Let's Play Prime Ministers

THE YOUNG MAN SINGING ON the stage in the Geneva auditorium could easily have been Egyptian. His face would not have been out of place on the streets of Cairo, yet his name was Aviv Geffen and he was singing in Hebrew. The sound was wonderful, the song was for peace, and the audience was made up of a few hundred Palestinians and Israelis, men and women of all ages gathered in this lovely Swiss city to proclaim their common commitment to peace and brotherhood. I should have been moved. I wasn't.

The rhetoric was overflowing with noble sentiments and virtuous purpose. The ceremony was perfectly choreographed, with American actor Richard Dreyfus, an archetype of the liberal Jew if ever there was one, acting as a highly congenial master of ceremonies. In big bold letters to the left and right of the stage, the parties to the agreement defiantly declared, "There is a partner; there is a plan." And, in a clear departure from Palestinian–Israeli negotiating traditions, the two sides were represented by two good-looking and articulate leaders, Yasser Abed Rabbo and Yossi Beilin, who concluded the ceremony with emotive and well-presented speeches, and with hands held high in solidarity and brotherhood. Yet, the whole spectacle failed to convince, producing a sense not so much of falseness as of unreality.

Before arriving in Geneva on what turned out to be a frantic day trip during which I attended, along with a small Egyptian group led by presidential adviser Osama El-Baz, the ceremony launching the much-celebrated, much-maligned Geneva Accord, I had read the text of the agreement. It may have been realistic, it may have been the best possible deal 'under the circumstances,' yet it was definitely not the stuff of which dreams of a bright and peaceful future are made.

For one thing, it was candidly iniquitous. In its most rudimentary sense, equity implies formal, legalistic equality, the kind of legal equality shared by a male millionaire with a PhD from an Ivy League university and an illiterate peasant woman, at least in terms of their voting rights or freedom to stand for public office. Yet, even on this crude level the Geneva Accord makes no pretence of providing equality between the two states, Jewish and Palestinian, stipulated and mutually recognized in the agreement.

Take the least contentious of this and all other proposals for a final peace agreement between Israel and the Palestinians: the question of arms. It is almost everywhere taken for granted that the fledgling Palestinian state must be demilitarized while Israel remains in possession of one of the most advanced military machines in the world, including some two hundred nuclear bombs and God knows what kind of stockpile of biological and chemical weapons.

That there is no question whatsoever of any future Palestinian state achieving military parity with Israel is not an issue. I do not believe that it is at all desirable for any such state ever to attempt to do so. Yet, to stipulate that Israel enjoys rights that are denied the Palestinian state in a formal and not just in a substantive sense is to acknowledge that the Israeli state should enjoy an intrinsically more elevated legal status than its Palestinian counterpart, and that it should do so in perpetuity. Such implications run throughout a document within which the imperatives of realpolitik, the language of power, constantly undermine the rhetorical stabs at brotherhood and equality.

And here's the rub. My sense of unreality was not motivated by the iniquities of the Geneva document as much as by the fact that it was being issued by the 'civil society' of Israel and Palestine. The whole document was a much trailed 'virtual' peace treaty and both Beilin and Abed Rabbo have been at pains to explain that they "only want to show that a peace agreement is possible," as Beilin put it.

This served simply to extend any sense of unreality to encompass Palestinian and Arab reactions to Geneva, as well. What's all the fuss about? After two years of intensive discussions, Abed Rabbo, Beilin, and their respective teams could have given us a much-needed document setting out the principles on which a truly equitable peace agreement between Israelis and Palestinians might be founded. This, after all, is the job of intellectuals and civil society organizations. Instead, they played prime ministers and gave us a virtual peace treaty. The worst that could be said about it is that the concessions made by Abed Rabbo should be taken considerably more seriously than those made by Beilin, as the Palestinian delegation was actually more official than 'civil.' Beilin's Meretz group, after all, stands next to zero chance of getting its way, even under a Labor government.

The real issue, however, is that both the Geneva document and, much more seriously, the failed 'factions talks' in Cairo this week bring into sharp focus something that both the Oslo process and the Intifada have managed to keep hidden for so long, and this is the profound crisis afflicting Palestinian strategy. In last week's issue of *Al-Ahram Weekly*, Graham Usher astutely observed that the dissent among Palestinians over the Geneva Accord's stipulations vis-à-vis the right of return actually betray an ambiguity at the heart of Palestinian strategy, as under a two-state solution it might be assumed that Palestinians would want to return to a Palestinian and not a Jewish state.

This is just one, albeit major, aspect of the strategic choices Palestinian political forces have so far preferred to avoid. They can no longer do so. If the Geneva exercise has served any purpose at all it is to reveal what has been from a Palestinian perspective the 'best-case scenario' of the peace process launched in Madrid a decade ago. And that, by implication, is enough to tell us that the best we can now expect from that 'peace process' is considerably less than the accord reached with a fringe group within Israeli 'civil society.'

*Al-Ahram Weekly*, December 11, 2003

# Losing Is Losing Is Losing

"SHARON IS SHARON IS SHARON" was the title given by *Haaretz* to a 'comprehensive' interview with the Israeli prime minister last week. A short introduction to the text of the interview summed up its salient points in this way:

> Only those who believe that there is a "new Ariel Sharon" and that only
> he will bring about peace have the right to be surprised: Sharon is the
> same Sharon and for him the War of Independence hasn't yet ended. In a
> comprehensive interview, the prime minister describes the main points of
> his plan: Jerusalem, the Jordan Rift Valley and the Golan Heights are ours.
> Not even one of the settlements will be evacuated because they all have
> strategic and Zionist value. It is impossible at this time to bring about the
> end of the conflict, nor is separation from the Palestinians a viable concept.
> What then? Time is on our side.

With time, the Palestinians will concede their enslavement and dispossession; the Arabs, by virtue of sheer force, will submit. This is the crux of Sharon's plan. And, it is noted in the interview, his popularity within Israel is unprecedented for it. The "war of independence" is, ironically, revealed for what it always was: the usurpation of the land from its original inhabitants, their dispossession and enslavement. There are no British occupation forces on Palestinian territory at the moment, as far as I know. And that particular war is not over.

Regional war? Sharon may or may not be itching for one. But a war needs an adversary, and as many gauntlets as Sharon may throw down, there do not seem to be many takers across the borders. The most obvious scenario is a strike against Syrian forces in Lebanon, which could develop into a full-scale war with Syria. The strike against the Syrian radar station seems to point in that direction. But the Syrians have always shown a great deal of 'self-restraint' on similar occasions in the past. They continue to do so. And the Americans would not like it. This is not totally to discount such a possibility—the Israelis always manage to find a pretext for a 'defensive' war, and the Americans, the Europeans, and their media always manage to swallow it—but it's unlikely.

Reoccupation of the self-rule territories? Even more obvious: it's already happening. But again, I believe it's unlikely. It would entail massive bloodshed and destruction on such a scale as to make even the western media's steely cynical heart flutter, however faintly. Moreover, it would bring an end for all time to the possibility of having Palestinians police Palestinians on Israel's behalf. And, it would upset the Americans. U.S. State Secretary Colin Powell, while making sure to blame the Palestinians for "provoking" the "hostilities" in Gaza (as he had Hizbullah for those in Lebanon), nevertheless remonstrated with the Israelis for their "excessive and disproportionate response" and called upon them to withdraw from the territories ceded to Palestinian self-rule by virtue of the Oslo Accords. Reuters quoted an unnamed U.S. State Department official as saying that the Israelis "made an agreement to withdraw and they should not reoccupy." For their part, the Israelis stated that they "pay very close attention to what is said in Washington. It is very important to us," as Sharon's adviser, Dore Gold, put it in an interview with CNN.

For the moment, then, Sharon is fighting a war of intimidation, a brutal, vicious, and inhuman war that is moreover creating even more facts of occupation and dispossession while wreaking havoc on Palestinian life and livelihood, but a battle of intimidation nevertheless. Its fundamental objective remains what Oslo is essentially about: to force the Palestinians and the Arabs to accept a Palestinian bantustan under Israeli military, economic, political, and security hegemony.

And he's winning it. The prospect of another war in Lebanon or a reoccupation of the self-rule territories, or even aggressive winks in Egypt's direction (with accusations of cross-border arms smuggling and Israeli soldiers' bullets increasingly finding their way into the Egyptian section of the divided city of Rafah), have got the Arabs, to put it mildly, flustered. Our top goal at the moment is to prove to the Americans, the

Europeans, to anybody who will listen, that we're good guys, have no aggressive intentions, and desire with all our hearts an end to the 'violence,' practically at any cost.

And, as I have argued before, Sharon has already won a decisive part of the battle by totally shifting its terms. We are no longer fighting to regain more occupied Palestinian territory but to avoid losing the territory over which we already have some semblance of control. No longer is the struggle about greater Palestinian sovereignty; it's about winning back some of the paltry prerogatives handed over under Oslo's "transitional" self-rule agreements. And the Intifada has become "violence." The battle for Palestinian independence has been conceded as part of a cycle of violence that must be broken. "Security cooperation" has become the be all and end all of the "process," to which even its most ardent advocates are shy to attach the word "peace."

Security cooperation, too, means one thing and one thing only: ending Palestinian resistance to the occupation. Hundreds have been killed, thousands wounded, and thousands more made homeless; olive and citrus groves have been bulldozed; the dismembering and plundering of Palestinian land has gone further and faster; and more settlements and more and wider connecting roads and byroads have been built. Still, the 'process' would have us cower in silence and docility in our ever-shrinking 'areas,' so that, maybe, we can get some of the tax money due to the Palestinian Authority under Oslo, which Israel has been withholding for the past seven months.

We're in for the long haul, and it's time to recognize it. The accent is on time. To put time on our side, not Sharon's, is what a new Palestinian strategy must be all about. Two absolute conditions for winning back time, in my view, are to turn our backs on the 'process' once and for all (what in heaven's name are we waiting for?) and to fight on a terrain of our own choosing, not Sharon's. When we bargain with Sharon to stop the 'violence,' we lose. And when we try to challenge him with his own bloodthirsty methods, he wins hands down. When we juggle the two, we lose twice. The writing is on the wall, let's read it.

*Al-Ahram Weekly*, April 19, 2001

# Meanwhile, Back at the Bazaar

LET'S FOR A MOMENT TAKE the peace process at its word. The Palestinian–Israeli struggle is not predicated on the fundamental fact of one people oppressing and dispossessing another. It is not a question of repression and resistance. Rather, we're haggling in a bazaar. The commodity we are trying to purchase is called land, and we want to pay for it in a currency called peace. Here, we can disregard the fact that we are buying stolen goods; that the seller did not come by his merchandise by legitimate means; and that, as it happens, it was stolen from us. All of these facts are firmly established by the law of the land, namely, in our case, the Geneva Conventions, the Universal Declaration of Human Rights, and a host of United Nations resolutions, including even the partition plan for Palestine of 1948.

But, as our luck would have it, the *muhtasib*, or market inspector, is crooked. He has an arrangement, of a strategic kind, with the other party to the supposed deal. Never mind also that the worth of our currency is highly dubious. If it was ever worth anything at all, it now looks more and more like the Lebanese lira during the last days of the civil war.

What we are interested in here, however, is the haggling itself, which seems to have attracted a large crowd, some of whom, including the crooked *muhtasib*, involve themselves in the bargaining in different ways. It is a sight to behold, for the contenders are breaking every rule of bargaining ever known to man or woman. This is one bizarre bazaar.

I am, I must admit at once, very unskilled at the art of bargaining. Usually, I either buckle too soon or walk away in disgust, possibly missing out on what someone with more skill would have made a very good bargain. But even I know that when the Khan al-Khalili merchant I'm buying spices from begins with 20 to my offer of 10, the next round should be somewhere around 18 and 12, possibly closing the deal at 15. What that next round cannot be, by any stretch of the imagination, however, is one in which I concede the full 20 only to be told that the item in question is now worth 30; I concede the 30, and the price goes up to 50. I am, meanwhile, being held down by the *muhtasib*, whipped by the merchant, and jeered at, nudged, and prodded by most members of the crowd, including a few members of my own family, who are supposedly standing around to help me strike a good bargain.

Prostrate on the ground, bruised and bloodied, a man I've often observed strutting and preening around the souk cloaked in an *'abaya* identical to that of the *muhtasib*, kneels down beside me and whispers in my ear that all this is only fair; after all, I must be punished for having missed out on the previous offer. (If you are not already bored to tears by Mr. Thomas Friedman's presidential 'memos,' see the *New York Times* of March 27, 2001. I, unfortunately, have to make a living as a journalist, and in this profession alienated wage labor takes such forms as being obliged to read Mr. Friedman, watch CNN, etc.)

I am not about to review the dismal history of the Middle Eastern bazaar called the peace process. Let us merely observe the bargaining since Ariel Sharon came to power in Israel less than two months ago. For a time we had the line that any Palestinian–Israeli negotiations must begin where they left off at Taba. Allegedly, according to Palestinian officials, Taba's nonagreement "reflected" (I never understood exactly how) the achievements of the Intifada. Taba then disappeared. Anyone who has the most cursory familiarity with the Palestinian–Israeli peace process should be fully familiar at this point with this now-you-see-it-now-you-don't aspect of Palestinian and Arab stances toward the process. It was back to Sharm al-Sheikh, which—if anyone still remembers—was essentially aimed at "restoring" the situation to what it was before September 28, that is, before the Intifada. But Sharm al-Sheikh has also disappeared.

The next rabbit out of the Arabs' hat, as I understand it, is going to be a lulu. Arafat, it has been whispered, is being advised by fellow Arabs to call on Palestinians to halt the Intifada for a four- to six-week period, during which six months of negotiations will be launched on interim and final status issues. It is, in my view, a very unlikely bid. Arafat cannot do it, and even if he does make the call, no one will heed it.

But let us assume for argument's sake that it happens and negotiations are launched. The 'final' will be the first to go. Sharon will have got everything he demanded: a halt to the Intifada and negotiations around so-called long-term interim agreements. By then, of course, he will have upped the ante some more. Long-term interim agreements will require shorter-term interim agreements, and each agreement will require implementation agreements, more guarantees of Israeli security, more security coordination, and more repression of Palestinians in the occupied territories. Meanwhile, settlements will continue to expand 'organically' and otherwise, the land will keep shrinking, even as the bypass roads, military checkpoints, and the like eat up more and more olive groves and citrus trees and destroy more Palestinian lives and livelihoods. Soon enough, Arafat will be demanding 'a return' to a long-term interim agreement, and Friedman will be writing yet another memo.

*Al-Ahram Weekly*, April 5, 2001

# History's Nightmare

ACCORDING TO THE ISRAELI PRESS, one of the first sentiments expressed by Ariel Sharon's new education minister, Limor Livnat, upon taking office was her resolve to expurgate the country's school curriculum of the 'New Historian' influence. The alleged New Historian influence in the Israeli school system is also one of Prime Minister Sharon's pet 'demons,' to use *Haaretz*'s Hana Kim's word. The columnist, however, reassured both Sharon and Livnat that, in fact, there was no New Historian influence in the school curriculum or, for that matter, outside it; that almost half of Israel's students do not study history at all; and that a passing reference in a single textbook to the Palestinians having been driven out rather than leaving of their own accord does not count as New Historian influence.

The extent to which ideology can subsume, manipulate, and condition memory is always astounding. In our part of the world, the battle over memory is no less vital to a just and human solution to the Israeli–Palestinian/Arab struggle than resistance actions on the ground. And the battle lines are drawn not just along the Arab/Israeli divide but within each 'camp,' and across them.

Take the New Historians' revelations about the founding massacres of the Jewish state. These, no doubt, would have found an appreciative audience among most Palestinians and Arabs had they been adequately popularized by the Arabic press, instead of the usual rubbish about AIDS-exporting Israeli tourists and sexual-depravity-enticing Israeli chewing gum. We have always held that the Palestinians were driven out of their land, though it took the work of Israeli historians to reveal the gruesome

160

truth of that version of Palestinian/Israeli history. It is something else altogether to conclude that more than a few of us share their critical attitude toward our common history. Indeed, I am continually amazed by the complicity and mutual reinforcement of the Zionist and prevalent Arab versions of that history.

Dismissing the Sharon/Livnat New Historian demons, *Haaretz*'s Kim recounts the following story: "Several years ago historians Dr. Ilan Pappe, Dr. Benny Morris and Prof. Avi Shlaim shared a car from Tel Aviv to Jerusalem. Pappe insisted on driving. 'I know how you two drive,' he said. 'If God forbid we crash—Israel's new history would vanish into thin air.'" Our equivalent, no less sadly, would probably fill a small van at most.

"The tradition of all the dead generations weighs like a nightmare on the brain of the living," wrote Karl Marx in that most 'un-Marxist' (in any conventional sense) of tracts, *The Eighteenth Brumaire of Louis Bonaparte*. When a fair section of 'the dead generations,' thanks to modern medicine and hygiene, is also alive and killing, the 'nightmare' is even more difficult to shake off.

And it is not just the 'facts,' though we do share—with the Zionist version of our common history—quite a few of those, too, most notably the myth that the Arabs actually fought for Palestine. (When was that exactly?) No less important, however, is the reading of those facts. Take Saddam Hussein's attempt to liberate Palestine via Kuwait. One would have thought that anyone who had the least recollection of Nasser's May 1967 'bluff,' and its disastrous consequences, would immediately have recognized Saddam's escapade for what it is: history repeating itself, the first time as tragedy and the second as farce (to use Marx's *Brumaire* once again), or merely as the bad sequel to a dubious blockbuster, to use the more contemporary Hollywood-influenced parlance. That ten years on some of us are willing to be taken in by the Iraqi leader's 'Jerusalem Brigades' boggles the mind. Memory, rather than an instrument of learning, becomes one endless nightmare.

And the nightmare, as nightmares often do, continues to generate ever new and variously repulsive phantasms. Palestinians in the occupied territories are, according to the International Red Cross, on the brink of starvation; the Israeli army and rampaging settlers continue to do their deadly work on a daily basis (a ten-year-old Palestinian child has just been beaten to death by settlers). And rather than underline the full horror of the killing of hundreds, some of us would like to make common cause with those who would try to belittle the killing of millions. In Beirut, from March 31 to April 3, 2001, a conference on "Revisionism and Zionism" is to bring together a motley crew of European and American neo-Nazis and anti-Semites, presumably to give further evidence that the Nazis killed three rather than six million Jews.

But, thankfully, we, too, have our share of 'new historians.' Edward Said, Mahmoud Darwish, Adonis, Mohamed Harbi, Jamel Eddine Ben Sheikh, Mohamed Berrada, Dominique Edde, Elias Khoury, Gerard Khoury, Salah Stetie, Fayez Mallas, Farouk Mardam-Bey, Khalida Said, and Elias Sanbar (fourteen Palestinian, Lebanese, Syrian, Moroccan, and Algerian intellectuals) have issued a statement declaring, "Arab intellectuals are outraged by this anti-Semitic undertaking. . . . We wish to warn Lebanese and Arab public opinion about this and call on Lebanese authorities to ban this inadmissible conference."

The Zionist Organization of America, which among other Jewish and Zionist organizations has been demanding that the Beirut conference be banned, is also, as Israeli writer Israel Shamir noted in a recent article, the publisher of a booklet called *Deir Yassin: History of a Lie*. Shamir protests, "I do not want to repeat the gory tale of sliced-off ears, gutted bellies, torched men, bodies dumped in stone quarries, or the triumphal parade of the murderers. Existentially, all massacres are similar, from Babi Yar to Chain Gang to Deir Yassin."

A car or a van, no matter. There is hope so long as there are among us, whether Arabs or Jews, people who will look to memory as an instrument of learning and salvation rather than of denial and repression. The nightmare can be shaken off yet.

*Al-Ahram Weekly*, March 22, 2001

# Whining and Dining

"THE TIME HAS COME TO listen to the people," sneered the Arabs' erstwhile great white hope, Shimon Peres, to Labor Party opponents of a "national unity" government under Ariel Sharon. A rowdy meeting of the Labor Party's Central Committee has confirmed by a two-thirds majority that it will be joining Sharon's government, responsible for the key portfolios of foreign affairs, defense, and settlements (euphemistically called "infrastructure"), among a total of eight seats of the twenty-eight in Cabinet. Peres, who has accepted the post of foreign minister, will be bonding with bomb-the-High-Dam-and-"transfer"-the-Palestinians psychopaths Avigdor Lieberman and Rehavam Ze'evi, among twenty other representatives of Israel's extreme right wing, all under the leadership of Sharon, "the butcher."

And 'the people' (at least those who went to the polls) have overwhelmingly chosen as their leader a war criminal, whose fundamental message is that Israel's survival is contingent upon the shedding of Palestinian blood.

The matter is settled, then. Everybody seems to recognize that Labor Zionism, whose one remaining distinction from the right was its allegedly dovish position on Arab–Israeli peace, is in its death throes. The Palestinians are to be confronted by a politically monolithic Israel, which has effectively released itself from all obligations established by eight years of the Oslo peace process and has unilaterally halted negotiations with the Palestinians. Its foremost mandate is to crush the Intifada, whatever it takes.

With the Intifada entering its sixth month and its cost in Palestinian blood and suffering rising by the minute, such dramatic changes in Israel, one would expect, should have encouraged some original thinking among the Palestinian leadership. The sense that a creative response of some sort is required was, at the very least, felt. No such luck. The Palestinian Authority's one response is to hang on to a lie, and our credulity is to be tested to the point of total idiocy. What was patently impossible to achieve in Camp David in July, in New York in September, and via Bill Clinton's last-ditch 'bridging proposals' in December–January was, we are now being told, "almost" achieved in six days of negotiations in Taba, held on the very eve of Israeli elections. The Intifada was raging. Israel was busy assassinating the leading cadres of its "peace partners." Helicopter gunships, artillery, tanks, and dumdum bullets continued to sow death and destruction. Palestinians' homes were being bulldozed, land they had been cultivating for centuries was being destroyed, and their towns and villages were subject to a deadly siege. Meanwhile, Ehud Barak and Yasser Arafat were engaged in a last, desperate, and futile, effort to forestall a Sharon electoral victory. Taba, as almost everyone recognized even then, was nothing but a bungled public relations exercise.

What was achieved in Taba, anyway? The two sides set down, in familiar vague terms, their areas of agreement and disagreement. The first amounted to the Palestinians conceding "a limited state" whose alleged sovereignty is exercised always "in coordination" with Israel, conceding, in principle, that there will be no full withdrawal from the West Bank; that there will be some sort of shared control over Arab East Jerusalem; and that Israel will annex the major settlement blocs in occupied Palestinian territories, effectively cutting the fledgling Palestinian state into three Israeli-besieged sections. The second amounted to the Palestinians objecting to the extent and form of withdrawals, settlement annexation, and shared control of Jerusalem. Some sort of "language" was apparently reached with respect to the right of return, but nothing about implementation. In short, nothing.

And, as per standard peace process logic, the Palestinian side, clinging to 'the letter and spirit' of the latest almost-agreement, established its concessions as a new ceiling for any future negotiations.

Now it's United States Secretary of State Colin Powell's turn to be told that Arafat, if he agrees to the latest set of concessions demanded of him, risks being assassinated by his own people. This time around, the argument is being put forward with respect to Sharon's position that a final-status agreement should be given up in favor of a long-term interim agreement. Indeed, the Palestinian leader is now saying that it is not a question of whether he will be assassinated but when. I don't know which of Arafat's bungling advisers fed him that assassination line. Whoever it is, he should be arrested and investigated, preferably by the notorious Force 17, for being an Israeli agent. And even if found innocent, he should still be shot for the crime of extreme stupidity.

The argument is shameful. It purports to scare the Americans and the Israelis into contemplating the chaos that would beset Palestinian society upon Arafat's demise. But it is testimony to an administration that is at once extremely authoritarian and totally inept, threatened by collapse the moment the leader passes away, whether by an act of God or man. And it is so easily answerable. Arafat's Israeli and American negotiators could just as well promise him elite guards—the best trained Central Intelligence Agency and Mossad operatives—to protect him day and night. And the European Union can always foot the bill. In public, they could berate him, as Barak used to do, by citing the example of such 'true leaders' as Yitzhak Rabin and Anwar Sadat, who paid for peace with their lives. And what sort of a freedom fighter is so afraid for his life anyway?

It was the Intifada that brought down the Oslo peace process. The Israelis now recognize that Oslo is over, and so do the Americans. It is about time the Palestinian leadership did. And the "symbol of the Palestinian people" should not whine, at least not in public.

*Al-Ahram Weekly*, March 1, 2001

# The Beginning at the End

THE POINT OF DEPARTURE FOR the long and tortuous road of the peace process was an attempt to move away from the fundamental fact of Palestinian dispossession, to avoid a settling of accounts with the colonial and racist nature of the Israeli state.

Mr. Yaacov Hayman, an American Jew from Hollywood, would thus continue to enjoy an unlimited right of 'return' to the land of his Biblical ancestors, whenever whim or inclination took him that way. Why he would do so is irrelevant. It could be a failed marriage, a brilliant career that never quite took off, mere anomie, or an intense bout of Zionist zeal. Twelve years ago, Mr. Hayman did 'return.' When we first learn of his existence, it is on Itamar, a Jewish hilltop settlement near Nablus in the West Bank. Palestinian peasants had been dispossessed of their land and livelihoods so that Mr. Hayman could find a nice home waiting, with a well-watered lawn and perhaps a little swimming pool, on this parched land. Then there are the massive byways, connecting roads, and security installations, for Mr. Hayman must come and go as he pleases in his ancestral homeland, his 'security' protected from its faceless inhabitants.

When Mr. Hayman appears on the world stage, the al-Aqsa Intifada is in full swing and the Itamar settlers have just shot and killed a Palestinian peasant working in his olive grove at the foot of the settlement. He does not hate the Arabs, Mr. Hayman from Hollywood tells the British *Independent*'s correspondent on that grim occasion, he just does not want to 'share' the land with them.

At an early stage in their peace trek, the Arabs adopted the "land for peace" formula as a slogan and a founding principle for the resolution of the Arab–Israeli conflict. This catchphrase-turned-founding-principle of the peace-settlement-turned-peace-process clearly embodies the fundamental flaw in that process, all the more so as it is the Arab side that holds it as a mantra, while Israel appears to concede it reluctantly. In the 'land for peace' spin, the slate is wiped clean, the reality of Palestinian dispossession erased, and the 'conflict' made to begin in May 1967, at most. The June War becomes a defensive war, and Israel's occupation of Arab land is motivated not by expansion and colonial conquest but by a desire to live in peace with its neighbors. The Arabs become the aggressors, who must be made to pay the price. Israel wants peace; the Arabs seek the land Israel occupied, to promote peace, in June 1967. The fundamental fact— one people oppressing and dispossessing another—is made to disappear. All we have is a bazaar: so much 'peace' for so much 'land.'

The brilliance of this spin lies in that, while fully affirming the Zionist myths about the origins, history, and nature of the conflict, it has given the Arabs a stake in perpetuating these very myths. The Arabs had fought for Palestine; they could go on bemoaning and/or boasting of the 'sacrifices' they made for the Palestinian cause, blame it for the many ills of their regimes, and, even as they were surrendering the Palestinian cause piece by piece, go on using the Israeli threat as justification for an authoritarian imperative of 'national unity.' Moreover, they had an effective bargaining card, which presumably Israel had been seeking desperately from its very inception: they could give it peace.

Because of the overwhelming preponderance of ideology over reality in the construction of the Arab–Israeli conflict, such obvious rubbish has been all-pervasive. The Arabs never fought seriously for Palestine (at least not outside the realm of rhetoric and dissimulation) and Israel never seriously wanted peace (not, that is, outside the same realm). The 'peace' part of the apparent barter was, in fact, a code word signifying a large package of concessions. Recognition of Israel's 'right to exist' became contingent not only upon conceding for all time the dispossession of the past, but also upon 'guaranteeing Israel's security' into the future. Insatiable and ever precarious, Israeli security, it would become increasingly clear, was contingent upon reaffirming, consolidating, and legitimizing the colonial and racist nature of the Zionist state and project. To deny it would be to deny Israel's right to exist, and to deny Israel's right to exist as a colonial and racist state would be to deny the Jews' right to exist, to threaten them with another Holocaust. Peace, ultimately, signified security and legitimacy for a colonial and racist project. Land, however—and here is the rub—is an essential security guarantee for a colonial project. Hence Mr. Hayman's 'return.' The trade-off turned out to have been a tautology.

In 2000, weary and dispirited, we reached the end of the road. Lo and behold, that which we had been moving away from for over a quarter of a century was sitting there waiting. The colonial and racist nature of the Zionist project was staring us in the face.

The real question is not one state, two states, or a federated state. A Palestinian/Arab strategy that does not directly come to grips with the racist and colonial nature of Zionism is doomed from the start.

*Al-Ahram Weekly*, January 25, 2001

# Ordinary Monsters

THE TWENTY-SOMETHING SOLDIER FIRST notices the huddled father and child fleetingly, his attention as yet focused on the source of intermittent rifle fire from a handful of Palestinian security men. And as fleetingly, an impression registers in the soldier's mind, almost subliminally at first: he has seen the look of terror on their faces, the child's panic, baffled and uncomprehending, for, like all children, he is yet unresigned to the monstrous cruelty of which human beings are capable. He is afraid of being hurt, afraid of his father being hurt and knowing how inadequate he is in providing help, afraid most of all, perhaps, of finding himself alone amid the madness, bereft of his father's protection. A single thought dominates the father's fear: he wants his little boy safely home, unhurt.

The impression grows gradually in the young soldier's mind. He takes other brief glances at the two, recognizing the desperate desire underlying their terror, of seeing this over, of somehow coming out of it all safe and unhurt, each in his own mind wishing the two of them home, seeing them with his mind's eye surrounded by family members, recounting their encounter with danger, in the past tense.

It's fun playing God, however. And as if that singular horror were not enough, we know from eyewitness testimony that it was not just one twenty-something soldier who was playing but a whole bunch of them—a regular turkey-shoot, insistently targeting an unarmed father and his little boy. So insistent that even the ambulance man who tried to come to their help is shot dead.

Which of the two did each of the young soldiers decide to aim at first, one wonders. The father, to see, however briefly, helplessness and utter terror seize the little boy in their grip? Or the son, for the satisfaction of registering, however momentarily, the man's unbearable grief, his loss and shame at having failed in the prime task of a parent, to protect his child? In short bursts, the automatic rifles unload bloodshed. Twelve-year-old Muhammad Jamal al-Durrah lies dead; a new batch of nameless monsters is born.

It couldn't have happened that way, some will no doubt protest. It's crossfire, unintended and unpremeditated, they will assert. Some, despite all the evidence, will even hold on to the farcical official Israeli claim that the shooting that injured the father and killed the son came from the Palestinian side. Not, mind you, that Israel's much-boasted military machine is supposed to be incapable of hurting Palestinian children. Not even the most zealous Israeli propagandist can make such a claim, however much he banks on the goodwill of Israel's many powerful friends in the world media. Israel's killing of children should not be so graphically illustrated, however. The victims should remain, as much as possible, faceless numbers. They're Arabs, after all, faceless numbers almost by definition.

It may not have happened exactly that way. But it damn well could have. A few short weeks ago, a number of Israeli soldiers were disciplined for brutally beating three Palestinian workers as they were trying to pass through an Israeli border checkpoint. The beatings were totally unprovoked. The soldiers concluded their brutal extravaganza by forcing the Palestinian workers to lie on the ground—all at gunpoint, naturally—and taking snapshots of each other pressing their boots on the prone Palestinian workers' faces. It couldn't have happened that way? Well, it did. This story at least was fully acknowledged by the Israeli authorities.

What does it take to transform a human being into a monster; not a freak, the Son of Sam or Jack the Ripper, but an ordinary everyday monster, with family and friends, someone who enjoys jazz, perhaps, fusses over how he takes his coffee, and likes to go dancing on a weekend?

But then, what does it take to occupy a family's home and land, consign its members to destitution and humiliation in a refugee camp, and feel not a twinge of guilt that maybe something in all of this is wrong? What does it take to bulldoze homes, enjoy the pool and the sprinkler-sodden yard of your settlement house, while the people whose land this used to be just a very short while ago go thirsty? What does it take to break children's arms, to humiliate, abuse, dispossess, and constantly beat into the ground a whole people for over fifty years? It takes as much as it took for a young soldier to aim at a frightened child and, unmoved by his terror, even thrilled by it, to pull the trigger.

Monsters, ordinary or extraordinary, are not short on rationalization or self-justification: "Given the chance, they'd do the same to us; they want to throw us into the sea; we've suffered the horrors of the Holocaust; this is our historic land . . . ." None of this provides an explanation, however, because what it really takes is a relationship of oppression, the arrogance of unchecked power, and the profound, dehumanizing contempt in which the oppressor holds those he oppresses. It is this that ultimately defines and creates humanity's ordinary monsters. And, strangely, the monsters are not beyond redemption: they can be humanized, paradoxically, not by the submission of the oppressed but by the growing strength of their resistance. Look at the United States' African-Americans, South Africa's blacks, Vietnam. Look at Palestine, in a few years' time.

*Al-Ahram Weekly*, October 5, 2000

# Religious Pathos and Pathetic Politics

I AM NOT ABOUT TO MAKE LIGHT of the various religious 'sensitivities' toward Jerusalem, even while recognizing that though the sacred is held to be everlasting, religious sensitivities of all sorts invariably reveal a decidedly conjunctural nature. The fact that Jews, Christians, and Muslims (by virtue of their common religious descent) hold Jerusalem holy and certain sites and shrines within it sacred nonetheless gives none of them a claim on the city beyond that of enjoying fairly free access to these sites and the freedom to perform whatever religious rituals their respective religions require. And, one might add, access is never 'unfettered' but is everywhere regulated and ultimately controlled by sovereign (political) states, even in the Vatican itself. Need we remind anyone of the kind of 'access' Palestinians, not to speak of other Arabs, Muslim and Christian alike, have been enjoying to this most holy of cities in the past thirty-three years?

The patently obvious fact about Jerusalem that has been drowned out by the raucous peace process rhetoric is that it is a Palestinian Arab city. Until fifty-two years ago, all of Jerusalem was a Palestinian Arab city (the prospective site of the American embassy was the home of a Palestinian family). Until today, East Jerusalem remains a Palestinian Arab city. It is a miracle that it does despite thirty-three years of economic and physical strangulation and the gradual but unwavering policy of ethnic cleansing pursued by an occupying power that boasts one of the most effective war machines in the world.

It is testimony to the indomitable ordinary heroism of the Palestinian people that they have not been 'cleansed' from Jerusalem; that they have been able to withstand the invasive spread of Jewish settlements into the very heart of their city in what Benjamin Netanyahu used to call "organic growth" but what any student of elementary biology would recognize immediately as cancer. For, despite the unbearable oppression, the arm-breaking, the arrests and detentions without charge or trial, the legal and extralegal torture, the house demolitions, and the countless daily humiliations by a virulently racist settler population and its military guardians, East Jerusalem has remained a Palestinian Arab city. Pakistani Muslims, American Jews, and European Christians may be as 'religiously sensitive' as they wish about Jerusalem. The Palestinians' right to their city is derived simply from the fact that it is theirs—an immutable spiritual and physical bond between a people and their land.

It is typical of the distortive effect that lies at the very heart of the 'peace process' that this most fundamental right of a people to their own land has been transformed into a question of reconciling the religious sensitivities of the world's three great monotheistic religions, including such disparate communities as Pakistani Muslims, American Jews, and European Christians.

The obfuscation has been so thorough in the case of Jerusalem as to open a Pandora's box of sheer garbage, what with Ehud Barak offering us such profound arguments in support of Israel's claims to Arab East Jerusalem as that there were no mosques around when Jesus walked the streets of the city two thousand years ago and with the Americans proposing 'divine sovereignty' over the Dome of the Rock. Not to be bested in the religious sensitivity free-for-all, Yasser Arafat reportedly suggested to Bill Clinton (during their latest meeting on the sidelines of the Millennium Summit in New York) that sovereignty over the site be given to the Jerusalem Committee of the Organization of the Islamic Conference.

Distortion and concealment of the fundamental facts of usurpation, dispossession, and oppression have made up the cardinal logic of the peace process. The Palestinian leadership's complicity in this distortion in the case of Jerusalem is not merely a function of its irrevocable entanglement in that process, however. There is an additional 'perk,' which for some mysterious reason Palestinian negotiators seem to believe is their strongest bargaining chip. The question of religious sensitivity conjures up the specter of militant Islamism. In trying to outbid the Israelis in underlining the intensity of Muslim, as opposed to Jewish, religious zeal concerning Jerusalem, Palestinian negotiators hope to paint a sufficiently horrifying picture of fanatical hordes unleashed in a rampage of terror and destruction.

It is not a threat that is even dignified by the implication that those who are making it intend to put into effect, failing a just peaceful settlement of their cause. Rather, they openly state that they will be its first victims. Barak recently derided Arafat for allegedly whining to world leaders that he would be killed by his people if he accepted what the Americans and Israelis are putting before him. Reminding Arafat that both Anwar Sadat and Yitzhak Rabin had been killed "for the sake of peace," Barak quipped that "we know of no attempt on Arafat's life."

In an interview with the London-based *al-Hayat*, Salim al-Zaanoun, the head of the Palestine National Council, revealed that a thoroughly dispirited Arafat had, in the course of Camp David II, told Clinton, "Don't forget to walk in my funeral, Mr. President." The statement was intended to be dramatic. Strange, then, that it sounded pathetic instead.

*Al-Ahram Weekly*, September 14, 2000

# The Archaeology of "Land for Peace"

THE ARABS AND PALESTINIANS HAVE been lambasting Benjamin Netanyahu almost daily since he came to power nearly a year ago for dumping the "land for peace formula," which is often also called the "land for peace principle." Even before Netanyahu, the Labor government, under both Yitzhak Rabin and Shimon Peres, was often criticized for allegedly trying to wriggle out of its commitment to that very formula/principle, which was established by the 1991 Madrid conference as a basis, or framework, for Middle East peace.

Meanwhile, the Israelis, backed by a massive battery of American and other think-tankers, commentators, columnists, and more, have been giving the Arabs the runaround by floating alternative tradesmen's euphemisms: land for security; peace for peace; security for security; peace for security. The Arabs have angrily reiterated their insistence that there will be no retreat from the "land for peace" formula/principle/basis/ framework. In turn, the Americans and Israelis have duly responded by reaffirming their own commitment to the same, albeit according to different interpretations.

Such word games have been an outstanding feature of the Arab–Israeli peace process. The most notable of these plays on words, of course, is the term 'peace process' itself, which in all likelihood was first coined in the Middle East and has since been offered to the world at large. While the words were never innocent and are invariably rigged against Palestinian and Arab rights, they always found an easy prey among our word-loving intellectuals, who set about elucidating, explaining, and interpreting their terms. I recall a speech made by the late President Sadat in which he stumbled, searching for an Arabic equivalent for the word 'momentum.' Apparently Henry Kissinger, who had a special flair for word games of this sort, had convinced the Egyptian president a few days before that "we had to maintain a momentum for peace."

"Land for peace" was formulated as a sort of explanatory footnote to United Nations Security Council Resolutions 242 and 338, the first of which was issued in the wake of the June War in 1967 and the second, basically reaffirming the first, in the wake of the October War of 1973. Who coined the formula, and exactly when, I confess to having failed to discover. I strongly suspect that it made its appearance, along with a whole barrage of other catchphrases such as 'peace process' and 'momentum for peace,' sometime in the mid-1970s, the time when Kissinger was busy talking in the Middle East even as back home the wheels were turning that would ultimately and dramatically end his career of having listened when he shouldn't have. Whether the famous formula is another of 'Dear Henry's' cynical contributions to posterity, I do not know, though it definitely has a Kissingerish feel.

What is truly amazing is that no one seems to know. I have looked up various references, asked numerous Egyptian experts, and went so far as to "Ask Israel" using the email service of the Israeli Foreign Ministry by that name. This column, I hope, will eventually generate an answer from someone with a better memory and/or research abilities than mine, but the paucity of information on the origins of "land for peace" is in itself truly remarkable in light of the buzzword's countless appearances in official statements, commentaries, analyses, and so forth.

But for all the Arabs' devotion to "land for peace," it could not have originated in the Arabic language. *Al-ard muqabil al-salam* smacks of translation and has none of the catchy finesse of today's media-conscious English usage. Indeed, from the mere ring of it, the formula is unlikely to have been invented anywhere else but in some U.S. think tank.

And a most insidious invention it is. What, indeed, can be more insidious than to heatedly defend, day-in day-out, something that was not yours to start with, that is inherently rigged against your interests, debases your fundamental rights, and, not least, is a chimera with no basis in current or past reality?

No less than the very notion of the peace process, "land for peace" trades off fundamental rights. It debases the very essence of the Arab/ Palestinian–Israeli confrontation from one of dispossession, usurpation, and unabashed racial and national oppression to one in which the oppressor and the oppressed are equated, each having something that the other wants. Much more pernicious, however, is the underlying assumption that Israel wants peace so much it would surrender Arab/Palestinian land, accept Palestinian self-determination, and the like in return.

By saying this, the Arabs and the Palestinians are in fact conceding the totally distorted Zionist version of the history of the conflict: poor, small, beleaguered Israel wanting to live in peace with its neighbors, surrounded by fanatical, war-crazed Arab hordes bent on its destruction. Land in this equation is no longer Palestinian or Arab land, it is mere earth, something base and material. The people, their dispossession and subjugation, are made to disappear. The Arabs, backward, sensual, and greedy, seek mere acquisition, while the Israelis, western and civilized, seek something intangible and noble: peace. With little more than a ditty, history, truth, and morality are turned upside down.

Conceding history, principle, and fundamental rights, this banner of the Arab peace offensive is without practical implication, even within the terms of the peace process. Since the disengagement agreements on the Egyptian and Syrian fronts in 1973, nearly a quarter of a century ago, the Arabs have had no peace to offer Israel. What they have been offering is "normalization," yet another Israeli construct that, when translated into real terms, means conceding sovereignty over such things as with whom to trade, what to sell or buy, whether or not to exchange diplomatic, political, cultural, even security ties, and so forth, in return for regaining sovereignty over your own territory.

In the various Israeli–Palestinian agreements from Oslo to the now-defunct Abu Mazen–Beilin secret understanding, the whole so-called trade-off takes on farcical proportions, whereby the Palestinians are given formal sovereignty over some of their territory in return for conceding overall sovereignty in military, security, and economic relations and foreign policy affairs. In return for this, the rest of the Arabs are supposed to coax Israel by offering yet more, if less flagrant, concessions on their own sovereignty over the conduct of their foreign policy, economic ties, and so on.

In the latter case, the Israelis are not dealing with the Arab states' commitment to Palestinian territorial rights. Rather, they are banking on the real need felt by the regimes of several Arab states for a 'positive' Israeli contribution to safeguarding their precarious security. No trade-off is involved; what is needed is merely some face-saving deal that would allow these regimes to make arrangements with Israel palatable to their peoples.

Moreover, the Israelis know that as far as such immediate and influential neighbors as Egypt and Syria are concerned, 'normalization' will always be highly unstable and precarious, irrespective of the kind of deal they make on the 'Palestinian track' and of any other bilateral and multilateral arrangements, for reasons that are inherent to the national security concerns of these two states. And if they can't guarantee Egypt, in particular, everything else they reach beyond it or behind its back, remains a house of cards.

What remains, then, of the alleged trade-off? The Arabs have no peace to offer Israel, for to offer peace you must have the alternative option of war. 'Normalization' translated in real terms as concessions to Israel's hegemonic ambitions in the region is, first of all, not really the Palestinians' to give, depends on needs that have little to do with the restoration of Palestinian rights, and remains, beyond the short term, a highly unstable and precarious prospect. If it is a Palestinian/Arab card, it is a very poor one, indeed.

So why are the Palestinians and the Arabs clinging so tenaciously to "land for peace"? Gullibility? Not quite. They realize that the fundamental logic of the peace process is one of submission to United States/Israeli dictates, with bargaining limited to the degree of submission. They realize, moreover, that their only real bargaining card in this respect is their own security, that is, the threat that the lack of a face-saving settlement will destabilize them to the extent that forces 'less moderate' and less friendly to U.S. and western interests will take over. In the current Arab reality, these forces are none other than the 'Islamist threat.' Knowing that in terms of the peace process, their one source of strength is their vulnerability, that Arafat's negotiating 'muscle' lies precisely in Hamas' potent ability to dislodge him and take over command of the Palestinian people, they have an interest in perpetuating the illusion that they have something of worth to trade.

The problem, of course, is that neither the Americans nor their Israeli allies take the 'Islamist threat' very seriously. I tend to agree with that assessment.

*Al-Ahram Weekly*, May 1, 1997

# THE SAMSON FIASCO

THE SECOND INTIFADA WAS SUBVERTED, hijacked, and effectively destroyed by Hamas's so-called martyrdom operations. Rather than being mobilized and organized in an ongoing popular struggle that could only triumph by winning over sympathy and support from among the Israeli people, the Palestinian people were reduced to, ultimately, handfuls of desperate, hopeless youths, their very bodies turned into homemade bombs. Suicide operations, hailed and sanctified throughout the Arab and much of the Muslim world, were symptomatic of the deep malaise that was overtaking the Arabs, and through them spreading out to Muslims everywhere. Critiquing 'martyrdom operations' was taboo, but then taboos are made to be broken.

# Butchers and Bulldozers

THE SENSE OF DÉJÀ VU cannot be ignored. Ariel Sharon's trouncing of Ehud Barak has induced the uncanny feeling that we are witnessing an almost exact replay of the Peres/Netanyahu episode.

Then, as now, Peres, with a view to teaching the Arabs yet another lesson in realism and pandering to the long-term shift to the right in Israeli society, launches the Grapes of Wrath onslaught on South Lebanon. The atrocity of Qana is committed and furiously defended by the 'dovish' prime minister: it's the Arabs who should be held responsible for the indiscriminate massacre of Arab civilians, children and adults, men and women. The hostage takers' argument finds readily receptive ears in the western media, with Robert Fisk and a few others dissenting. Nevertheless, after the usual expressions of official Arab outrage, the Arabs desperately campaign for Shimon Peres in early Israeli elections. ("Netanyahu would wreck the peace process, spell war and devastation in the region.") Israel's Palestinian citizens display a mind, and a sense of dignity, of their own. They punish Peres at the polls. Peres leads into Benjamin Netanyahu. The Arabs, with a sense of misgiving, a summit conference, the usual appeals to the revival of Arab solidarity, and a couple of vaguely worded warnings to the 'hawkish' premier, decide to give him a chance to reveal his true intentions toward peace. Campaign rhetoric, we are told, should not be taken very seriously and, after all, "we are dealing with a state, not a prime minister." The Americans and Europeans urge self-restraint.

It's not just more of the same, however. True, Fisk continues to find himself in that lonely wilderness of human reason and conscience, amid a media jungle where heartless ignorance reigns supreme. Otherwise, despite the eerie resemblance between them, the difference between the Peres/Netanyahu and Barak/Sharon episodes is as great as that between the process and its fulfillment. The difference between a train station and the end of the line is not, after all, just one of scale.

The journey lasted over a quarter of a century, but the point we were trying to escape from was there, waiting for us at the end. There was no escaping the colonial and racist nature of the Zionist project and state; 1948 is back, and it has a face. There is something gruesomely fitting in that this face should be Sharon's, a man alternately described as "the butcher" and "the bulldozer." Butchery and bulldozers was how it all began.

To wait on the pleasure of the "king of Israel" is demeaning, and to engage in ominous reading of signs and portents of future devastation at his hands is futile. Both spell impotence, as does our inevitable penchant for empty swaggering and braggadocio. "Three hundred million guns await you, Sharon," screamed the banner headline of an 'independent' Egyptian newspaper this week. If only to avoid the sheer boredom of endless repetition, we must attempt to think in a new way of a new strategy.

Which just might bring us to the subject of guns, not the fantastical 300 million guns from which Sharon has supposedly been cowering in fear ever since he was hit with the apocalyptic headline a few days ago, but the few real guns in Palestinian hands, with which they have been fighting an extremely unequal battle against what is arguably one of the most sophisticated, and brutal, fighting machines anywhere in the world. Are they useful in the context of a strategy of liberation? With an eye on the next parliament, Egyptian editors can afford to send fanciful hosts into battle, grandly hailing the hundreds of thousands of martyrs they are so willing to offer to the Arab and Muslim nations' greater glory. The Palestinians, fighting tooth and nail for their survival, can ill afford to partake of such spurious luxury. The sordid and dehumanized indifference that certain Arab political figures and intellectuals show rhetorically for the lives of their own peoples, Israel puts into effect in reality. The question is pertinent in an immediate sense, since the armed character of the Intifada has been assuming greater weight in past weeks. Although the suicidal act of a lone bus driver in Tel Aviv could hardly qualify as armed struggle, it underlines the Intifada's increasingly desperate tendency to move away from popular protest actions toward individual acts of violence.

It is not, in my view, a good development.

But let me first make one thing absolutely clear. For Palestinians to resort to violence against their Israeli tormentors is the most natural thing in the world; it is knee-jerk and, yes, totally human. A couple of weeks ago, *Haaretz* carried in graphic detail the story of a Palestinian family's heart-rending struggle to take their sick child to hospital. The girl needed an appendectomy, a twenty-minute procedure that the most inexperienced of hospital interns could perform. Their little girl in horrible agony, the family rushed from one Israeli checkpoint to the other, begging for their daughter's life and being subjected, at each stop, to the heartless sneering of the soldier boys of the self-appointed master race. Their towns and villages were 'closed.' The girl died in excruciating pain.

I have a nine-year-old son who is as precious to me as I have no doubt the little girl was to members of her family. I've given this a lot of thought: let anyone harm him the way this Palestinian girl was harmed and I would want to find someone to kill.

You don't want Palestinian violence, get out of their land. It's as simple and as blatant as that.

It is beside the point, however. Desperation and anger, and the totally human need to hit back at one's oppressors, do not on their own make for successful resistance. And absolutely nothing justifies the harming of a child, be she Jewish, Arab, or of any other religious, ethnic, or national group on this planet.

*Al-Ahram Weekly*, February 15, 2001

# A Bloody Amnesia

THERE WAS A PERIOD OF TIME, albeit a short one, when the Palestinians had set themselves the goal of creating a secular democratic state for both Palestinians and Jews in all of Palestine. This strategic goal was to be accomplished through (and this may sound jarring to post-Ronald Reagan ears) a "protracted people's war"—the Vietnamese, after all, were in the process of winning just such a war. It was a consensual strategy upheld (at least nominally) by every Palestinian organization, from Yasser Arafat's Fatah to al-Hakim's Popular Front for the Liberation of Palestine. Israel had yet to give a helping nudge to the creation of its eventual nemesis, Hamas.

Why, with the missiles flying, human and car bombs exploding, and the Egyptian–Jordanian/Saeb Erekat initiative floating, unearth such an historical curiosity from the obscurity to which it has been consigned for over a quarter of a century? Simply because memory is important. Perpetual amnesiacs, who seem to begin each day with a clean mental slate, are as constitutionally incapable of formulating a strategy as they are of passing a first-grade exam. The fact that Arab and Palestinian 'elites' seem to suffer from this strange malaise is, however, a product of social rather than physiological determinants. It's an affliction of the heart, not the mind.

"Sixty-two Israelis dead and wounded in Palestinian suicide attack," shouts the banner headline of the Egyptian opposition *al-Wafd* newspaper. In the 'independent' *al-Usbu'*, the editor dedicates his front-page editorial (this, a telling peculiarity of the Egyptian press) to a cloying elegy of the heroic suicide bomber. The suicide bombing in Kfar Sava, a Tel Aviv suburb, in fact killed one Israeli, a fifty-four-year-old doctor. All but two of the sixty-one wounded were released the same day after treatment. A fourteen-year-old boy was reported to be in critical but stable condition, and a lightly wounded pregnant woman was being held in hospital for observation. This is not armed struggle, let alone a "protracted people's war." It is sordid, pathetic, aimless. It is tragically wasteful, and the waste is counted in human lives.

And there is no heroism in it, though a suicide bombing by a Palestinian, young or old, may make perfect sense, may be perfectly understood as a response to the half-century of unbearable oppression and humiliation to which the Palestinians have been subjected. Such is the warped reality that has come to govern people's lives.

I am a peasant whose life has been spent tending the family's olive grove. It's a hard life and it may not provide a prosperous existence but it is feeding many mouths and it's providing my loved ones with a home, and, no less important, a sense of self-respect. And then an Israeli settlement springs up almost overnight on a hilltop overlooking my land. The well, which for generations has provided water for my olive trees, is confiscated by the Israeli army. The water is to be used for the swimming pools and lawn sprinklers of the few dozen gun-toting, trigger-happy settlers who have recently 'returned' from somewhere in America. My olive trees die of thirst while, I'm told, the Israeli prime minister gives interviews in which he elaborates on the wonders of the olive tree. Then one day the bulldozers come. The grim-faced soldiers are unmoved by our appeals and beseeching. The settlement needs a byroad and my life and those of my family members is shattered forever. What happens to me in the afterlife is the least of my worries. I want retribution in this one.

I am the father of a six-year-old girl and one night she begins to complain of stomach pains. The pain gets worse. It's an obvious case of appendicitis. She must be taken to hospital immediately, but there is a blockade on. We rush from one Israeli army checkpoint to another. The cries of my child make not the least impression on the soldiers. Neither do my tears, my beseeching, my begging for my daughter's life. She dies in horrible agony. Whether it's heaven, hell, or nothing at all that waits for me in 'the afterlife,' someone, anyone must pay in this one.

Just two stories among thousands. They go on and on and on. And no one seems to care. I need only imagine myself a Palestinian living under Israeli occupation and becoming a suicide bomber becomes the most natural thing in the world.

It is not, however, heroic. It is not heroic to risk your life when you seek death, but only when you love life.

And against all odds, the Palestinians continue to fight for life. Hamas may boast one hundred suicide bombers; there are millions of Palestinians. And their very will to struggle for liberation and to live in order to bring it about is the truly heroic aspect of the Palestinian people's condition.

I may fully understand, even sympathize with the suicide bomber. I have nothing but scorn and contempt for the 'leaders' who build their political influence on the desperation and hopelessness of their supporters. As for the Cairo editors who seem to wallow in the blood of Palestinian martyrs, they are merely ridiculous.

Transforming liberation fighters into walking bombs is wasteful and sordid. Killing and injuring civilians is immoral. The massive imbalance in the ability to exact violence makes a mockery of the so-called 'armed operations.' A struggle for liberation, not mere futile, desperate, and aimless retribution, is a conscious act of will—a plan, a function of experience and learning, of the ability to assess critically the history of the struggle as it happens. These are the tasks of people who would be political leaders, intellectuals, and writers. Amnesiac windbags are no help at all.

*Al-Ahram Weekly*, April 26, 2001

# Arms and the Man

NEARLY ONE YEAR AFTER ITS INCEPTION, the Intifada is now almost wholly identified with suicide bombings, which have become more frequent and more devastating. It is Hamas and Islamic Jihad that are now calling the uprising's shots. The process of reduction has been going on for many months. Is it one of advancement or degeneration?

We need to recap:

The Intifada was launched as a popular uprising, a spontaneous mass movement involving the active participation of tens of thousands, nurtured and enthusiastically supported by a whole people. Such sudden outpourings of mass energy are among the mysteries of human history. They can be explained only in hindsight. Political movements can help prepare the ground for them, provide them with leadership and direction once they take place, but they can never actually instigate them. Why, how, and when do people—ordinary everyday people who have children to raise, a daily living to scrape together, and ordinary everyday lives to lead—suddenly decide that they can bear no more; that the business of coping with hardship, oppression, and humiliation is no longer possible? Many may claim to have the answer. I don't believe anybody does, really. Sure, there are always a great many reasons why people should rebel, but more often than not they just cope, weaving day-to-day acts of resistance, subversion, and adaptation into highly complex and subtle survival strategies.

The distinction between popular sentiment and its phenomenal forms is something that the oppressors and their hosts of publicists are incapable of understanding. It implies an admission of the fundamental fact of oppression. Hence the ever-repeated question: "Who's behind it?"

Nearly twelve months ago, the al-Aqsa Intifada's one fundamental feature was the spontaneous resolve of the Palestinians in the West Bank and Gaza to refuse to live with Israeli servitude and humiliation any longer, whatever the cost. The forms such resolve takes, in the Palestinian as in any other popular uprising, depend on leadership, strategic direction, organizational capability, tactical proficiency, or, indeed, the lack or extreme weakness of all of these elements.

Contrasting the second Intifada with its 1980s precursor might prove useful in explaining the forms the ongoing uprising has taken over time, drawing it further away from its first installment, so much so that the two are now comparable more in name than in any other recognizable element.

Consider their three fundamental differences. The most significant, if least obvious, is the fact that while the first Intifada epitomized the Palestinian struggle for a two-state solution, the second Intifada was a response to that solution's collapse. It is this that lies at the heart of the 'endgame' character of the confrontation on both sides; there simply is no 'middle ground,' either in practical, objective terms or in imagination. From the very outset of the Intifada, the endgame quality of the confrontation found expression, on the one hand, in unprecedented levels of Israeli repression (coupled with the virtual collapse of the Israeli 'peace camp') and, on the other, in a profound strategic crisis on the Palestinian side.

To grasp the extent of the crisis we need to note that the Palestinians' two-state strategy was from its inception a 'peace strategy.' It was grounded in the supposition that a negotiated Israeli withdrawal to pre-June 1967 borders was imminent. So imminent, indeed, that when Popular Democratic Front for the Liberation of Palestine leader Nayef Hawatmeh (writing, with Yasser Arafat's behind-the-scenes blessing, as early as 1972 under the byline of 'a Palestinian leftist') presented the first-ever version of a Palestinian two-state strategy, his main concern was not how to achieve a Palestinian state on the West Bank and Gaza, but how to forestall Jordan's King Hussein from grabbing the West Bank again once it was returned. As such, the crisis in Palestinian strategic thinking was and remains much more profound than would be explained by the crisis of the Palestinian Authority's disastrous negotiating strategy as elaborated in the Oslo process.

The second and third distinctive features of the al-Aqsa Intifada are more obvious. They both derive directly from the Oslo process. These are, respectively, Arafat's PA and the availability of arms. Several years of PA self-rule had devastated Palestinian popular organizations as only a 'national' authority could. These organizations had been developed and greatly refined during the first Intifada and survived both Israeli repression and the Intifada's 'exhaustion' (the first Intifada, we might note, had all but fizzled out by the time of the Gulf War, which was the true forerunner of the 1991 Madrid peace conference). They were unable to survive (except as mere shadows of their original selves) a national leadership armed with a ready-made bureaucracy well practiced in the arts of authoritarian control—that optimal combination of direct repression and soft coercion, populism and patronage, nepotism and corruption that has been among the more prominent success stories of post-independence Arab regimes.

These very conditions had contradictory effects, however, which the collapse of Oslo brought into sharp focus. The PA's authoritarian control was contingent upon its maintaining a 'national' character. The struggle for independence was yet to be won, or even to appear to have been won. Only a Yasser Arafat, bolstered by his Palestinian Liberation Organization bureaucracy and erstwhile freedom-fighting security forces, could have enough influence to protect 'Israeli security' while allowing Israel both to maintain its overall dominance over Palestinian land and people and to avoid the 'demographic nightmare' of seeing the Jewish state dissolve in a sea of Arabs. But these were the very same reasons that made it extremely difficult to transform a Yasser Arafat into a full-blown quisling and his erstwhile freedom fighters into Israeli gendarmes. With Camp David and the outbreak of the Intifada, the contradictions came to a head. Israel, deciding that the Palestinians needed another major lesson in 'realism,' sent the missiles flying. Palestinian arms, for what they're worth, could only turn toward the national enemy.

"Contrary to the Israeli account" of the Intifada, writes Palestinian scholar Yezid Sayigh, Arafat's behavior "since the start of the Intifada has reflected not the existence of a prior strategy based on the use of force, but the absence of any strategy. His political management has been marked by a high degree of improvisation and short-termism, confirming the absence of an original strategy and of a clear purpose, whether preconceived or otherwise."

The second Intifada's recourse to arms was not a strategic choice, nor is it a sign of strength. It was practically preordained, an outgrowth of Oslo as much as of its collapse. For its part, armed struggle has been reduced to what we are now calling 'martyrdom operations' (presumably in deference to the Saudi mufti). These, irrespective of their moral standard or strategic and tactical ramifications (all of which are highly dubious, to say the least), are merely the easiest course of armed violence under conditions of extreme imbalance of military force.

The Palestinian struggle for liberation could not, and should not, remain the captive of chance.

*Al-Ahram Weekly*, August 16, 2001

# Suicide's Not Painless

THE STATE OF THE ARAB world today, and especially of Egypt, is such that reasoned debate is next to impossible. The process of reducing the Intifada (in people's minds, if not yet fully on the ground) to 'martyrdom operations' is almost complete. Thus, if you criticize such operations, you open yourself to accusations of playing into American hands, of acting to bring an end to the Intifada. The matter becomes even more sensitive given that Arab governments, under United States pressure, are doing just that, with considerable Palestinian Authority complicity, and we have yet to draw attention to the vulgarity, viciousness, and slanderous accusations that have characterized the debate of such 'sensitive' issues in Egypt.

Here, I might point out that I'm fully aware of the dubious advantage that this column gives me. My little bit of partially liberated territory (we're talking armed struggle, so we might as well use military metaphors), being in English, is safer than most. That, however, is a privilege I do not welcome. I would like to think of this column as sniper fire, but I'm the first to admit that my "safe haven" or "foco" (as Che Guevara/Régis Debray might have put it back in the 1960s) may well be so safe that the bullets are not hitting any worthwhile target.

Let me first of all underline a certain dilemma that faces all of us in addressing the issue of suicide operations. It is, like many other issues in contemporary Arab life, a debate under siege. In this case, the blatant hypocrisy of the western world—its political leaders and media—in its views on the Israeli–Palestinian confrontation tempts one to shout "a plague on all your houses, we will do our best to be the vicious, heartless beasts you make us out to be. Our children are no less precious than yours, our lives no less sacred, our dignity no less worthy of preservation." I need not cite the multitudinous examples of the flagrant double standard. They're only too familiar.

I could cite one of the less flagrant examples of this double standard, however, which struck me as especially poignant just for being so. It is the statement made by German Foreign Minister Joschka Fischer at the time of the Tel Aviv disco bombing. Expressing his horror at the suicide bombing, he said that it conjured up the image of his own teenage children, who also queue up to go into discos. It struck me at the time that Mr. Fischer (a nice, left-wing social democrat who would be horrified at the suggestion that his body harbors a single racist bone) would never think of drawing a similar parallel in the case of Palestinian children and teenagers, who are being killed and maimed daily, and in much greater numbers. Some of them would even frequent discos if they could find them.

Mr. Fischer, who was in Israel at the time, is supposed to have 'saved the day' by rushing to Yasser Arafat and pressuring him to declare a unilateral ceasefire immediately. It was this declaration, we've been told, that stayed Sharon's hand from carrying on with the Israeli military's plan to reoccupy parts of the self-rule territories and destroy the PA. But that is another story.

I have described armed attacks against Israeli civilians as "immoral." I realize that this is a particularly weak aspect of my argument, not because there is no such thing as an Israeli civilian but because the 'masters of the universe,' in Washington and elsewhere, have made a total mockery of any humanitarian moral standard. Even organizations mandated to uphold the humanitarian moral standards that have been codified into international law (such as the International Red Cross) have conspicuously failed to do so in any consistent manner.

The purely arbitrary nature of horrified condemnations of certain military acts against civilians, and the approving justification of others, seems to deny the existence of a moral standard of any kind in this matter. This is especially true because we know that sanctioned killing and maiming of noncombatants claim so many more victims and cause far greater human suffering than operations that give rise to horrified condemnation of the sort expressed by Mr. Fischer.

I do believe, however, that humanitarian moral standards do exist, that they express something fundamental about our human nature, and that they are subject to historical development, essentially through struggle. Take racism, for example, if only for the sake of the forthcoming conference in Durban, South Africa.* In moral terms, humanity has come a long way over the past fifty years toward recognizing racism for the abhorrent monstrosity it always was. There is no doubt in my mind, moreover, that this 'moral development' can only be understood as the outcome of the anticolonial struggles of the peoples of the south and of ethnic minorities (particularly African-Americans) in the imperial north. That such struggles do not merely lead to the defeat or weakening of particular structures of racial supremacy but also are conceptually appropriated and expressed in general terms as a rejection of any and all forms of racism is what human moral development is all about.

The Palestinians' is a liberation struggle. Theirs is a supremely moral cause. And it is from the morality of their cause that they derive their greatest strength. Is it not worthwhile, then, for them to take the moral high ground that is theirs by right, and suit their means of struggle to the substance of their cause?

*Al-Ahram Weekly*, August 23, 2001

---

\* The UN World Conference Against Racism of 2001 was held in Durban, South Africa on August 31–September 8.

# Ultimate Sacrifice

ARIEL SHARON, "THE BUTCHER," did not kill the Intifada. It committed suicide, thanks largely to the suicide operations of Hamas and Jihad, the seemingly incontrovertible foolishness that has increasingly characterized Arab political and intellectual life for over two decades, and a tenacious determination to block out experience, to learn nothing at all. To put it simply, the oppressor's practices (brutal, barbaric, and inhuman as they doubtless are) cannot justify the failure of an uprising against oppression. Attempts to use them to that end beg the very question the uprising seeks to answer: how to win?

It used to be that the Palestinians' slogan of struggle was "Revolution until Victory." Revolution—or, in today's terms, Intifada—until death is not an attractive option. The Biblical Samson strikes a ridiculous, rather than heroic, figure, not to mention that our attempts to bring down the temple over the heads of our enemies as well as our own invariably miss the enemy altogether. Not only do we manage to lose a great many more heads than does the enemy, but (and by now this should be starkly clear to the blindest of us) killing civilians (few or many, innocent or not) does nothing, absolutely nothing, to weaken the enemy. It makes him stronger and more voracious. Sharon, we all seem to agree, practically wills Palestinian suicide operations. Yet, many of us continue to praise these operations, finding perverse virtue in insisting on the very tactics into which the enemy relentlessly attempts to corner us. It is, to say the least, a peculiar mindset that may best be exemplified by the bewildering circumstance that those who welcomed and/or justified the 9/11 outrage as a blow against major symbols of American economic and military hegemony were more often than not the very same people insisting that the Israeli Mossad had done it (on 'who benefits the most?' grounds).

But the alternative is there. In mid-December, a number of prominent Palestinian intellectual and political figures (including such luminaries as Haidar Abdel-Shafi, Edward Said, Mustafa Barghouthi, and Mahmoud Darwish) issued a declaration outlining some of the salient features of an alternative strategy to the submission of Oslo and the abhorrent suicidal tactics of Hamas and Jihad. Soon after, Barghouthi organized a nonviolent international solidarity action involving over five hundred Europeans who traveled to the occupied Palestinian territories at their own expense and joined Palestinian activists in a variety of highly creative forms of peaceful resistance.* Not surprisingly, the Israelis arrested Barghouthi twice in the course of the campaign and, with typical brutality, used rifle butts to smash his knee. The good doctor, who heads the Union of Palestinian Medical Relief Committees (a creation of the first Intifada that has resolutely and miraculously survived both Oslo and the Palestinian Authority) struggles on, however, fighting with his comrades against enormous odds (nearly a thousand Palestinians have been killed and twenty-six thousand injured, a great many of them left with permanent disabilities, since the beginning of the Intifada).

Yet, here in the 'mother of the world' it seems that only folly trudges along. Last week, about a thousand political and intellectual figures gathered in a Cairo five-star hotel under the dubious banner of the 'independent' weekly newspaper, *al-Usbu'*, famous for its (partially successful) campaign to have democracy activist Saad Eddin Ibrahim hanged in a public square (instead, a responsive state security apparatus sentenced him to a mere seven years in jail). The attendants valiantly braved hail and snow (well, a spell of inordinately cold weather and a little rain) to make it to the downtown hotel where they proclaimed their determination to fight to the death against American hegemony and Israeli occupation. I did not attend this particular function, but, having taken part in dozens

---

* Edward Said, "Emerging Alternatives in Palestine," and Mustafa Barghouthi, "The Amazing Power of People," in *Al-Ahram Weekly*, January 10, 2002, and Fayza Hassan, "Diary of an Occupation," *Al-Ahram Weekly*, January 17, 2002.

of similar exercises in futility, could have easily scripted the event.* It was more of the same: the same heated speeches, the same ranting and raving, with each political and 'intellectual' figure trying to outbid the others in ornamentation of language, fierceness of avowals, and dearth of thought. As ever, there was the 'close down the Israeli embassy in Cairo' nod—a worthy goal, if only anyone bothered telling us how to go about it. And, just in case anyone was hoping that there might be something, anything, new under the sun, there was the inevitable, hysterical appeal to the attendants to 'go out on the street,' which invariably ends in everyone, not least the appellants, going home to a good night's sleep. (Street demonstrations and marches are banned under emergency law, in force in Egypt since practically forever.)

The star of this particular show, however, seems to have been the suicide operation. "Painful operations and suicide attacks . . . this is the only road," declared one of the speechmakers, reportedly to resounding applause.

Last May, I described the then-newly resurgent suicide operations as sordid, wasteful, and futile, and warned that these operations were a recipe for destroying the Intifada. In response, a friend wrote me an email harshly taking me to task for criticizing, from the privileged comfort of a middle-class Cairo existence, an action taken by Palestinians suffering the ravages of a heartless occupation. Better that, I would suggest, than urge horribly suffering Palestinians to their death, the destruction of their homes, and the defeat of their struggle for liberation, from the privileged comfort of a downtown Cairo five-star hotel. We have had enough of the foolishness, the strutting, and the preening. We've had enough of empty rhetoric, hypocrisy, and wastefulness. We've had enough of defeat and, most of all, we've have had enough of this sordid attachment to death.

A word to other middle-class Cairo 'armchair Intifadists' like myself: you want a suicide operation? Go do it yourself.

*Al-Ahram Weekly*, January 17, 2002

---

\*    See: Amira Howeidy, "Five-Star Steam," in *Al-Ahram Weekly*, January 17, 2002.

# Hamas in the War of Civilizations

WHAT IS HAMAS' STRATEGY, and will it succeed? Wrecking the Israeli–Palestinian peace accords seems rather a narrow objective, which, indeed, Hamas appears close to achieving. But what does this have to do with correcting the grave injustice that these accords have installed as law, to virtually universal approval and celebration? I believe, nothing.

Having said this, however, one cannot dismiss the recent wave of suicide bombings. Jerusalem, Ashkelon, and, a week later, Jerusalem, then Tel Aviv, as a mere exercise in destructive fury. The highly selective euphemism, 'terrorism,' provides an easy solution for the need to explain. It evokes images of mindless and bloodthirsty fanaticism, which for a western audience are loaded with a deeply ingrained, and daily reproduced, racist view of Arabs and Muslims.

Hamas violence, in this view, is self-explanatory, inherent in the very nature of the suicide bombers as Arabs and Muslims. A 'profound' explanation, deriving from this, will tend to lecture on the 'fundamental' concepts of jihad and martyrdom in Islam, neglecting to mention that similar operations were until some time ago—and occasionally even now—conducted by both Christian and Muslim fighters of such Marxist Palestinian organizations as the Popular Front for the Liberation of *Palestine* and the Democratic Front for the Liberation of *Palestine*. Indeed, neglecting to mention that it was none other than the late Wadie Haddad, a Christian and a Marxist with close links to such 'intrinsically' European groups as the German Bader-Meinhoff group and the Italian Red Brigade, who established the tradition of Palestinian 'terrorism.'

A first and starkly obvious level of explanation for the bombings lies in the fact of continuing occupation and national oppression. What is remarkable here is not the lack of evidence but the insistent blindness of almost everyone in the face of overwhelming evidence. Apartheid, whose presence in South Africa was universally condemned for decades, is being hailed in Palestine as a triumph of peace and understanding between nations. It has been equally remarkable during the past week that in the frenzy of moral indignation following the Hamas operations, the Israeli reaction, billed as "Israel's war against Hamas terror," has evoked little concern for anything but the 'peace process.'

Western commentators and journalists, who do not hesitate to criticize human rights violations in states' confrontation with Islamist militants in such countries as Egypt and Algeria, did not even seem to recognize the fact that mass administrative detentions, curfews, arrests of relatives of suspects, and the sealing and destruction of homes involve human rights issues. No one seemed to notice that, as far as Israel is concerned, there is not even the pretense that the Palestinians are anything but a subject population with whom the occupation state can do as it pleases, and as its security considerations make "necessary."

Only racism can explain this particular blindness, which is made considerably easier to maintain by the fact that anti-Arab, anti-Palestinian racism helps alleviate the purely western guilt of a previous and bloody racism against the Jews.

For the Palestinians, this virtually universal blindness to their suffering makes that suffering doubly intense. It creates a psychological climate whereby you either address Israel and the west in their own terms, through the 'peace processing' discourse, thus conceding that Israelis are much more equal than Palestinians, or you do not address them at all. When the price of Israeli and international sympathy is the denial of one's own human dignity and right to equality, everything else seems equal.

Equally, it sets an ideological climate for such tendencies as Hamas and Jihad, whose denial of the 'other' is practically a knee-jerk reaction to that other's incessant denial of Palestinians and Arabs. Israeli and western responsibility is no solace, however. Armed attacks against civilians, as I noted before, are immoral whether they are made by the oppressors or the oppressed, and irrespective of the blatant hypocrisy with which world media and governments grade their level of indignation depending on the perpetrator.

But besides their inherent immorality, such attacks imply bad strategic choices, whether they are successful or not. And this brings us to a second level on which Hamas' strategy can be understood. For these are not merely individual acts by desperate, brutalized, and humiliated men who, driven by a deep sense of injustice, lash out viciously and indiscriminately against their oppressors. The latter may explain the personal, and bewildering, act of the suicide bomber but it fails to explain the choices of political leaders who order these acts and who issue statements claiming responsibility for them.

On this level, I believe Hamas' strategy to be cynical in the short term and abhorrent in the long term, and that in both the short and long terms it brings the Palestinian people no closer to winning their liberation and fundamental national and human rights.

Wrecking the Oslo Accords cannot be an aim in itself. The criteria for assessment of the bombings, from the perspective of the Palestinian struggle for liberation, is whether wrecking Oslo in this manner brings that struggle closer to fruition. The mechanism Hamas is depending on to destroy Oslo makes the answer to this question patently negative. For it is not the Palestinians who are being called upon to abrogate Oslo by winning wider rights and power than those stipulated by the agreement, but the Israelis, and this not through eliciting greater Israeli sympathy for the Palestinian cause but by strengthening the hand of racism, arrogance, and oppression within Israeli society.

I do not believe that Hamas' leaders are so naive as to believe that strengthening the Likud and the extreme Israeli right is tantamount to improving the chances for Palestinian self-determination, especially as there is no question that such acts will equally strengthen the Palestinian people's level of consciousness, organization, and struggle so as to offset the vicious repression and hatred unleashed against them by Israel. On the contrary, such individual acts of violence tend as a rule to politically disarm an oppressed people, transforming them into helpless and demoralized bystanders suffering the indiscriminate wrath of the oppressor without the ability to resist increased repression, not to speak of escalating the struggle. This is even clearer in the case at hand, with the Hamas bombings coming at a time when the majority of Palestinians in the West Bank were, for better or worse, emitting a collective sigh of relief over the reduction of direct Israeli military oppression.

This, in fact, leads me to the conclusion that the wrecking of Oslo was not really the main short-term objective of Hamas' leadership. Rather, it seems to me that Hamas is first and foremost concerned with making political cash out of its ability to act the spoiler. They appear to be attempting this in two ways. One—which seemed to be confirmed by last week's statement declaring the Qassam military wing's decision to surrender its arms and explosives to the Palestine National Authority—is to improve Hamas' bargaining position vis-á-vis the PNA. A big gamble was obviously involved here, and, in view of the massive campaign unleashed against Hamas and the Sharm al-Sheikh summit, it has backfired terribly.

For the moment at least, and most likely for some time to come, Yasser Arafat will be in no position to deal with Hamas or give it greater space within the power structure of the self-rule territories. Rather, the opposite is true.

A longer, and surer, plan seems to have been the creation of a situation where the whole Oslo formula is either so grossly violated by Israel as to become redundant or it collapses with a Likud victory in the coming elections. Oslo, however, is here a necessary victim for the real objective, which is to discredit Arafat and the PNA, to identify them completely with the Israeli occupation and with Israeli repression, even to bring about their downfall, thus creating new and expanded space for Hamas' political and ideological influence in Gaza and the West Bank. The strategy is thus one of using Israeli mechanisms to achieve purely intra-Palestinian objectives.

In both cases, the Hamas leadership reveals a considerable degree of political cynicism. Not surprising when one recalls that Hamas, after all, was first nurtured by the Israeli occupation authorities with the aim of offsetting the nationalist and leftist trends that set the terms for the Palestinian struggle throughout the 1970s.

In the long term, the Hamas project is the flip side of the Zionist project. It takes Israel at its word, as an embodiment of Jewish identity, and pits against it an equally religious and no less mythical Muslim identity. Muslims around the world are to be pitted in perpetual war against Jews around the world. A Muslim identity stands in ever-lasting confrontation with a Judeo-Christian identity.

As it happens, the so-called Judeo-Christian world is immensely more powerful than the Muslim world and likely to remain so for decades to come. Thus the only practical manifestation of this 'war of civilizations' will be to set the stage for Islamist takeovers in Muslim countries. The United States, its western allies, and Israel use the heaven-sent 'Islamist threat' to flex their muscles, unleash poll-winning punitive campaigns, seal shut the cracks within their own societies and among them, and intensify their dominance, military, economic, and political, over the Arab and Islamic worlds. The Islamists point and say, "We told you so."

The great paradox in this scenario is that such potential Islamist takeovers will not unleash the 'holy war,' so dreaded by western commentators, against Israel and the west. Rather, I have not the slightest doubt, the 'two sides,' while maintaining their mutual ethnic, cultural, and religious antipathies—each affirming the other's dearly held 'identity'—will, eventually, come to do business.

This is merely a scenario. It is not inevitable. Precluding it will depend, among other things, on the ability of the Palestinians, with their inexhaustible reservoirs of courage and determination, to evolve a strategy that provides a genuine alternative both to capitulationism and to ultimately futile and morally reprehensible exclusivism. Such a strategy, in my view, implies winning the support of large sections of Israelis, through struggle not through capitulation, through a discourse of liberation and not one of 'peace processing,' through an assertion of our common humanity, not of our allegedly insurmountable differences and opposition.

Admittedly, all this seems something of a utopian vision at the moment. Not more so, however, than seeking genuine liberation and justice through either the Oslo or the Hamas path.

*Al-Ahram Weekly*, March 14, 1996

# CRISIS OF THE INTELLECT, OR YET AGAIN, A CRITIQUE OF ARAB REASON

AFTER 9/11, EVERY TOM, DICK, AND HARRY became an expert on the 'Arab mind.' Dressed in learned scholarly garb, a Pandora's box of racism, bigotry, and sheer stupidity was let loose on the world. There was an inherent rejection of modernity in Arab/Muslim culture, defined for its part in religious terms. It was this rejection of modernity that was the underlying cause behind the Arabs'/Muslims' failure as states and societies, their lack of democracy, their fundamentalism, and their terrorism.

Ironically, the racist notion of an 'Arab mind' was a recycled, mistranslated concept coined by Arab intellectuals in the wake of the devastating Arab defeat at Israeli hands in June 1967. Students of Marx and Hegel, these late 1960s Arab intellectuals were actually speaking of critiques of 'Arab reason,' wherein reason, in Hegelian language, denotes dominant ideology, modes of thought, paradigms, and such. Retranslated back into European languages, Hegel gave way to the Ku Klux Klan, reason to stupidity. But the fact remains that the task begun in Beirut some forty years ago remains, to use a jihadist term, 'an absent duty.' Not only are the flaws in 'Arab reason' that the intellectuals of the 1960s and 1970s set out to critique and demolish still around, they have been compounded hundreds-fold.

Identifying, exposing, and thoroughly demolishing these flaws through relentless, courageous, and, indeed, ruthless criticism remain fundamental conditions for movement on all levels of contemporary Arab life, political, economic, cultural, and social.

# Leaps of Logic

THE CONSPIRACY THEORY IS doing the rounds already: the Mossad's done it, or the Central Intelligence Agency. It might even have been the two, acting in cahoots. The thinking may be more convoluted than usual this time around, but it is no less popular for all that. There is a peculiar logic at work here, since the proponents of this and similar conspiracy theories (the 9/11 incarnation being the most widely known) are invariably the very same people who will point out vehemently that "what goes around comes around."

They will go to great lengths to show, quite rightly, how United States and Israeli violence and brutality bear the majority of the responsibility for all and any counterviolence. But they will go even further to deride those among us who would condemn such instances of 'counterviolence' as being insensitive to the enormous suffering of our own people, even as we allegedly toady up to the west by expressing abhorrence for attacks on civilians, kidnappings, and videotaped butchery.

One would have thought that the one line of thinking cancels out the other. Either the act of violence in question was the cynical and villainous work of insidious intelligence bodies (*à la* Reichstag Fire), which would make it doubly repugnant. Or, it is the partially, or wholly, justified reaction to a much greater and much more terrible violence, which, presumably, gives it some legitimacy. Yet, the same people seem to have patently little trouble suggesting both arguments at once.

There is logic, of a kind, in the apparent incoherence, however. In both arguments, 'we' stand blameless, saved the onerous, distressing task of critically examining structures of thought and ways of being that are prevalent among 'us.' More significantly, perhaps, such thinking helps us to avoid stumbling onto the potentially frightful realization that there is no 'us' in any real, ideological, or political sense, that a shared cultural, national, or religious identity by no means makes Arabs and Muslims an undifferentiated mass, a monolith with a single body and one mind.

Not surprisingly, this preposterous notion of a distinct Arab/Muslim 'mind' is in great vogue on the other side of the 'civilizational fault line,' where, in fact, its origins are deeply rooted. Once again, we may expect a host of American, Israeli, and other 'western experts' soon to begin pontificating on the Arab mind's propensity for conspiracy theories. This is no more than half-baked orientalist garbage, the kind of racist nonsense that in today's world is permissible only where Arabs and Muslims are concerned. It is no less racist for the fact that some Arab 'intellectuals' have zealously undertaken the role of 'witnesses for the Crown,' providing elaborate testimony as to the inherently backward and irrational characteristics of the minds of the rest of us.

But first, let us consider yet another significant thread in the conspiracy theory tapestry. This has to do with the classic whodunnit question: who stands to benefit? But here, again, there is a rather peculiar logic at work.

If anyone had any doubts at the time, it is now glaringly evident that George W. Bush and his neocon cabal jumped at the 9/11 atrocity as a "golden opportunity" to pursue their "new American century" strategy, both at home and abroad. And as the current presidential campaign has demonstrated overwhelmingly, not only are the Republicans' prospects of another term in the White House almost wholly dependent on milking 9/11 for all its worth, but also, and more dangerously, the neocons have had astounding success in setting the terms of the American debate, possibly for a long time to come. However consistent John Kerry's criticism of the war on Iraq may or may not be, it is amply evident that the neocon "war on terror" agenda of fear at home and 'preemptive' aggression abroad dogs the Democratic mindset no less than it does the Republican one at the current stage of U.S. politics.

Such recognition of the 'benefits' derived by neocons in particular and those driving for militarized U.S. global hegemony in general from 9/11 and the hobgoblin of 'Islamist terror' is by no means sufficient reason to conclude that it was the neocons themselves who have '*done*' 9/11. For that you need concrete evidence, not mere speculation, as even Hercule

Poirot would tell you. (Pearl Harbor provided Franklin D. Roosevelt with a 'golden opportunity' to renege on his electoral promise to stay out of the Second World War, but there is very little doubt, I would think, that it was in fact the Japanese who conducted the attack, even if they were goaded into doing so by Roosevelt, as some U.S. historians suggest.)

In fact, the much more obvious (logical) conclusion to be drawn from such recognition is that the strategy and tactics openly adopted by our marauding jihadists, whether they are affiliated with al-Qa'ida or not, do great service to the enemy. Reason enough, one would think, to denounce it on political/strategic rather than just moral grounds.

But to acknowledge that such acts of violence render great service to imperial and Israeli designs—to the point of accusing the beneficiaries of having committed the acts themselves—while at the same time expressing various degrees of sympathy for these acts is to fly in the face of the most basic rules of logic and coherent thinking.

This brings us to the blame debate—a most ridiculous debate if ever there was one. Since 9/11, western pundits have not tired of hectoring Arabs and Muslims to stop blaming the west and Israel for the rampant ailments of their 'failed' societies and to start looking critically at themselves. Arab neoliberals have taken up the call with typical zeal. The Taba bombings, no less than 9/11, the suicide bombings in Israel, the butchery in Iraq, and so forth are all to be attributed not to American and Israeli invasions, occupations, violence, and brutality, not to indiscriminate bombings, assassinations, torture, and horrible humiliations, but to the Arab/Muslim rejection of modernity. On the other side of the barricade, these facts of American/Israeli violence and oppression are offered as justifications of acts of counterviolence, however morally horrifying and politically damaging. Ad nauseam, the refrain is repeated: "Why is our blood so much cheaper than 'theirs'?"

For all its overwhelming preponderance, this is a debate over nonsense. Social and political phenomena are explainable. This is a fundamental tenet of rationalism, be it of western or *Mu'tazilite* roots. But to identify causal connections between particular events or phenomena implies very little, if anything at all, in terms of justification, whether on moral, legal, or political grounds. If the relentless, tedious debate testifies to anything, it is to the failure of both the western and the Arab/Muslim 'minds.'

It so happens that the Taba bombings are directly and most profoundly connected to the ongoing butchery in Palestine and Iraq at Israeli and American hands. It also so happens that, brutal, horrifying, and morally repugnant, last week's bombings, which took the lives of scores of civilians, including at least ten Egyptian youths, mostly of working-class origins, contribute nothing at all to the cause of Palestinian, Iraqi, or Arab liberation and a lot to the perpetuation of their oppression.

*Al-Ahram Weekly*, October 14, 2004

# The American Mind

WHERE WOULD YOU EXPECT conspiracy theories about 9/11 to be disseminated in Cairo? A coffeehouse in Sayyida Zeinab, al-Azhar, or any of the multitude of so-called 'popular quarters of the city,' filled with shisha smoke and permeated by the smell of molasses-soaked tobacco (otherwise known as *mi'assil*), mixed perhaps with the subtle whiff of some other rather more expensive substance?

Where does the supposed propensity of the 'Arab mind' for conspiracy theory come to its own and propagate? Could it be in the scruffy offices of local newspapers, regularly slammed by a certain Mossad-led, United States–based media monitoring organization as dens of anti-American, anti-Semitic incitement, which the U.S. government, the European Union, and nearly everybody with some aid money to disburse is doing their utmost to help reform? (God knows, the need is great, even if the path, in this as in every other area of our contemporary life, is shrouded in mystery.) Possibly, but the most lucid, indeed the most erudite and comprehensive argument to the effect that all was not what it seemed with 9/11 was to be had in none of these.

Certainly, I've come across several versions of 'what really happened' on that fateful day in September 2001 over the past five years. There's been my friend and colleague, an expert on political Islam, who throughout continued to insist that al-Qa'ida didn't do it, almost totally unfazed by my taunting him with each growingly more blunt admission to having indeed 'done it' by Messrs. Bin Laden and al-Zawahiri. We've all heard the one about the three thousand Jews who failed to show up at the

World Trade Center on the day of the atrocity. And though many have written to expose this story for the myth it has always been, much of the Egyptian public continues to believe it—just, one may add, as their more prosperous and literate American counterparts went on believing in that other 9/11 urban legend, courtesy of Mr. Cheney, the one about Saddam's links to al-Qa'ida.

My absolute favorite 9/11 conspiracy theory, however, was told to me by that most ubiquitous source of information vis-à-vis the mood on the 'Egyptian street,' a taxi driver. (In the absence of any sort of political life in the country outside a narrow and isolated political elite, both local and foreign journalists have come to rely on the taxi driver as the ultimate authority on what the 'ordinary Egyptian' thinks or believes.) According to my source, both Osama bin Laden and Saddam Hussein (who was yet to be captured) are CIA agents and were, in fact, tucked away by their handlers somewhere in the United States. This particular theory had the ingenious merit of fusing all the conspiracy theories in one: Bin Laden did it, so did Saddam, and so did the Americans. How far that particular theory was reflective of the word on the Egyptian street is anybody's guess. I had a lot of fun with it, nevertheless, imagining Saddam and Bin Laden, clean shaven, sharing a little house in some Midwestern American city, posing, perhaps, as a gay couple?

I had to wait five years to listen to a 9/11 conspiracy theory I could not easily laugh at or shrug off. The setting was as incongruous as were the parties to the discussion, largely one-sided, my interlocutors talking and me, skeptically, listening. Sipping cold Stella beer, munching on antipasti, and enclosed in the courtyard of the Italian Club, a surprisingly idyllic spot discreetly hidden from the hustle and bustle of one of the busiest streets in town, my friends and I could not have been more securely insulated from the Egyptian street.

Nor could my friends be accused, by any stretch of the imagination, of suffering from that most dangerous disease, endemic to the region and differentially diagnosed as the 'Arab mind.' My friend had lived a large chunk of his adult life in the west. His recipe for solving Egypt's multifarious political, economic, and social problems is to entice Egypt's erstwhile foreign communities (the Greeks, Armenians, Italians, Jews) back into the country. (I am, I might add, particularly enamored of the idea of enticing the Jews back, since it would have the additional potential benefit of emptying Israel of nearly half its Jewish population.)

The third party to our little group on that particular summer evening was my friend's American wife, a lovely, tall Texan with long auburn hair. They had been recently married at the foot of the Pyramids in what my American-pop-culture-savvy wife informed me at the time was a New Age ceremony. Extremely vague about what 'New Age' anything actually denotes, I was nevertheless quite impressed by the insouciance shown by my friend's large Egyptian Muslim family toward the flower-bordered ankh within which the bride and groom exchanged their conjugal vows.

Having gone to considerable effort to absolve my companions at the Italian Club of any suspicion of being blighted by, God forbid, an 'Arab mind,' I might now reveal that they were the source of the most persuasive 9/11 conspiracy theory I had yet come across. It was all about steel structures and impossible cell phone calls and an unlikely hole in the Pentagon and a disappeared fourth, or was it fifth, plane. I was referred to websites and to American scholars who have organized to question the whole edifice of reasoning and evidence presented by the official investigation.

I remain highly skeptical, for a number of reasons. The first may be discounted as sheer pigheadedness. As soon as I learned of the attack on the World Trade Center, my first guess, accompanied by intense dread (I could already see the 'war of civilizations' being launched), was that it was Bin Laden and Co. who'd done it. Something of the sort seemed to be coming ever since the jihadists had reached the conclusion (eloquently expressed by our good doctor, al-Zawahiri, in a famous autocritique) that battling the far enemy (Crusaders and Jews) was a far better strategy in terms of winning Arab and Muslim hearts and minds than focusing on the near enemy (apostate Arab and Muslim regimes), which they had been doing to no avail for nearly two decades. Later developments, needless to say, seemed to amply confirm my initial guess.

The second reason for my skepticism is rather more compelling. I find it very difficult to believe that a secret on such a heinous and grandiose scale could be kept secret. Whatever the loopholes in the findings of the official investigation (and obviously there are loopholes), it is nearly impossible to assume a coverup that must have involved the complicity of at least several hundred people in a whole array of branches of the government bureaucracy at a great many levels, and in the deliberate murder of more than three thousand American citizens by an American intelligence body. Such an assumption makes the Kennedy assassination (presumably at the hands of Lyndon B. Johnson, J. Edgar Hoover, the CIA, the Mafia, and Cuban émigrés) seem pretty tame. And while I have few illusions about the greatness of American democracy, there is little doubt in my mind that the U.S., despite the best efforts of the American right, is in fact a democracy, however imperfect.

My third and indeed most compelling reason is that grand conspiracy theories present us with something in the nature of divine and/or other forms of supernatural intervention. Simply, they place major historical events and processes at the mercy of whim, beyond prediction or reasoned analysis. A corollary of such an assumption is that human beings are ultimately no more than puppets on a string and that the choices we make are exercises in futility.

It so happens, however, that we need no conspiracy theory, grand or small, to learn that both President Bush and his neocon cabal no less than the Prince of the Faithful of Tora Bora and his band of global marauders had been, on the eve of 9/11, chomping at the bit to instigate a great, bloody, and perpetual 'war of civilizations.' It has served them tremendously well over the past five years. It's the rest of us who have to suffer the devastating fallout.

*The Daily Star Egypt*, September 18, 2006

# New Year's Resolutions

THE YEAR 2003 HAS BEEN described as the worst year in modern Arab history by some pundits, on par with or even worse than the two prime catastrophic events that have largely shaped the contemporary Arab world: the *nakba* of 1948 and the equally crushing defeat of the Arabs at Israeli hands in June 1967. Yet, as the year drew to a close, such assertions—made in the heat of the fall of Baghdad, the seat of the Abbasids and birthplace of the glorious reign of Harun al-Rashid—appear to have lost much of their force. The anticlimactic capture of Saddam Hussein and the somewhat comic confessions of Muammar Qadhafi, coming within a week of each other in December 2003, seemed to point to an alternative perspective on the year's drama. Rather than being measured against 1948 and 1967, it would be more useful perhaps to see 2003 as underlining the fact that, strange as it may seem, contemporary Arabs continue to harvest the bitter fruit of their two 'founding' catastrophes, indeed, continue to replay them in forms that are ever more absurd, if not as immediately devastating.

Nowhere else in a postcolonial Third World is the psychological and intellectual legacy of colonial domination as manifestly alive or as compelling as it is in today's Arab region. Nearly half a century after independence, the nationalist zeal of the 1930s and 1940s seems to sustain the fervor of its vigorous youth. This is no inherent cultural or religious trait of the facile 'why do they hate us?'-type formula. Rather, it is the perfidies and ravages of the colonial world that have managed to survive in this region long after their demise everywhere else. After all, the Balfour

Declaration was issued in 1917, yet the process of Palestinian dispossession continues, unabated, to this day.

There is, nevertheless, something terribly wrong about a nationalistic zeal that has long passed its dotage. Stagnant, easily reneged upon, but rarely subjected to a serious critique, pan-Arab nationalism has been in a state of decay so protracted as to produce something akin to the 'living dead' of horror fiction. In different ways, Saddam, Qadhafi, and even Osama bin Laden have all provided testimony to a pan-Arab nationalism in extreme putrefaction.

If one were to look for symbolic significance in Saddam's degraded capture and Qadhafi's droll turnabout at the end of 2003, one might be tempted to see them as crystallizing the final demise, the stake through the heart, of decadent pan-Arab nationalism (of which militant Islamism is one particularly virulent form).

Things are never that simple, however, and structures of thought, just like the social structures they both reflect and help shape, tend to remain in place until they're actually removed by acts of will. The fall of Saddam Hussein will certainly not prove to have been the final nail in decadent pan-Arab nationalism's coffin, just as neither 9/11 nor the fall of Kabul signaled the demise of militant Islamism in 2001–2002. Indeed, the resilience shown by these two defunct systems of thought and practice over the past decade has been in great degree a function of their ability to merge one with the other, with Islamist militants increasingly adopting nationalist rhetoric and Arab nationalists quoting ever more freely from religious texts.

If anything, 2004 will witness even more intense, if ultimately misdirected and futile nationalist/Islamist zeal, even as feelings of hopelessness and despondency sink ever deeper into the popular Arab consciousness. (These seemingly contradictory emotional reactions have not proved mutually exclusive in the past and are unlikely to become so anytime in the near future.)

Indeed, if the last days of 2003 are anything to go by, there is nothing for the Arab peoples to look forward to in 2004. Doubtless, Arab regimes will continue to talk a lot about reform while doing their utmost to keep any reforms they do enact at as purely a cosmetic level as they can get away with—and they can get away with a lot. Democracy is in the eye of the beholder, and he happens to live in Washington, D.C., where war criminal Ariel Sharon is a man of peace and Colonel Qadhafi, leader of the

Libyan revolution, is even now being awarded his democratic stripes for total transparency, not with the Libyan people but with secretive Anglo-American weapons inspection and intelligence teams.

In Palestine, it is highly unlikely that 2004 will bring any mitigation of the dreadful reality that continues to unfold there, as Sharon's apartheid wall rises higher and extends further afield, rupturing Palestinian lands and lives. Meanwhile, the Palestinian Authority, hapless, deeply divided, and petty-minded, is clearly inadequate to the Herculean task of uniting the Palestinian nation around an effective strategy of resistance, one that is not satisfied with futile acts of vengeance but aims at winning genuine liberation.

And the most conspicuous alternative to the PA continues to be Hamas and Jihad, who offer a strategy that parodies, ad nauseum, the sins of the Arab nationalist regimes toward the Palestinian cause, that is, by manipulating it as an instrument for expanding their domestic hegemony. Three years into the suicide bombing strategy, it must now be obvious that while it may enhance the ideological and political influence of Islamists among Palestinians and in the Arab world, the strategy does the Palestinian cause itself nothing but harm.

Nor does the picture look any less grim in Iraq. We'll have an indigenous Iraqi government in 2004, but the prospects for a return to peace and stability under continuing American tutelage and military occupation are less likely there than they have been in Afghanistan, which two years after 'liberation' by American forces seems to be heading straight back into the Taliban's arms.

Zooming out to the global village, I've christened 2004 year two of the "second American century." Saddam's final crime may prove to have been giving the world, through his contemptible capture, another four years of the neocons. All in all, and on the basis of today's available data, it does not look much like a happy new year.

Yet, there is always the unfathomable dynamic of the choices people make. Ultimately, that is what it is all about. When and how do people decide that they've had enough of a particular historical configuration and choose another? The question has always been a source of perplexity, and the only answers we come by tend to rely heavily on hindsight.

In 2003, Edward Said died. He was mourned by thousands in Palestine, in the Arab world, and, indeed, in almost every country in the world. In a column I wrote some years ago, I likened Edward Said to John the Baptist, lamenting the fact that his powerful message—combining unyielding rejection of oppression with the most profound humanism—was that of "a voice crying in the wilderness."

Edward later told me that he liked the article but disliked the metaphor, protesting that many people agreed with what he had to say. Many people do. But regardless of how many they are and how much influence they may have, the most significant fact about Edward Said's legacy is that an alternative, a truly powerful and compelling alternative, does exist. Our options are not as impoverished as to have been reduced to the choice between subjugation and death, between Bushes and Bin Ladens. The alternative is there, all we have to do is choose it. And like every choice, that requires an act of will.

*Al-Ahram Weekly*, January 1, 2004

# Myth Laid Bare

WHY IS IT THAT ABSURD CHOICES ARE consistently presented as the only ones available? Why are local tyrants manufactured into the only alternative to global tyranny? What if some of us think there is absolutely nothing to choose between imperial hegemony and national humiliation and oppression on the one hand and nationalist/Islamist despotism on the other? Why is it that supporting Hamas and Jihad's morally abhorrent and politically ruinous suicide bombings is posited as an inescapable expression of our solidarity with the Palestinian struggle for emancipation from the daily horrors of a heartless and brutal Israeli occupation? And why, for that matter, shouldn't I join millions of Iraqis in celebrating the capture of the murderous thug called Saddam Hussein?

"Hegel remarks somewhere that all great world-historic facts and personages appear, so to speak, twice. He forgets to add: the first time as tragedy, the second time as farce." The celebrated quotation from Marx's *The Eighteenth Brumaire of Louis Bonaparte* has been lingering at the back of my mind ever since Saddam Hussein embarked on his geographically muddled venture to liberate Palestine via Kuwait. Let me explain why.

Arab peoples' experience with Nasserism has been tragic in every sense of the word. Gamal Abdel Nasser, it can be argued, is the very archetype of the tragic hero.

And it does not take too great a leap of the imagination to see in Saddam Hussein's 1990–91 invasion and occupation of Kuwait a caricature—a farcical repetition, even—of the crisis that culminated in the June War of 1967. Simply replace American/Israeli baiting and provocation with American/Israeli/Kuwaiti baiting and provocation. View Saddam's posturing as a caricature of Nasser's attempts to use the crisis to enhance his bargaining position vis-à-vis his adversaries on the one hand and his hegemonic stature at home and within the Arab world on the other. The absence of any genuine preparedness for battle, as evidenced by the swift collapse of both armies, is an obvious point of overlap, as is the manner in which the doors to any possible compromise were systematically closed while the baiting and provocation intensified, making any retreat impossible. The inevitable results followed: war and humiliating defeat. The similarities are obvious, even if superficial, making of the later events a farcical reenactment of the earlier.

The point, however, is that having passed through the tragedy of Nasserism, we should have become immunized against the farce that was Saddam in 1990–91. We were not.

Not only that, but for more than a decade we have been replaying Marx's addition to Hegel's words, insistently repeating the farce as ever greater farce, recasting, in our endless and futile search for a resurrected Salah al-Din, our illusions about the heroic figure of Nasser as ever more ridiculous delusions about despicable thugs such as Saddam Hussein and maniacal criminals such as Osama bin Laden and Ayman al-Zawahiri.

To have been taken in by Saddam in 1990–91 is folly enough; to be fooled by Bin Laden in 2001 and again by the very same Saddam in 2003 suggests a denial of experience that might be explained by an advanced case of Alzheimer's, or total idiocy.

But the explanation, of course, lies elsewhere. Ideology is a powerful weapon, and our intellectual classes have for almost three decades now been adamant in their refusal to settle accounts with the intellectual heritage bequeathed by June '67. Interestingly, it's been a catch-22 situation. The Arab world is blighted by its proximity to Europe, by its strategic geopolitical importance, by its oil wealth, and by the fact that even as the Arab countries were embarking on the postcolonial era, a Spartan-style settler colonial state, armed to the teeth, was being implanted in their midst, dispossessing a whole people and eradicating a nation even as it was being born.

It is the intensity of the national oppression and degradation to which the Arabs have been exposed in the last half-century of 'postcolonialism' that provides an explanation for their persistent, and increasingly humiliating, failures to achieve national emancipation and dignity. In our national zeal, we have placed our struggle with 'the west and Zionism' above every other aspect of our social and spiritual existence—above citizenship, class, gender, and ethnicity. Ever wary of foreign penetration, we are continuously reinforcing those red lines beyond which our thought and practice cannot venture, lest 'the enemy' be allowed to enter, reproducing new authoritarianisms and reviving old ones.

The great irony of it all is that it is this very nationalist zeal that rather than strengthening our ability to fight national oppression and humiliation has enfeebled it to such a degree that we have become the preferred punching bag of the U.S. as it sets the stage for a new imperial American century.

My initial reaction to the capture of Saddam Hussein was, as I found out later, shared by millions of Arabs. It was anger, anger at why he did not die fighting, at why he did not kill himself. In his degradation, the tyrant had degraded us all. Such feelings lasted only a few moments. On second thought, I found myself delighted at the way the tyrant had fallen, exposed as a coward, as a rat in a hole.

It is time that the myth that gave us Saddam, and continues to give us his like, be similarly exposed.

*Al-Ahram Weekly*, December 18, 2003

# United We Fall

ARAB LEADERS, MEETING AT SUMMIT level this Saturday, presumably in a final bid to prevent a disastrous war against Iraq, are faced with an insurmountable dilemma: to convince Bush Junior and his band of global thugs that an American invasion of Iraq will impact disastrously on regional stability, opening a Pandora's box for America's many Arab friends. This, after all, is the Arabs' only bargaining card vis-à-vis the United States. In their weakness is their strength. And God forbid that the Arab regimes' warnings to Washington involve any suggestion that they would themselves act against it if it goes ahead with its invasion and military occupation of Iraq.

Oil and other similar weapons are things of the remote and much-repented past. Increasing oil production so as to offset the effects of the American-inspired capital strike against Hugo Chavez in Venezuela, so as to save the American economy from the recessionary effects of an oil price rise caused by the American administration's concerted attempt to overthrow a democratically elected government in Latin America, that is much more our style these days. Only after doing so, only after swearing eternal fealty to American interests in the region and everywhere else do we whimperingly warn that our very future is at stake. The only threat the Arab regimes can make to Washington concerns fears for their survival. Their message is that American actions will bring about their collapse.

But the regimes are beginning to realize with increasing alarm that the current U.S. administration has a more than cavalier attitude toward the survival, let alone stability, of its Arab friends.

The 'weakness weapon' is flawed in a much more fundamental sense, however, irrespective of how much regime change the U.S. administration's "chicken hawks" (as Edward Said so aptly calls them) would like to see in the Middle East. This is due to a very simple and starkly obvious fact: the Arab regimes have a vested interest in rendering the only effective weapon they are able to deploy against U.S. (and Israeli) hooliganism in the region ineffectual. Hitherto they have met with remarkable success in doing so. During the past couple of weeks the whole world has risen up in opposition to the war in Iraq. Millions took to the street, from Los Angeles to Seoul; everywhere, that is, except the Arab world. None put it as bitterly and as succinctly as the *Independent*'s Robert Fisk: "One million demonstrate in London, but the Arabs, faced with disaster, are like mice."

The paradox is deeply ironic, for the Arab regimes' fear of the effects of an American invasion of Iraq upon their peoples has ensured that they adopt iron-fist tactics against any mass movement opposed to that invasion. Meanwhile, the success of their repressive measures undermines their howls of protest directed to the U.S. and the international community, warning of the dire consequences to themselves and hence to regional stability.

Ultimately, however, Washington's contempt for the Arab masses is not very different from that which Arab regimes seem to have for their own citizens. The experience of the past quarter of a century has apparently convinced them that Arabs will accept just about anything: authoritarianism, eternally stalled political reform, the institutionalization of torture and a host of other human rights abuses, economic failure, attacks on economic and social rights, rampant corruption, impoverishment, oppression—you name it, and it's on offer. The list goes on and on. Why then should these very same masses be expected to rise up now, especially when all the evidence seems to indicate that they have no intention of doing so? Indeed, to all appearances, Arabs are just as frustrated and angry as Fisk described them: mice.

And, sorry, I don't buy the repression excuse. It begs the question why people, in the Arab world and elsewhere, have risen up in the past against repression. It also gives too much credit to Arab regimes to grant them sole responsibility for the sorry state of the Arab masses. Why should they have succeeded with such apparent finality when other, more violently authoritarian regimes (for example, Latin America's many military juntas) have failed?

There is, I believe, an even greater irony in store for us. I would suggest that the fundamental reason behind the Arabs' abject failure to confront the most humiliating national oppression in their history—to be instituted and symbolized by American military rule in Baghdad even as Ariel Sharon continues his butchery in Palestine—is a function of their having put nationalism above every other aspect of their political and social lives for more than half a century.

Three million Italians came out on the streets of Rome to protest the American-led war on Iraq. But millions of Italians had earlier taken part in a general strike and mass demonstrations throughout the country against a new labor law detrimental to workers' rights. It is because they were able to do the one that they were able to do the other.

*Al-Ahram Weekly*, February 27, 2003

# Passion, Torn to Tatters

I CONFESS I HAVE AS MUCH TROUBLE figuring out exactly what 'our' culture, values, and (the grander and even more fashionable-sounding) civilization are as I do with those of the 'west.' Still, if ignorance, hypocrisy, and a penchant for losing, refined to an art form, are aspects of any or all of these (they are certainly predominant enough), then we may rest assured: the west's alleged onslaught on our civilization has been a dismal failure. If anything, each B-52 sortie and every Ariel Sharon-driven massacre seem to strengthen our resolve to cling even more tenaciously to these apparently precious cultural and civilizational attributes.

Blaming the oppressor for the ignorance and stupidity of the oppressed, no less than for their legitimate anger and/or futile acts of desperation, is valid enough. It is woefully inadequate, however, when we are trying to identify ways in which the oppressed can achieve liberation and not just plead their cause before some ethereal court of global conscience. Ehud Barak, followed soon after by Sharon, literally pushed the Intifada to armed violence. The degradation of Palestinian armed struggle into the ubiquitous suicide operations of Hamas and Jihad was practically ordained by both the incalculable imbalance of the antagonists' capacity to deploy armed violence and the infinite brutality and lawlessness of the Israeli occupation. "Why are their children, their lives any more precious than ours?" The rhetorical question is bitterly genuine, especially bitter in view of the hypocrisy and racism that so clearly governs the responses of the world's masters to 'our' pain and suffering as opposed to 'theirs.'

These arguments have been raised over and over again, and not just by Arabs. The evidence is out there, for all to see (available, in the age of the Internet, at the click of a mouse), exposed and passionately argued by Palestinians from the occupied territories and outside them, by courageous Israelis from across the Green Line, and by many 'alternative,' if besieged, voices in the west. It has been eloquently and tenaciously expressed by that unique embodiment of human civilization, British journalist Robert Fisk, who, having been beaten almost to death by Afghan refugees last week, was nevertheless able to say that he understood their anger.

Sharon could not have expected more of the latest wave of Hamas and Jihad suicide operations had he ordered them himself. This fact, glaringly obvious to anybody who is not totally blinded by vested interest, bigotry, stupidity, or a combination thereof, says a lot about Sharon and the Israeli occupation. It also says a lot about Hamas and Jihad, and about the rest of 'us' as well. Hamas and Jihad, Israel's 'archenemies,' carry out Sharon's will, and 'we' applaud. When we're not applauding, we're ranting and raving at the unfairness of it all; and when we're not ranting and raving, we're apologizing and rationalizing, all the while taking cold comfort in the justice of our cause.

The Intifada is all but lost. Yasser Arafat, besieged and humiliated, is on death row, his very life hostage to Sharon's whim and a hitherto reluctant go-ahead from Washington. Sharon has finally been able to get in on the "war on terror," with America's blessing. The Palestinians are on the edge of civil war. The Arab regimes, cowering in fear of the next blow (the destruction of the Palestinian Authority, phase two of the "war on terror," or both—the prospects of chaos and mayhem are too horrific to conceive), are unable to hold a foreign ministers' meeting.

But hey, what else could we do? They've forced us to it.

Meanwhile, we are supposed to look forward to Egyptian 'character actor' Mohamed Sobhi performing no fewer than fourteen roles in a television serial dramatizing the "Protocols of the Elders of Zion," which apparently has had millions spent on it and is to be broadcast in many parts of our glorious Arab nation. The casting is apt. Sobhi is symptomatic of 'the state of the nation,' or is it civilization? Several years ago I had to suffer through a Hamlet performed by this man, hailed as one of our great actors. I'm no drama critic but even I could recognize that Sobhi's acting skills seem to lie precisely in "saw[ing] the air too much with . . . [his] hands" and "tear[ing] a passion to tatters." Little wonder, perhaps, that he is so well admired; tearing a passion to tatters seems to be a particular predilection of 'our' civilization these days.

The "Protocols of the Elders of Zion," as any moderately intelligent person who has taken the time to look it up knows, was invented by the Russian secret police to divert the masses' anger away from the viciously oppressive tsarist regime and toward the Jews. It is an age-old trick, and is currently being deployed with much greater sophistication against Arabs and Muslims, western capitalism's Jews of choice at the beginning of the twenty-first century.

Sharon is murdering more Palestinians than ever before. Dubya is itching to expand his "war on terror" by targeting more Arabs and Muslims. The Arab regimes are cowering in fear and the masses are seething in futile anger. The region is poised over a precipice of chaos and mayhem. But hey, we cling to our civilization. Funny that we should do so by reproducing one of the ugliest products of the west's.

*Al-Ahram Weekly*, December 13, 2001

# Making One's Mark

FOREVER BEMOANING THE 'CRISIS OF THE INTELLECTUALS,' the Egyptian intelligentsia seems nevertheless content to allow vulgar demagogues, self-seeking hypocrites, and generally the most ignorant, opportunistic, and empty-headed of its members to set the terms of debate for everyone else. The power of intimidation that this group enjoys is as bewildering as it is phenomenal. Some of its members literally reek of petrodollars, of both the revolutionary and conservative varieties. Others are known to have developed their meager, if invariably mawkish, writing skills drawing up secret reports about their colleagues for various security bodies.

To these two routes of self-advancement, the past years of economic liberalization have added the apparently lucrative avenue of what we might call intellectual entrepreneurialism. This largely takes two forms. The first is for the enterprising 'intellectual' to ally himself with this or that network of businessmen/bureaucrats (such private–public networks are essential for doing good business). As its 'literary representative,' he or she is then charged with the task of singing his or her patrons' praises and, more important, maligning competing networks with as much mudslinging, slander, and abuse as his or her 'literary' and tabloid-journalism skills allow.

The second form of intellectual entrepreneurialism is to play the field. It goes something like this: pick a 'network' and start throwing some restrained mud—a little investigative journalism, a few large ads, and maybe something under the table. Later—surprise!—you discover that the target was the victim of vicious slander and is in fact a shining example of bureaucratic entrepreneurialism (or entrepreneurial bureaucracy), not like some others we could name. Nudge, wink, and on to the next target.

All three methods of making one's mark on the world, as Gustave Flaubert might have put it, are usually pursued in unison, as if the one course of self-advancement (report-writing usually begins while one is still an aspiring undergraduate) led quite naturally to the other.

Such people may be of interest to writers of fiction (from Honoré de Balzac to Naguib Mahfouz), but for our purposes here, they tend to be extremely predictable and eminently boring. My real interest is in the disproportionate influence they seem to exercise today among a fairly large group of people who, by and large, possess a fair share of talent, intelligence, and integrity (even if these are subject to the double bind of authoritarianism and a market economy).

I am hardly looking for consensus, though, whether among the intelligentsia or in society as a whole. It's debate that we need and it's debate that we continue to lack, at least on any level that could be designated an intellectual one. Nor is there a shortage of real gems out there. The monthly *Kutub: wughat nazar*, to cite one prominent example, has been a breath of fresh air in Egyptian intellectual life, and it is produced by Egyptians, not *khawaga*s. Invariably, however, the gems can hardly be seen for all the muck and, worse, original and sophisticated intellectual production is determinedly neutralized by being completely ignored or reduced through an often vicious process of omission and willful misrepresentation, to fit within the already established, crude, and vulgar terms of the debate.

Take two prominent examples: normalization and the so-called nongovernmental organization (NGO) movement. The simple fact that these two 'issues' have, for several years now, been major (indeed, the major) arenas of fierce debate and contention among Egyptian intellectuals is telling in itself. Has anyone wondered recently whether normalization, or rather antinormalization, is really as crucial to the Arab peoples' solidarity with the Palestinian struggle against Israeli occupation as it is made out to be, let alone to the urgent task of drawing up an overall strategy of Palestinian liberation?

Is it not time to move on to something even a little more energetic than merely abstaining from meeting with Israelis? In the heyday of Egyptian–Israeli treaty making, the government was leaning hard on intellectuals to 'normalize,' and refusing to do so was an act of resistance, albeit of a rather modest nature. Who's leaning now? The antinormalization movement (and I was present at its birth) was the creation of a dejected intelligentsia at once outraged by Anwar Sadat's about-face and horrified to discover that the majority of the people welcomed what it saw as an act of 'historical treason.' Has anyone bothered to notice that things have changed massively since then, in particular with respect to the Egyptian people's sentiments?

And what of the raucous uproar over NGOs? The debate, after all, is not about the alleged fifteen thousand civil associations in the country, nor is it even remotely interested in Egyptian 'civil society,' the bulk of which is to be found neither in these thousands of state-controlled organizations nor, for that matter, in the handful of advocacy groups on which the whole hysterical commotion is centered.

Contrary to the postulates of fashionable liberal dogma, civil society in Egypt is not weak but extremely complex and sophisticated and, rather than acting as a force for democratization, is joined at the head to the authoritarian state bureaucracy and functions essentially on the basis of patronage—one of the fundamental survival strategies of the Egyptian people.

The absurdity seems to strike no one. The health of the nation, its independence and integrity, and the future of its democracy hinge on some two dozen groups accounting for no more than a couple of hundred harassed people who are, moreover, as hopelessly 'isolated from the masses' as everyone else.

Keep it crude and vulgar, that seems to be the golden rule of 'intellectual debate' in Egypt these days. It is well suited to the knaves and imbeciles among us. Why should it satisfy the rest?

*Al-Ahram Weekly*, June 21, 2001

# Spots, but Still a Tiger

EGYPTIAN INTELLECTUALS HAVE BEEN SPEAKING of the 'crisis of the intellectuals' for years. This general 'crisis' subdivides into a host of others related to intellectual production, including the crisis of the press, scientific research, education, cinema, publishing—the list goes on. And then, of course, there are the related crises of political life in general and party politics in particular, of civil society, of democracy, and so forth.

Almost everybody admits that the Egyptian intelligentsia is embroiled in crises. Explanations of various sorts are provided, ideas for solutions are put forward—and nothing seems to happen. If anything, it get progressively worse; the Egyptian intelligentsia had more vitality a decade ago than it does today, and was more vigorous still twenty than it was ten years ago.

Is it fate? Most explanations of the crisis, or of this or that particular crisis, seem to indicate that intellectuals are subject to ironclad conditions beyond their control: authoritarianism, Islamic fundamentalism, the corrupting influence of petro-dollars, or foreign funding, globalization, privatization, and other forms of foreign 'penetration.'

Most quaint of all is the generation theory. Although I'm one of the potential beneficiaries of the proposition, I fear I've been a great disappointment to my old friends and colleagues from the student movement of the early 1970s as far as advocating our common interests is concerned. According to this proposition, we're still 'youth' (though we've had more than our fair share of heart attacks and/or bypass operations, and are already past middle age); therefore, if only the old geezers of the 1940s and 1950s would relinquish their monopoly over the country's political and cultural life and hand it over to us, the so-called 1970s generation, they would help solve all the above-mentioned crises and others besides. A recipe for self-advancement if I've ever seen one.

Irrespective of the explanatory validity of any or all of the above propositions, however, none of them even considers the agency of intellectuals themselves. It's a chicken/egg dilemma for, whether it's authoritarianism, fundamentalism, or even the 'geezers' monopoly,' the activism of intellectuals is necessary to challenge it.

Why is the Egyptian intelligentsia, although it includes highly talented and cultured people, incapable, as a body, of engaging in general debate except at the crudest and stalest levels? Why, indeed, when it comes to the 'big issues' of the hour, do such highly talented and cultured people surrender leadership to their most vacuous and empty-headed peers? Why, in a country where there is no political life to speak of, is intellectual debate hostage to political expediency, and political expediency reduced to the most vulgar populism and demagogy? Why is an intelligentsia that has spent nearly half a century totally isolated from 'the masses' so obsessed with suiting its intellectual production to various (extremely vague) notions of what the masses are capable of understanding and responding to? And why this insistence on a 'national consensus,' which invariably stifles debate and criticism, but also predicates 'intellectual inquiry' on the search for a 'common denominator,' which means that anything sophisticated, original, or creative must be thrown overboard so as not to rock the 'national' boat? Our national consensus, then, is to be defined by the stupidest, least critical, and most ignorant among us.

Why is nothing problematized? Why is there so little reflection or self-criticism? We've had some Marxists and Nasserists turn zealous liberals, others turn fervent Islamists. We've been able to observe a 'reconciliation' between the two archenemies of Arab ideological and political development during the last century: pan-Arab nationalism and Islamism. Yet, none of these transitions is achieved via a thorough critique of our intellectual heritage. They come about as largely unexplained 'moments of enlightenment.' Structures of ideas are not criticized but rejected en masse. It's a question of apostasy and belief, rejecting one religion for another.

Observe the state of the Egyptian press and publishing. Once upon a time, the tiniest of cracks in the authoritarian monolith would have been filled immediately with some of the most original and subversive of intellectual production. People were challenged to read between the lines, look for the nuances of Salah Jahin's latest cartoon, find a profound political and ideological critique in a short story in Gallery '68. Tarek al-Bishri would write about political life in Egypt between 1945 and 1952, and everyone would read this 'history' as a scathing critique of the Egyptian political system after the July 1952 revolution.

The tiny cracks have become gaping holes—filled largely with garbage. The space for pluralism of expression is mostly used for vulgarity, slander, and extortion, with each platform doing its absolute best to incite the state to shut down all the others.

The Egyptian intelligentsia has yet to transcend its original state of sheikhs and effendis. Much has been made of this division since the 'Islamic renaissance' some quarter of a century ago, yet few have observed the fundamental resemblance between the two. For both (and there's been a lot of functional crossover between them), the people are an object, not a subject, of history. One has the function of 'enlightening' the people with the fruits of modernity, and the other of 'instructing' them in the truth of their religion and the glory of their tradition. Both seek to steel the (Egyptian/Arab/Muslim) nation to withstand the onslaught of the developed west.

The 'people's' needs and desires are never an issue in themselves; the glory, strength, and advancement of the 'nation' (however defined) are the only goals. At heart, we're all descendants of al-Afghani and Muhammad Abduh. Liberals, Islamists, Marxists, and Nasserists, the problematic is the same. Perhaps it is time for the problematic itself to be put into question.

*Al-Ahram Weekly*, June 14, 2001

# Banking on Bombast

LAST WEEK, DURING YET ANOTHER RALLY, the opposition parties decided to open a bank account so as to be able to accept donations to support the Palestinian Intifada. It is very unlikely, though, that such an account will be opened. Even as I write, the idea has probably already been consigned to that mountain of forgotten resolutions, dire warnings, and good intentions that make up the collective subconscious of Egyptian political society.

Whether or not the bank account materializes is not, however, the point. More significant, and far more bewildering, is the fact that no one seems to find it in the least embarrassing that the idea should be suggested a full seven months after the outbreak of the Intifada.

Last week's was the second joint opposition rally in support of the Intifada. It was, predictably, as dull and vacuous as the first, held shortly after the outbreak of the Palestinian uprising. The first, however, had the dubious distinction (especially if you have a taste for the macabre) of resurrecting from oblivion the dim-witted notion of 'driving Israel into the sea,' and this by the then-new leader of the ('liberal') Wafd Party, no less.

There is a double irony in this. Under Gamal Abdel Nasser (who, despite the widely held belief, never actually made that particularly gruesome and patently impossible call), veterans of the then-defunct Wafd whiled away the years of their enforced political (and often, economic) retirement at the Gezira Club's Lido, Groppi's, and other hangouts of the (temporarily, as it turned out) impoverished rich, bemoaning how Nasser's foolhardy bellicosity toward Israel and its American allies was ruining the country. For a Wafd leader to adopt radical Nasserist rhetoric is irony in itself; for him to adopt the extravagantly exaggerated version of that rhetoric, mediated by both the 1960s Sawt al-'Arab Radio and the Zionist propaganda machine, smacks of burlesque.

The real point, of course, is that none of it is serious. The Wafd leader, I am certain, has not given a minute's thought to how exactly we're supposed to throw Israel into the sea, and, even worse, no one really expects him to. Rhetoric is all, and the more bombastic, irrational, and vacuous the merrier. It's no different than the 800 million guns that one Egyptian newspaper promised Ariel Sharon soon after his election, in a banner headline, or the (I don't know how many) other tens of millions of human bombs that our Jihadist friends keep threatening to unleash against the Jews and their crusading allies. It's no different, for that matter, from the calls for a general Arab/Islamic war against the Zionist enemy. In each and every Arab–Israeli war during the past fifty years, Israel has had more forces in the field of battle than the combined Arab forces. Yet, we—no less than the Zionist propaganda machine—love to reiterate that hundreds of millions of Arabs (even Comoros at the other end of Africa is a member of the Arab League) and Muslims are supposedly at our beck and call for a final showdown with the enemy.

It goes on and on. The same drab, unbearably hot, and smoke-filled conference halls. The same aged and aging leaders (with the odd minor change, at the hand of God) lined solemnly, if somewhat ungracefully, behind panels that are often too small to accommodate either their numbers or girths. The same overheated 'youth' activists, shouting the same slogans. And everyone enacting the same, long-rehearsed farce.

Usually, it goes something like this. The youth (many of whom are now well past middle age) eventually begin to insist hysterically that the few hundred attendants should 'march out on the street,' presumably to 'awaken the masses,' most of whom—this particular drama usually takes place around 11pm—are getting ready for bed or are already in it. The older and allegedly wiser party functionaries insist, no less hysterically, that emergency law is in force and that to go out 'on the street' would be adventurism and provocation in the extreme. Shouting matches are engaged in, accusations hurled, the odd scuffle breaks out. And yet, for all its heatedness, both parties to the fracas must be fully aware that it is futile.

Everyone is playacting, including the state. The streets around the party offices hosting the rally are a battle zone, except that there is no battle. Truckloads of helmeted anti-riot squads are everywhere. Other police trucks hold dozens of civilian dress-clad, stick-wielding 'special' anti-rioters, who appear even more fearful, if only because they are better nourished and less bewildered than their black-uniformed counterparts. Walkie-talkies gripped tightly in their hands, police officers, from generals down, move hither and thither, looking grim and busy. And, of course, there are the inevitable plainclothes State Security Intelligence officers, sitting around, smirking, and exchanging the odd joke with passing activists.

The few hundred solidarity rally activists like to think of themselves as 'the vanguard of the nation' and, as such, take themselves extremely seriously. The police, for reasons of their own, are happy to oblige. They tend to deploy something in the order of two dozen anti-riot personnel per potential demonstrator. There is a bitter irony in all this. Arguably, the Egyptian people's solidarity sentiments with the Palestinians have never been stronger than they are today. The energy expressed by university and high school students during the first weeks of the Intifada and the general sentiment on the street until today have been without parallel since the early 1970s—and then it was occupied Egyptian territory rather than solidarity with the Palestinians that topped people's concerns. The nation's political and cultural intelligentsia could not hope for better conditions to organize an effective and powerful solidarity movement. Seven months after the outbreak of the Intifada, though, it continues to show a decided preference for hot air.

*Al-Ahram Weekly*, May 10, 2001

# What Is Terrorism?

TERRORISM IS THE ANTITHESIS OF self-determination. But let's stop here for a moment. I've used the 't' word and I need to qualify it at once. Omnipresent even before 9/11 and the global "war on terror" ("the urgent task of our time," according to George W.), it was rendered totally meaningless a long time ago.

Overlook, for the moment, the competing definitions (for example, the difference between terrorism and legitimate armed resistance). Set aside also the various dated and updated lists of terrorist organizations and terrorism-sponsoring states ordained by the United States.

Look for designation. Ask yourself such apparently outlandish questions as, for instance, why the groups in the Northern Alliance in Afghanistan are not considered terrorists? They are nonstate armed groups; some of them, indeed, are backed by Iran (a notable member of the U.S. list of terrorism-sponsoring states); they are engaged in armed violence against the government (abhorrent as it may be, but there are plenty of despicable regimes); and, if it is atrocities against civilians you're looking for, they've committed their fair share (both during the anti-Soviet "jihad" and after), as recently underlined in a statement issued by Human Rights Watch.

Why was Osama bin Laden a *mujahid* when he was fighting the government-supported Soviet military presence in Afghanistan and a terrorist when he was fighting the government-supported U.S. military presence in Saudi Arabia? Who decides which governments are "puppets" and which are not, which are legitimate and which are not?

And what of atrocities? The capacity of states to commit atrocities is invariably much greater than that of nonstate groups. Why are state-committed atrocities less morally reprehensible? Recall such U.S.-backed monsters as Indonesia's Suharto, Zaire's Mobutu Sese Seko, Cambodia's Pol Pot, Israel's Ariel Sharon. And, if you insist on nonstate groups, what of the Contras in Honduras, the Israeli settlers in Palestine? Why are the Kurds terrorists in Turkey and freedom fighters in Iraq?

U.S. and British officials have described the "war on terror" as the greatest military operation since the Second World War. Yet, the enemy, "terrorism," is knowable only on condition of a total surrender of our minds and critical faculties to Washington and London bureaucrats and their slavish, self-interested media friends.

What is terrorism? I have no intention of debating definitions set out in dictionaries and international legal compendia, or of offering a 'definitive' definition of my own. I will, however, for the purposes of this discussion, use the term in a very old, very strict, and largely value-free sense, as, for instance, we would use 'war' (the most bellicose of warmongers would acknowledge that 'war is a terrible thing,' while most peace-minded people would concede that, 'sometimes, war is the only option'). The objective is not to convince the reader that my usage of the dread word is the correct one, but rather to explain what I mean when I do use it. Terrorism here is strictly a noun, not an implied adjective. I see it as a particular mode of armed violence to which nonstate political movements resort, aiming not to defeat the enemy militarily (as in armed revolutions or liberation wars, for instance) but to serve propaganda purposes, including intimidation, psychological attrition, declaring the movement's objectives, winning popular support, and so on.

As such, two qualifiers immediately come to mind. One, not all terrorisms are the same. Terrorism by fascist groups, state-linked paramilitaries, or colonial settlers is qualitatively different, morally and politically, from that pursued by, say, South African blacks fighting apartheid, Algerians fighting French colonialism, or Palestinians fighting Israeli occupation. Two, terrorism need not imply atrocities. Indeed, attacks against civilians are, historically, a fairly recent terrorist tactic. Many resistance movements have sordidly internalized the cynical disregard for the lives of noncombatants shown by states via two world wars, the Nazi Holocaust, two nuclear bombs, and countless genocidal campaigns. But in the nineteenth and early twentieth centuries, terrorist movements like the Russian Populists or Egypt's Black Hand (an underground terrorist group affiliated to the Wafd Party in the early 1920s) would target only especially hated state/colonial figures and symbols.

Having said this, I could now argue that terrorism as a form of resistance by the oppressed (I'm not interested here in the terrorism of the Contras, or Jewish settlers) is both politically ruinous and morally abhorrent. Fundamentally, the one salient feature of terrorism (irrespective of the relative legitimacy of the cause in defense of which it is pursued) is its antidemocratic nature. Its point of departure is the political apathy of the oppressed people whom the terrorists set out to 'liberate.' The people are called upon not to act but merely to cheer on the heroic 'saviors' acting on their behalf, sacrificing their lives to 'awaken' them. Intrinsic to a terrorist political strategy is a deep contempt for the people's ability to appropriate knowledge and political awareness, let alone to determine their own future.

And, by its very nature, terrorism works to reproduce the ignorance and political apathy it takes as its point of departure, on an ever-expanding scale. It appeals to people's emotions and baser instincts (such as retribution, spectacle, hero worship) rather than their capacity to reason and make choices. The people, indeed, are not called upon to make choices of any kind, save to deliver some of their number, as individuals, to the ranks of the self-sacrificing 'heroes.' They are made spectators to a horrific battle between largely faceless underground fighters and gigantic state machines whose capacity for untamed violence on a massive scale seems to lie just beneath the surface in the most democratic and 'civilized' of nations. Little wonder, then, that terrorism is the strategy of choice for intrinsically authoritarian political movements.

Atrocities are not a necessary corollary of terrorism, but it slips so easily into atrocity. The purely military logic of using armed violence against an immeasurably superior armed force obliges the terrorists to seek ever easier targets. Eventually, in Pakistan today as in Egypt several years ago, the heroes of the Islamic revolution end up shooting defenseless and impoverished Christian fellow citizens in the nearest village.

Terrorism is a product of intense oppression (and the deep feelings of humiliation and injured human dignity that such oppression generates) and, at the same time, of political helplessness and desperation. It begins from a point in which all avenues for popular self-determination appear closed, and it works to shut them tighter still. Can it be very surprising, then, that terrorism has gained such prominence in today's Arab world?

*Al-Ahram Weekly*, November 8, 2001

# In Search of Meaning

"WITH YOU TILL ETERNITY, AND after eternity."

This offense to logic and language was not the outcome of a teenager's fumbling attempt at an overamorous Valentine's Day card. In fact, I came across this particular travesty while on a short visit to Lebanon a few years ago, painted in bold letters underneath a massive billboard portrait of President Hafez al-Assad. I was reminded of it this week as Ariel Sharon put the final touches on his national unity government, and as Israel prepared to escalate levels of slaughter and devastation in the occupied territories. The Israelis have been talking strategy. It may be immoral, monstrous, and ultimately self-defeating, but it is strategy. The Arabs, for the most part, seemed to insist on talking nonsense.

*Ma'ak ila-l-abad wa ba'd al-abad* sounds even worse in Arabic than in my English rendering above. Yet, the ignominious billboard went virtually unnoticed by my Lebanese friends, whose education system, unlike Egypt's, continues to produce people who are more or less literate in their mother tongue. We've become immune to nonsense, the manipulation of language into an instrument of equivocation, ambiguity, and sheer mumbo-jumbo.

I was struck by this piece of illiterate groveling simply because, as a visitor, I was looking from the outside in. In context, however, I, no less than my Lebanese friends, have stopped expecting to make any sense out of the greater part of the barrage of official, semiofficial, and oppositional words to which we are exposed day and night, on the streets and through the media. Language, in this case, has become an increasingly impenetrable code, a series of subtexts that have to be deciphered. You look for messages, rather than meaning. And this, as even the least educated Egyptian will tell you, applies just as much to the weather forecast as to the prime minister's statements on the state of the economy. And so well trained have we, as a people, become in this art that on occasion the hidden message is understood as the exact opposite of the outward meaning. Thus, for instance, when an official pronounces Egypt free of mad cow disease, Egyptians immediately start stocking their freezers with poultry.

The Israelis are talking of widening the scale of 'liquidations' of leading Palestinian political figures, tightening and perpetuating the starvation siege of Palestinian towns and villages, reoccupying parts of the self-rule areas, and generally escalating the level of armed violence against the Palestinian population in the West Bank and Gaza. We, on the other hand, seem intractably bound—"till eternity, and beyond"—to prevarication, ambiguity, and mumbo jumbo. Behind all the bombast, empty rhetoric, the gnashing of teeth, and the inevitable whining, however, we can identify two equally futile and squalid categories of response: those who are excited by suicide bombings and Saddam Hussein's "Jerusalem Brigades," and those who would cynically try to use them as bargaining cards.

The one group would have us believe, without the least attempt at rational elucidation, that killing two or three old men and women in a Tel Aviv suburb and transforming Palestinian youths into walking bombs will somehow liberate Palestine. The other, despite enormous evidence to the contrary, and again without the least attempt at explanation, would have us believe that the Americans and Israelis are sufficiently frightened by the 'threat' of Hamas, Jihad, and Saddam that they will somehow awaken to the realization that they must offer a less humiliating deal to the moderates of the Palestinian Authority, and keep Yasser Arafat alive.

Both camps exhibit a total disregard for Palestinian lives and suffering. And both fall on two sides of a more basic if no less vacuous divide: the 'peace is a strategic option' camp versus the *sira' wugud wa laysa hudud* (a struggle of existence and not borders) camp. The very meaninglessness of these two fundamental, and allegedly opposing, slogans is exemplified by the fact that nothing that pertains to a coherent strategy can be inferred from them. They serve, in fact, as pretexts to persistently dodge the task of elaborating such a strategy.

"Glory to the martyrs" and "Long live the Intifada" may express legitimate feelings of solidarity with the Palestinians and anger at Israeli oppression and brutality. But they remain little more than hollow senti-ments unless we are also willing to discuss the fact that aimless martyrdom is just death, and that the Intifada is, in fact, dissipating, as popular resis-tance gives way to armed attacks by individual guerrillas, armed attacks on military targets give way to attacks on noncombatants, and trained guerrilla fighters give way to bungling human bombs.

Suicide bombings are sordid. Armed attacks on noncombatants are immoral. And the story of the Biblical Samson is more farce than tragedy.

We fight to win, not to kill and be killed (in far greater numbers). The Palestinians' greatest strength is the morality and fundamental humanity of their cause; Israel's is its military might. We need to fight on a terrain of our choosing, not theirs.

*Al-Ahram Weekly*, March 8, 2001

# Mirror, Mirror on the Wall

THE MOST ACCURATE REFLECTION OF the bankruptcy of the Arab political and ideological landscape is to be found not in Palestine, nor even in Iraq, but in Darfur. In the first two instances the images reflected back at us are too busy, too complex for our ever-dimming perceptions. We cannot quite make out the barren wasteland that is contemporary Arab reality. In Darfur, though, the picture mirrored is stark. And it is horribly ugly.

Practically everybody has failed the test of Darfur, opposition movements and civil society organizations as much as Arab governments.

The bitter and raucous contest between the two ideological/political camps—the liberals and the nationalists/Islamists—that has passed as a lame excuse for intellectual and political life for years now has once again been demonstrating its vacuity. The picture is more pathetic than fearful.

Having stood by as a million of their close kin were being butchered, brutalized, and subjected to rape and ethnic cleansing, Arabs are now scrambling into action, or rather scrambling to give the appearance of action: the Americans are coming; Israel's pernicious machinations are working behind the scenes; Arab national security faces yet another dire threat; and yet another Arab country is falling prey to American domination and Zionist infiltration and they're after our oil.

And so we suddenly discover the humanitarian tragedy in Darfur. The discovery is a transparent ploy to placate America and, hopefully, to get Omar al-Bashir to "shave his own head," as the saying goes, "before having it shaved for him," à la Saddam Husscin.

Unlike Saddam, however, Bashir, along with Yemen's Ali Abdullah Saleh and Libya's Muammar Qadhafi, has been displaying ever-growing hairdressing skills since George W. declared his global "war on terror" and Saddam Hussein's dental examination was flashed across the world's television screens.

Bashir's problem lies in trying to balance the requisites of mollifying the Americans while maintaining the hegemony of his corrupt, theocratic, and viciously authoritarian regime during a period of intense domestic and regional crisis. This accounts for the equivocation, dillydallying, and the occasional displays of defiance, both 'popular' and governmental.

But what stands out in the whole mess is just how subordinated the terrible plight of hundreds of thousands of Sudanese—presumably as much 'our' people as the Palestinians and Iraqis—is to other considerations, whether these are defined as averting U.S. intervention in yet another Arab country by urging Khartoum's 'gradual' compliance, forestalling the same through protests and expressions of solidarity with 'the Sudanese people,' or proclaiming jihad against western imperialists.

And there is not an ounce of principle in any of it. We've been endlessly railing against the western media and considerable sections of western (especially American) public opinion, and rightly so, for the racism inherent in their attitude to Palestinian suffering. Why, runs the constant refrain, is Palestinian blood deemed so cheap?

But what of the blood of the Sudanese in Darfur? How cheap is that?

Since when did we become so skeptical of reports in the progressive western media and of international human rights organizations, the very same media and organizations for which we have expressed deep admiration for their honest and courageous reporting of the Israeli occupation in Palestine and of the American invasion and occupation of Iraq? Suddenly, in Darfur, we've discovered that they are western, with suspect (imperialist) agendas.

What has become of the democracy and human rights that every political and ideological trend in today's Arab world blazons across its banners (with the sole exception of the jihadists who, at least, are consistently loathsome)?

As far as Darfur is concerned, most of us are happy to feign ignorance, or the kind of skepticism that we fail to muster even in the face of the most outlandish e-rumors, as long, of course, as the rumors are to our taste. Remember the one about the three thousand Jews who didn't show up at the World Trade Center on 9/11?

There is no great mystery about Darfur. A corrupt, repressive, and backward regime plunders, impoverishes, and disempowers its peoples to such a degree that they are set against one another in the daily struggle for survival, for livelihood, for land. Under such conditions, whatever ethnic and/or tribal fault lines exist, however tenuous or even manufactured, can become chasms. The absurdity of the Arab/black African divide in Darfur is testimony to this. (It so happens they're all black and they're overwhelmingly Muslim.) The regime favors one tribal/ethnic group over other groups, arms them to the teeth, backs them militarily, and cynically mobilizes them in a ruthless, no-holds-barred fight to maintain its oppressive control over the whole population. This is the 'tragedy' of Darfur. It is a familiar pattern that has on more than one occasion descended into the horror we see today in Darfur, the butchery and ethnic cleansing of hundreds of thousands of people. Remember Bosnia, anyone?

It's not that no one in the Arab world has spoken out against the atrocities in Darfur. One of the few bright spots in this whole mess came from a most unlikely quarter. The Arab League Secretariat's fact-finding mission to Darfur last May, in a manner unprecedented in the history of the normally insipid pan-Arab organization, reported that massive violations of human rights had been committed by pro-government militias. Few at the time seemed to notice or care. After fierce Sudanese protests the report was shelved and Arab foreign ministers, meeting at the Arab League headquarters in Cairo this week, were silent on the atrocities committed by the Sudanese government in Darfur, though they emphasized their opposition to foreign intervention and, predictably, demanded the international community adopt a more gradual approach toward solving the crisis. Sudan's Islamist government, which has been fervently 'cooperating' with the U.S. 'war on [Islamist] terror,' has donned, for the moment at least, the moth-eaten mantle of pan-Arab nationalism. Beware Zionist machinations in Darfur, the Sudanese foreign minister warned his peers.

It's all horribly familiar. So recurrent is this sense of déjà vu that along with the recognition comes nausea.

By all means let us confront U.S./Israeli oppression and atrocities in Palestine and Iraq. But is it not also time that we came to the conclusion that our dismal failure so far in effectively confronting those atrocities is inextricably tied to our willful failure to face the monsters in our own midst? It's a simple lesson that recent Arab history has been drumming into our heads over and over again. How many Saddams will it take for us to finally learn?

There will be no replay of Iraq in Sudan. The dire warnings are so much posturing. The Americans will not intervene militarily, and Khartoum, with as much foot-dragging as it can get away with, will rein in its 'devilish' militias. Tens of thousands of people will have died; it will take years for the survivors to restore a semblance of normality to their lives, the scars possibly never to heal; and we will have learned, most likely, nothing at all.

*Al-Ahram Weekly*, August 12, 2004

# Public Secrets

I WAS REMINDED LAST WEEK of a very interesting study I read some years ago on the *harat*, the alleys or quarters, of Ottoman Egypt. The study, using documents of the period, provided a detailed physical and social description of these basic units of urban life in order to challenge the prevalent wisdom on the seclusion of women in Egypt and other Muslim countries. The author presented a powerful argument to show that seclusion was in fact the "privilege" of the rich and powerful, that "the Islamic house," with its enclosed courtyards, *haramlik* and *salamlik*, was the preserve of the few. Behind the gates of the *harat*, the majority of urban dwellers, men and women, lived a highly communal life in which little, if anything, could be hidden.

One aspect of the study I found especially interesting was the set of rules and regulations governing this communal life. For obvious reasons, exile from the *hara* was one of the worst punishments the community could inflict on members who had breached these rules. I was amazed to discover that among the transgressions calling for this supreme punishment was "gossip" about other members of the *hara*. The author drew attention to the apparently paradoxical character of this particular regulation, since the nature of life in the *hara* was such that there can have been very few secrets to be gossiped about.

The paradox had a very familiar ring to it, however. One has only to look at current social and political reality, in Egypt and the rest of the Arab world, to realize that 'public secrets'—things everyone knows about that are spoken of at the risk of ostracism—are a prominent feature of this reality, on the local and national levels.

245

At a two-day meeting in Amman, Jordan, last week, participants from several Arab countries dealt with one of the more 'sensitive' public secrets of our current reality: "The Christian Arab today." Taking the form of a *conversazione*, or discussion circle, and conducted in accordance with Chatham House rules, whereby participants' interventions cannot be quoted without their prior consent, the meeting was a sort of *hara* in reverse. Jordan's Royal Institute for Interfaith Studies provided the gates, and behind them around forty Christian and Muslim Arabs, journalists, academics, and political figures laid bare the public secret so strictly kept 'on the outside.' What was remarkable about the meeting was that by its second and last day both the participants and organizers, most of them veterans of many similar inter-Arab and international meetings, were unanimous about its exceptional success. Why? Again, the answer seemed unanimous: the meeting's candor.

That such a seasoned group of Arab intellectuals should feel exhilarated at mere honesty and outspokenness in expressing the grievances and fears of Christian Arabs, on the one hand, and the deep concerns both they and Muslim Arabs feel as to the actual and potential effects on their societies of these grievances and fears, on the other, this seems to be a reflection of how suffocatingly repressive our contemporary Arab political and cultural climate is.

On the 'outside,' red lines and forbidden territories seem to surround us on every front. To cross, even in thought, is to risk disintegration, strife, and the inevitable 'penetration' by foreign forces. Are we so vulnerable?

There is more to the problem. The public secret of the situation of Christian Arabs cannot remain secret very much longer. Public secrets are not all repression, after all. As in the case of gossip in the *harat*, they imply a level of complicity between oppressive structures and those who have a stake in maintaining them, and those who could encroach upon their boundaries. This is very apparent in those areas where public and private domains converge most closely. The family is a supreme example: women have for ages been adept manipulators of public secrets, feigning submission to patriarchal authority even as they act to subvert it.

In the case of Christian Arabs, however, a far more overtly political process is at work.

For many reasons, not least a real history of religious tolerance under Islam, Christian and Muslim Arabs entered the modern world united in the struggle against western colonialism. This was in spite of the concerted attempts of western colonial powers to manipulate the religious divide and to present themselves as protectors of Arab Christians.

One of the more interesting aspects of the meeting in Amman was to underline the extensive and underreported role Arab Christians played in forging modern Arab cultural identity, a role that drew extensively on the achievements and triumphs of Muslim Arab civilization, helping create the symbols that were to inspire the struggle against colonialism and for modernization for over a century.

Here again, though, we had a public secret. Joined in the battle for freedom, to forge a modern national identity and to establish nation states based on citizenship, both Christian and Muslim Arabs implicitly agreed to gloss over the only semi-secularist character of the national movement and the states born of it. Rights of citizenship would remain incomplete, certain levels of discrimination against religious minorities would continue, and more against national and ethnic minorities (Kurds, Berbers, etc.) would be tolerated; modern states would maintain a certain religious character, which by its very nature sets limits on the rights of religious minorities. Lebanon, of course, was the notable exception to this general trend, though the sectarian 'Lebanese formula' was by no means a way out of the dilemma, as a decade and a half of civil war were to show.

For the rest, the public secret was to be even more closely kept as the national movement adopted an increasingly authoritarian character. By the middle of this century, nationalism in the Arab world tolerated no differences among 'the people.' To admit to any contradictions, whether on the basis of class, religion, ethnicity, or gender, would be to open a breach in the national front, allowing in the forces of imperialism and Zionism. A single party under a single leader became the rule.

Christians, no less than Muslims, were active architects of this authoritarian model. After all, the godfather of the Arab Baath Party was none other than Michel Aflaq.

But, for years now, our public secret has been in a state of extreme crisis. The failure of the pan-Arab national project, defeat after humiliating defeat at the hands of Israel and its western backers, and the triumph of 'globalization' were the interconnected processes that made the secret no longer viable. In the Arab world, as elsewhere, globalization has pushed the nation state and citizenship into severe crisis. The not so 'hidden hand' of the global market is everywhere strangling the political sphere—that is, the sphere where self-determination is exercised—placing strict limitations on people's ability to make real choices and hence pushing them back into increasingly narrower tribal identities based on religion, ethnicity, or race.

In the Arab world, both Muslims and Christians are embroiled in the fallout of these processes. Intolerance, religious bigotry, and the tendency to put religious differences above shared national and cultural identity are increasingly afflicting Christians and Muslims alike. Muslims, however, are the overwhelming majority and as they come to identify themselves increasingly in religious terms, Arab Christians will be ghettoized in equal measure.

The meeting in Amman did not come up with definitive solutions. It revealed, however, that there is a will and a determination among Arab intellectuals, Muslim and Christian, to fight back, that, ignorant congressmen working out of the American Israel Public Affairs Committee's pockets and poisonous Mossad bunglers be damned, we can expose our own weaknesses and come out the stronger for having done so.

*Al-Ahram Weekly*, December 25, 1997

# ELUSIVE SPRING,
# ENDURING AUTUMN

By THE END OF THE twentieth century, nearly a quarter of that century had passed and still Egypt was being described as a political system in transition, from authoritarianism to democracy. In fact, something had transpired, and Gamal Abdel Nasser's populist authoritarianism had not been giving way to democracy, however gradual and slow-paced, but to oligarchy, a marriage of state and business, conducted behind political space and at its expense. As this became increasingly clear, hopes began to turn toward some sort of Orange Revolution. The reinvigorated political activism of 2005 triggered hopes of a Cairo Spring. Acknowledging that extant political space had indeed been revitalized, I contended that, vital or dormant, Egyptian political space had shrunk to a few acres, roughly the triangle stretching from downtown Cairo's Tahrir Square to the headquarters of the Press Syndicate (both favored demonstration sites) about a mile away. What we had been witnessing in Egypt between 2005 and 2010 had not been signs of a coming spring but indications of an enduring autumn. Between the elections of 2005 and those of 2010, it was not rebirth we were seeing but decay.

Then, of course, I was proven wrong.

# Stormy Elections Close
# a Turbulent Year

THE HEADLINE OF THE STATE-OWNED newspaper *al-Ahram* described December 7, 2005 (the last day of voting in Egypt's month-long, three-stage parliamentary election), as "the most violent day" of the election. The independent daily *al-Masry al-Youm* went a bit further. Under photos of mayhem that could have been shot in Nablus or Ramallah, the newspaper declared, "Egypt can now breathe a sigh of relief. The elections officially ended yesterday." Its tongue-in-cheek banner read in bold letters: "Ceasefire."

The November 9–December 9 parliamentary elections were to have been the pinnacle of a year during which political reform and democratization overwhelmingly topped the nation's agenda and dominated public discourse. They have proven anticlimactic to say the least. In terms of violence, thuggery, chaotic and manipulated voter lists, police repression, intervention and coercion by state bodies, flagrant vote buying, and vote rigging, this year's poll rivals the worst elections the nation has seen since the uniquely free parliamentary poll of 1976. And while ballot-stuffing has been rendered more difficult in general as a result of judicial supervision, there have been numerous well-documented instances of the most barefaced rigging of the results, on occasion with judicial complicity and more often in flagrant disregard for the judiciary, including threats of violence and actual physical attacks on judges.

The most prominent form of electoral misconduct this time around, however, was to attack the electorate itself. Hired thugs, many of them absurdly wielding swords, provided the overriding image of the 2005 poll. The evidence overwhelmingly pointed to candidates of the ruling National Democratic Party (NDP), including renegade members running against the official party ticket, as the real culprits behind the rampaging thugs. Invariably, the police stood by while the NDP-supporting thugs attacked and intimidated voters.

In the later stages of the poll, the police abandoned even the pretense of a neutral position. They prevented voters from casting their ballots by laying siege to polling stations, as well as to whole villages and urban districts in which opposition (mostly Muslim Brotherhood) candidates enjoyed strong bases of support, which led to violent confrontations between anti-riot squads and angry opposition supporters.

With at least ten dead and scores injured, one human rights organization compared NDP and police behavior in stage three of the election to Operations Desert Storm and Desert Shield combined.

Moreover, the results of the 2005 poll underline the conclusion that the Egyptian political system is in deep crisis. For the first time in Egyptian parliamentary history, the outlawed Muslim Brotherhood seized eighty-eight seats of the People's Assembly, accounting for 20 percent of a total of 432 races concluded so far (polling has been postponed by judicial order in six constituencies, accounting for the remaining twelve elected seats, and President Hosni Mubarak has appointed another ten members).

And although the NDP has maintained its overwhelming majority in parliament, easily crossing the two-thirds mark needed to pass constitutional amendments by seizing 311 seats (73 percent of the total), a closer look at the numbers reveals a ruling party that seems to be coming apart at the seams.

In fact, the official ticket of the NDP—notwithstanding the rigging, violence, and intimidation—met with resounding failure, with 287 NDP candidates having lost their races, giving the ruling party's official ticket a success ratio of 34 percent. The NDP only gained its majority by reinstating renegade members who ran as independents against official party candidates.

No less serious has been the equally resounding failure of the legal, secular (or semisecular) opposition, with the Wafd Party winning a mere six seats, the leftist Tagammu' two, and the Nasserist Karama (not yet licensed) two, and one seat going to a breakaway faction from the Ghad Party. All legal opposition party leaders failed to win back their seats, including the Arab Nasserist Party's Diaa Eddin Dawoud, Tagammu's Khaled Mohieddin, and Ghad's Ayman Nour.

Is Egypt's political future destined, then, to hang between the decaying and crumbling semisecular authoritarianism of the NDP and the rising, and considerably more vigorous, Islamist authoritarianism of the Muslim Brotherhood? It is too early to tell. For the time being, however, the proverbial Cairo Spring has proved to be just as fleeting as that much-sung season invariably is in our desert-besieged valley. As 2005 draws to a close, it is autumn—at the outset of which seventy-seven-year-old President Mubarak embarked on his fifth six-year term at the nation's helm—that seems to provide a more fitting metaphor for the paroxysms and transformations that grip the Egyptian polity.

It is in terms of decay, and not yet renewal—the twilight of an era, rather than the advent of a new one—that the sea change in the political life of Egypt over the past year can be made intelligible.

*Arab Reform Bulletin,* Carnegie Endowment for International Peace,
December 2005

# Big Trouble, Small Acres

"I ALWAYS HAD THREE SCENARIOS," the seasoned academic tells us in typically clipped tones, "Now I have none."

The same sentiment, expressed a little less pithily perhaps, is constantly to be heard among Egypt's intellectual community. Whether optimists, pessimists, or 'pessoptimists,' all find themselves unable to predict, with any degree of intelligibility, the course of political developments in the country over the next few months, let alone years. Everyone seems to agree that a point of no return has been crossed. The Egyptian polity, remarkably obdurate for the past quarter of a century and deeply rooted in authoritarian structures established more than fifty years ago, is apparently coming apart at the seams. Yet, beyond the breakdown, which until now has been accompanied with more whimpers than bangs, everything remains opaque.

On the most superficial level this opacity is merely a projection of the lack of transparency of a regime in obvious turmoil. This is made all the more glaring by the fact that even today, with presidential elections due in fewer than three months, we do not know whether we have an incumbent in the running. Certainly we are being teased with the prospect daily and campaigning of sorts—whatever our views of its efficacy—has already begun, which begs the question, why all the teasing? After all, it should have become clear by now that rather than whet the appetite this kind of teasing merely dulls it.

But then, opacity has been the defining feature of the government-led 'reform' process for a year now. The president readily acknowledged that his intention to call for the amendment of Article 76 of the constitution was initially known only to the speaker of parliament and five legal/constitutional experts. No less opaque has been the apparent struggle within the upper echelons of the ruling party. We are aware by now that the young versus old guard, liberal reformist versus conservative bureaucrat schemata, borrowed from the Soviet and Chinese experiences as read by the western media, is facile and largely inaccurate. But we can only speculate—wildly, and on the basis of the flimsiest of facts—about the real content of the struggle and, no less significant, about who is squabbling with whom.

That there is an intense crisis within the ruling elite is clear. What are the constitutive elements of this crisis? The real configuration of forces at the top of the state bureaucracy and the way in which it is unfolding continues to be a matter of speculation, rumor, and conjecture. And these have been running riot, no longer confined to whispers and political café gossip but splashed daily in banner headlines in the plethora of independent and opposition newspapers that in the past few months have left no red line uncrossed.

The most prominent subject of rumor is the 'succession.' But is there really anything behind all this speculation that Gamal Mubarak is being groomed to succeed his father? All we have to go on is the younger Mubarak's expanding political influence and the continuing seepage of political gossip, some of which seems to presume that those recounting the latest story heard it in the Mubaraks' living room.

What we are actually seeing are the outward, phenomenal expressions of the crisis at the top, and in such profusion, with such intensity, that the expression of the crisis far outstrips its presumed causes, whether they be the problem of succession, American pressure, Kifaya and other opposition movements, or internecine strife within the ruling elite.

While the opacity of the ruling elite in Egypt is nothing new, the fact that it has spread to envelop the country's political future in such overwhelming, inexorable gloom is a function not only of the intensity of the crisis but also, and perhaps more important, of the fact that it is very much 'a crisis from above.'

True, the rise in opposition movements and street activism in recent months has altered the political landscape, encouraging ever more vocal and radical dissent at home and drawing a great deal of attention abroad. Eyes—from Washington to Seoul, governmental and civil, sinister, benign, and well-wishing—have been trained with interest on what looked to be a Cairo Spring.

The political landscape of the country has been transformed in interesting, even exhilarating ways, and this in the span of a few months. Yet, we cannot but remind ourselves that this whole landscape is made up of no more than a few acres. A journalist friend put it very aptly, pointing out that in his estimation the whole political melee we've been witnessing of late involves no more than the readership of one of the more popular independent newspaper: seven thousand people. The rest of the country's population of 70 million are either unaware it is going on or content just to look on.

Will it all fizzle out? It just might, though with every passing day this becomes more unlikely. For behind the host of incidental elements feeding the current crisis lies its most compelling cause: age. A political system the most remarkable feature of which has been its longevity is finally giving up the ghost or, to use a more accurate metaphor, crumbling under its own weight.

It is neither American pressure nor the increasingly vociferous and media-conscious activism of a vocal political elite but decay that is, paradoxically, driving the revitalization of politics.

Where it will lead depends on how and when the Egyptian people finally enter the fray. Enter it they must, that at least is clear. A decades-old High Dam made up of fear, intimidation, and resignation is fracturing by the day; the waters of pent-up dissatisfaction will inevitably pour through.

What remains to be seen is whether 'the people' will make their entrance and put their stamp on the country's future, as an undifferentiated mass, potentially destructive mobs, who are the easy prey of demagogues, rogues, and fanatics, or as politically aware, self-organizing, and empowered citizens. It is the manner of their entrance that will determine Egypt's political future. And an obdurate, self-interested, and unyielding ruling elite and a self-involved, smug, and neglectful opposition could well ensure that we replace an aged, decaying authoritarian system with a younger and more vigorous variety.

Then, it will be "see you in 2030."

*Al-Ahram Weekly*, June 30, 2005

# Anatomy of a Downtown Cairo Demonstration

"BUT THEY ARE MY GRANDCHILDREN'S AGE" were reportedly among the last words uttered by seventy-two-year-old Ahmed Mostageer, geneticist, philosopher, and poet and one of Egypt's greatest contemporary scientists, as he watched televised coverage of the Israeli devastation of Lebanon from what was to prove his deathbed. Yet again, Arab children were being killed and mutilated, their homes destroyed, their brief lives robbed or shattered irreparably amid untold horror. And, if anything, the 'civilized' world looked on with even more callousness than usual.

It was with similar feelings of identification that I joined several hundred others in Tahrir Square, at the heart of downtown Cairo, to protest the Israeli attack on Lebanon. The outrage was heartfelt and profound; the identification with the pain and suffering of the Lebanese people was shared by millions of Egyptians and other Arabs everywhere. And yet I could not shake off a sense of the surreal that seemed to hang like a dim veil over the downtown demonstration, rendering me more an observer than a participant.

The fact that I'm a very infrequent demonstrator was certainly a contributing factor to this feeling of detachment (the last demonstration in which I'd taken part was in 2000, at the outset of the Palestinian Intifada), as was my formative experience of protest demonstrations. This was way back in the 1970s when to even contemplate going out on the street you had to count on a minimum of ten thousand or more demonstrators, and—dare

I say it—an abundant and readily accessible stockpile of stones. These are never in short supply in our great city, perennially a work in progress.

The wave of downtown demonstrations of the past few years has, therefore, continued to strike me as more theater than politics. A few hundred people, mobilized via text-messaging and e-mail, surrounded by ten or twenty times their number in anti-riot police, often left to their own devices and occasionally, and wholly unpredictably, pounced upon in paroxysms of police frenzy—none of it seemed to ring very true.

This is not to disparage the energy, genuine courage, and sheer persistence of this core of activists, who in 2005 captured the attention of the world media with their determined battle for democracy. Yet, for all that, I could not help but feel that the downtown demonstrations were not so much a function of the expansion of the democratic right to free expression and peaceful protest, as they were testimony to the protracted disintegration, over the past quarter of a century, of the very space in which such rights can have any meaning—that is, politics. It's not that more democratic rights have been won since the 1970s; they had merely been rendered insignificant.

"How many people do you think are gathered here?" a foreign television reporter was asking my old friend, a fellow veteran of the 1970s student movement and a leader of the Kifaya (Enough) movement that shot to international renown last year. "A few thousand," my friend answered unabashedly, to my utter amazement. I had estimated something in the order of five to seven hundred—an estimate I would have thought the reporter, with a camera crew at her back, could have made for herself.

I had already discovered that this was an 'invitation only' demonstration. At last, I felt, I had uncovered the full subtleties of the police counterdemonstration strategy. It was brilliant in its simplicity. Huge contingents of anti-riot police laid a tight siege to the demonstrators, who, squeezed into a small corner of the 'square,' were surrounded by wider circles made up of hundreds of civilian-clad and uniformed policemen. The encirclement was nearly ten tight circles deep.

Meanwhile, what must have been several thousand other policemen were spread out everywhere: reserve contingents of anti-riot squads placed hither and thither (occasionally being rushed from one spot to another for no easily discernible reason); high-ranking police officers, their shoulders heavy with stars, eagles, and crossed swords; little congregations of the slick, civilian-dressed officers of the State Security

Investigations department, cynical smiles perpetually plastered on their faces, as if in gleeful contemplation of the day they will have you in one of their torture dens in nearby Lazughli; and every kind of rank-and-file policeman you will ever have come across or handed a tip in lieu of a parking ticket, in their myriad of equally grubby uniforms.

A bird's eye view would probably give the impression of a middle-ages battle taking place below.

The 'invitation only' police strategy works this way: as you approach the tiny spot in which the early arrivals have been squeezed already, dozens of police officers will rush you along, and away from the site of the demonstration. When you insist on veering toward the demonstration in any case, you are told in no uncertain terms that it is "prohibited to go there." "But I want to go there," I say, pointing to the spot where portraits of Hizbullah leader Hassan Nasrallah, nervously joined by red and Lebanese flags, could be seen over the helmeted heads of encircling anti-riot police. A ranking officer then gives you a penetrating look, presumably assessing whether you belong to the "ordinary masses" (and thus have no business there) or to the self-styled "political elite," which does. Evidently, I passed the test. My trump card, which happens to be an outdated ID that identifies me as the editor of *Al-Ahram Weekly*, remains snug in the wallet in my back pocket. This process is repeated several times, and finally you come up against the wall of anti-riot police encirclement. Again, you are to seek, and be given, permission to wade through.

It is thus that the seeming anomaly of an 'invitation only' demonstration is made. Once inside the 'inner' circle, I found a wholly secularist crowd, chanting themselves hoarse in praise of Hizbullah, Hassan Nasrallah, and Hamas. Possibly half were women, but the ubiquitous headscarf was hardly in evidence. The svelte young woman in tight jeans, with a green Hamas bandana pulled around thick, flowing dark hair, proclaiming "long live the Islamic resistance," struck me as an apt metaphor for the incongruous position in which Arab democrats and secularists constantly find themselves by virtue of George W. Bush's endless "war on terror."

The chants go on and on, seemingly endlessly, even as 'the masses,' or at least those among them who have ventured downtown of an evening, presumably for shopping or the cinema, look on curiously as they are being hurried along to mind their own business. The demonstrators have only the besieging policemen with whom to communicate. This is done alternately by trying to provoke them or to convince them of the justice of our cause. Occasional scuffles break out, but tonight there are no orders to strike.

I'm not a chanter, never have been, even in the glorious 1970s, even when I liked the slogans being chanted, which on this occasion I did not. Back then I would have been concerned with the leafleting side of the affair (unknowingly training for what was later to become my profession). Now, I busy myself by conducting what, in my mind, I have called an anatomical study of a downtown demonstration—hence the title of this chapter. I wade in and out of the encircling police, each time having to seek permission to do so. I decide to try and get a definitive answer to a question that had been bothering me over the past few years: why the civilian-clad anti-riot contingent?

Initially I had believed that these slightly better fed and considerably more vicious members of our Central Security Forces were to play the role of 'angry citizens,' incensed by the demonstrators' verbal attacks on our beloved president or the leaders of friendly countries such as Messrs. Bush, Blair, Sharon, and now Olmert. But over the countless demonstrations of the past couple of years it became glaringly obvious that no such pretense was even being attempted. I went up to one of them and asked him. He gave me a wolfish kind of smile in reply. "The better to beat the ----- out of you, my dear," it seemed to signify.

Philosophically, I fell back on an answer I had reached earlier, after some thought. It was merely an affirmation of lawlessness, of brute force unbound by law, or the trappings of law that uniforms presumably signify.

Two or three hours later, I waded through for the last time. The more hardy demonstrators were still shouting slogans, still alternately trying to provoke or convince their besiegers. The gap between our feelings of anger, empathy, and solidarity and our ability to express them at all fruitfully yawned as widely as ever. As I walked away I recalled the lines from the beautifully haunting poem, "The Testing-Tree," by Stanley Kunitz. Some ten years ago, following the first Qana massacre, I had them printed out on a piece of paper I then placed under the glass top of my desk. It got lost when I moved last year, but the words were not forgotten: "In a murderous time the heart breaks and breaks and lives by breaking."

*The Daily Star Egypt*, August 28, 2006

# Sewage Street Story

Why now?

It is a question being asked in tones of anger and frustration by a great many people. And the reason behind their bewilderment at the sudden eruption of terrorist incidents in Egypt after years of calm should be obvious to all. For, however seriously, or not, we take the harbingers of Egypt's democratic spring, even the most pessimistic acknowledge that there is something new in the air, that decades of suffocating political stagnation might, just might, be coming to an end.

However skeptical one may be about the real extent of reform encapsulated in the proposal to amend Article 76 of the constitution, allowing for multicandidate presidential elections, there should be little doubt in that it represents a crack, a potentially devastating fissure, in at least one plank of a hitherto sacrosanct, if anachronistic, authoritarian constitution. The presidential elections may, as many critics suggest, in the end deliver little more than the old wine repackaged in a new bottle. But the simple fact that a few of the more serious opposition parties are being allowed to put up presidential candidates cannot help but enliven the political and ideological debate, opening up new vistas to a public demoralized by having been stuck for decades in the same old scene.

And while it is true that the increasingly vociferous tone of antigovernment opposition during recent months has been confined to what is, ultimately, a narrow political and intellectual elite with little or no popular base, the mere fact this elite feels it can voice its criticisms in such unprecedented terms is significant. Such boldness is contagious, encouraging more and more groups to join the fray.

The revival of street politics—however limited, however heavily under siege—was helping to create a new climate in the country, a climate in which other sections of the population were being encouraged to make their own entrances onto the political stage, shyly, hesitantly perhaps, but entrances nonetheless. It may have been too early to celebrate a nascent political vitality that remains, for now, too feeble and limited to convince that democracy is finally within our grasp. One thing, though, is sure. Acts of terror are guaranteed to set the whole process back. Hence the urgent question: why now?

That Cairo should have been the scene of three terrorist operations in less than a month is worrying enough. Far more frightening, though, than the rapid-fire recurrence and the targeting of tourists is the extreme youth of the perpetrators, the horrifying amateurishness of their attacks. There are millions just like them, inhabiting the depths of poverty and hopelessness, suicidal and desperate. The utter misery of their lives need not be so graphically symbolized as in the case of the Yassin family, by their living on Shari' al-Magari, or Sewage Street.

The culprits are, in a sense, victims, though to reduce them to such, to make them exclusively victims, reflects only the deep-seated contempt in which the intellectual and political class actually holds the poor and disenfranchised, viewing them alternately as a docile mindless mass and a blind force of seething, pent-up anger. The poor are objects, with no minds of their own. They are to be pacified, kept down, manipulated, distracted, or incited. They are never perceived as subjects capable of making choices.

But the Yassins and their group, in setting out on their murderous mission, were making a choice, however destructive and evil. It was a desperate choice, but it seemed the most attractive choice on offer.

Those responsible for limiting the horizons of people like the Yassins to the extent that death becomes preferable to living are manifold. They include the security bodies that the first annual report of the National Human Rights Council, established by none other than the president, portrays as an extralegal force on the rampage, responsible for wholesale roundups involving thousands and the routine torture and sometimes killing of suspects, including women and children taken as hostages. Need I say that the bulk of their victims are the poor and disenfranchised?

The security forces are ably aided and abetted by the contributions of the political and intellectual classes, both in government and the opposition. Have they not contributed to the Yassins' murderous choice by waxing poetic over or rationalizing away the equally murderous choices of Osama bin Laden and the video butchers of Iraq? Have they not, through official, opposition, and independent media, left millions of young Egyptians prey to the Internet-disseminated drivel of militant Islamists? In using religion as the ultimate distraction, they have made religious trivia the paramount subject of discussion. And what of their crude populist propaganda, the imminent threat to Islam, this war on Muslims that nonchalantly weaves together fact and fiction to create a Muslim flipside to the neoconservatism of Bush and his cronies?

What are the effects of incessantly celebrating death, of constructing vengeance and self-destruction as the only option available to the oppressed and disempowered? Busy squabbling over the terms and scope of political reform, has anyone given a thought to the people who live on Sewage Street? Does anyone try to make reform relevant to them? Does anyone make the least effort to engage with them? Is anyone interested in helping them find their own way onto the political stage?

That groups of fanatical, desperate, and poorly educated adolescents can hold a nation's future hostage is outrageous. But they can, and will continue to sprout like so many mushrooms as long as we have security bodies that round up and torture people in their thousands, and an intellectual and political class that is unwilling to ponder, let alone accommodate, the lives of millions of Egyptians, or to perceive them as anything more than objects of manipulation.

*Al-Ahram Weekly*, May 5, 2005

# Enter the Absent Actor

As the presidential bombshell was being thrown into their midst by their respective speakers, members of the two houses of parliament appeared, in turns, dumbstruck, glum, and half-heartedly cheerful. Like awkward adolescents, they seemed wholly unsure of how they were supposed to behave in a rather delicate social situation. Used as they are to fervently cheering and heartily applauding each and every presidential pronouncement that comes their way, Hosni Mubarak's landmark declaration had his party's legislators looking worried, bemused, and befuddled.

The sheer weight of the surprise may partially explain such a starkly untypical response.

During the second half of 2004, there was a feeling that significant changes were afoot. Longstanding National Democratic Party (NDP) bosses Youssef Wali and Safwat al-Sherif were abruptly removed from their Cabinet posts while the president was undergoing surgery in Germany. The ruling party's Policies Committee, headed by the president's son, Gamal, seemed on a roll.

The younger Mubarak, surrounding himself with a new breed of party cadre—young, bright, and modernist in outlook—appeared to have become an agenda setter of sorts for the regime headed by his father. The change of Cabinet that followed soon after fell short of the higher side of elite expectations but gave both the premiership and practically all of the government's economic portfolios to the 'Young Turks' of the Policies Committee.

And while the anticipated surprises that the NDP's September conference was presumed to have had in store were not forthcoming, no one could help but take note of the preeminent influence Gamal Mubarak wielded over the conference's televised proceedings.

Yet, by early 2005, the expectations curve seemed on a steep downward slope. The 'old guard' of the NDP—Soviet-style party bureaucrats who received their political training in Nasser's Arab Socialist Union—were not only as firmly entrenched as they ever were, it was also becoming increasingly clear how indispensable they actually were to the continued preponderance of the ruling party.

When it came to coopting the opposition, ensuring the NDP's fortunes in parliamentary elections, and doing the groundwork for the presidential poll, it was up to savvy veterans such as Safwat al-Sherif and Kamal al-Shazli (respectively, the secretary general and deputy secretary general of the NDP) to save the day.

No less significantly, the ruling party and the president himself seemed to have put the lid on the political reform debate as whole, and most especially on the question of a constitutional amendment. The 'national dialogue' with opposition party leaders, ostensibly launched to discuss domestic political reform, was effectively transformed into a 'united front' effort against foreign, particularly American, intervention in Egyptian affairs.

The opposition leaders easily conceded the postponement of the constitutional amendment until after the forthcoming presidential election. The arrest of Ghad Party leader Ayman Nour lowered expectations even further. By the time the second round of the 'national dialogue' was coming to a close, most observers expected little more than a few cosmetic changes to legislation governing political life and, perhaps, a backroom deal with the main opposition parties allowing them a greater share of parliamentary seats. Their current share is so meager as to allow the NDP considerable room for largesse.

Then came the president's bombshell. Little wonder, then, that the NDP's parliamentary majorities were stunned. One cannot help but suppose, however, that surprise was not the only, or even the most important, element behind the parliamentarians' obvious discomfiture. It's almost certain that there was a considerable number of very worried people among the halfheartedly cheering and applauding members of parliament.

The bombshell form with which the president's decision was announced is vintage Egyptian presidency. It smacks of the 'strategic deception' tactics adopted by Anwar Sadat in the prelude to the October War of 1973, and seems to explain some bewildering aspects of the mixed messages of the past few months, most notably the relative freedom allowed the Kifaya (Enough) movement to publicly protest the president's reelection.

Some analysts are describing the constitutional amendment put forward by Mubarak as heralding the birth of Egypt's 'Second Republic.' This assessment may well prove to have been apt. Yet, the big question is whether it will be a truly democratic republic. The answer to this question goes well beyond the current debate over the conditions for presidential nomination—how restrictive or otherwise. It also transcends the possibility that the president has other bombshells up his sleeve, such as, for instance, stepping down in favor of another NDP candidate, be that Gamal Mubarak or someone else.

It even goes beyond the currently infinitesimal possibility of a non-NDP candidate actually winning the presidency. After all, what guarantees do we have that a new popularly elected president will be more democratic than Mubarak or any of his predecessors of the First Republic?

The Muslim Brotherhood's Mohamed Akef recently declared the group's support for a fifth term for Mubarak on the ostensibly religious grounds that Muslims should show obedience to their rulers. Akef is the leader of Egypt's largest, and quite possibly only, viable opposition force at present and, notwithstanding the obviously tactical maneuvering involved in his statement, it behooves one to wonder about the extent of 'obedience' Akef would expect of us if he were to become our 'ruler.'

There is much more to democracy than multicandidate presidential elections, however free these may be. It is not even merely a question of recognizing and respecting—in law as in public sentiment—that even as we are citizens of the same country we have different and often widely divergent interests, inclinations, needs, and hopes. It is above all about people's ability to organize, balance, counterbalance, and peacefully negotiate these differences.

Neither the Americans nor the current opposition parties, nor even Mubarak himself, can guarantee that the Second Republic will be a truly democratic republic. Only the Egyptian people can.

Meanwhile, a stone has been dropped into the stagnant waters of Egyptian political life. Whether its ripple effects will help bring this hitherto absent actor onto the political stage remains to be seen. The future of democracy in Egypt, nevertheless, depends on it.

*Al-Ahram Weekly*, March 3, 2005

# Out with the Old

THE SOVIET MOGULS OF THE ruling National Democratic Party (NDP) are being squeezed out of office; at last, pundits have been saying with audible sighs of relief. Three weeks ago, Safwat al-Sherif, ostensibly the biggest mogul of them all, was abruptly removed ('resigned') from the remarkably powerful office of information minister—a position he held for twenty-two years—and 'elected' speaker of the Shura Council, the largely ineffectual consultative upper house.

And now we have a new prime minister who, at fifty-two, is the youngest Egyptian head of government for decades. Ahmed Nazif is widely held to be modern, dynamic, efficient, and possessed of considerable personal integrity.

Agriculture Minister and Deputy Prime Minister Youssef Wali, another old-timer (also with twenty-two years in office under his belt), the bête noire of many previous cabinets, is also out.

A new ministry, of investment development and the public business sector, has been created for thirty-nine-year-old Mahmoud Mohieddin, the rising economic star of the NDP's Policy Secretariat and a babe in the woods by Egyptian Cabinet standards. But Kamal al-Shazli, veteran of the Arab Socialist Union (ASU) and its Vanguard Organization and NDP political wheeler-dealer par excellence, retains his long-held post of minister of state for People's Assembly affairs, though with a somewhat truncated portfolio. The affairs of the upper house, the Shura Council, have been handed over to Mufid Shehab, former minister of higher education.

A mixed result, then, as far as the much-touted struggle between the NDP's modernist reformers, mostly gathered in the party's Policy Secretariat, led by Gamal Mubarak, and the ruling party's old guard goes. Al-Shazli, after all, is much larger than his Cabinet post, even in reduced form. As the man mainly responsible for keeping together the highly intricate patronage/client network that is the ruling party, he gives new meaning to the concept of party whip. Neither is al-Sherif out of the running yet. He remains secretary-general of the ruling party, though rumor has it not for long.

Others will assess the degree to which the new Cabinet shifts the balance between reformers and the old guard, or what it might herald of more dramatic shifts to come. (According to a friend much more in the know, this is the tip of the iceberg and the next few months will witness "very exciting developments.")

That may or may not be. There is, though, an interesting aspect to the reformer/old-guard polarity worth noting. Irrespective of the extent or real substance of the reformists' reforming zeal, one cannot help but wonder at the absence of politicians from their ranks.

All things being equal, it is easy to imagine the politically savvy ASU veterans, à la al-Sherif and al-Shazli, eating the young reformers whole for lunch. The new prime minister is a case in point. Nazif may well be all the wonderful things people are saying about him but a politician he ain't. And reforming a state is a somewhat different proposition from reforming a corporation or even a government department. The reformist ranks may be full of bright young technocrats but there isn't a real politician among them.

How far this will affect the reformers' political fortunes in the days to come remains to be seen. It is not as serious a flaw as it may seem at first glance, however. All other things are not equal, and, in any case, the role of the Cabinet in policymaking in Egypt is marginal, and has been so for decades.

I underline the absence of politicians in the latest reshuffle because it is symptomatic of a much larger phenomenon: the death of politics, of all politics, in Egypt There is a certain irony in the fact that the only politicians we have left are a moribund and now dying breed of Soviet-style party bureaucrats. What kind of reform can we speak of when a quarter of a century of 'liberalization' has failed to produce any liberal politicians worthy of note? When it has failed to produce political figures of any kind?

The most telling feature of this Cabinet change is the way it came about: whispers, followed by press leaks, followed by surprise appointments/removals, followed by more leaks, followed by more appointments/removals, with the nation waiting for the next surprise, or lack of one. Recently, the Indian people surprised the world by changing their government. We, on the other hand, are expected to be titillated and then elated when the surprises come from on high.

Having conceded many years ago that we have very little control over our collective fate, we've been reduced to a nation of observers, citizens/analysts possessed of various degrees of adroitness and left to exercise our analytical skills on a hodge-podge of fact and fiction, rumor and bizarre theories (often trussed up as facts), and lately, thanks to the communications revolution, whatever pickings come our way via the World Wide Web and satellite television.

So, let me beg the readers' pardon for yawning amid all the excitement, but the only government change I find of interest is one brought about by the people and the only reform that it is worth getting excited about is democratic reform.

The ball remains, as it always has, in our court, in the court of the people.

*Al-Ahram Weekly*, July 15, 2004

# Nasser and the End of Politics

THE REVIVED DEBATE ON EGYPT'S July 23 revolution on the occasion of its fiftieth anniversary has been as flat, lackluster, and uninspired as the fireworks that were set off along Cairo's Nile-side Corniche to mark it. It was largely a rehashing of the same tired old debate that followed Nasser's death in 1970 and has remained with us since: the revolution destroyed democracy and a vibrant civil society, setting the country on the road to political and economic disaster, or, alternatively, the revolution's democratic failings (now practically everybody agrees that 'democracy' is a good thing) were grounded in its times—the tasks of national liberation; the weaknesses of pre-1952 liberal democracy; the requisites of national unity in the face of external aggression and imperial pressures; and the emancipation of the working masses, effectively disenfranchised by the 'liberal age.'

Save for the surprising rehabilitation of Egypt's first and largely irrelevant one-year figurehead president, Muhammad Naguib, the official line, aptly expressed in state-organized celebrations, was as bland and muddled as it's been for three decades. Rather like someone who inherits a fortune from a disreputable ancestor, the Egyptian state is constantly torn between the need to vindicate its claim to the inheritance and to distance itself from the benefactor and his various radical antics.

Herein, in fact, lies the most interesting question about the July revolution. This is not the usual, superfluous question about when and how the revolutionary regime ended. The real question concerns the anomaly inherent in the fact that the state structure created by the revolution remains largely unchanged half a century later, despite sea changes in orientation and in every other conceivable area of life, domestically, regionally, and internationally. The revolution may have committed suicide, been assassinated, or simply passed away of old age; the state it created has been phenomenal in its obdurate capacity for survival, even as it mutates.

We might put the question in more concrete terms. For instance, how is it that a populist authoritarian state anchored—ideologically, politically, and institutionally—in a compact with the masses can maintain its fundamental structures largely unchanged once that compact has been torn to shreds and the corporatist bodies that embodied and instrumentalized it are effectively ruined? How is it that this can go on for over a quarter of a century, with no end in sight? To put it another way, how is it that decades of a multiparty system cannot produce a single political party worthy of the name? How can greater press freedoms not produce a free press? How is it that a much wider scope for free expression does not have the slightest effect on decision-making or political life and creates hardly any new social and political awareness? How is it that greater freedom of expression can become so overwhelmed by vulgarity and religious narrow-mindedness it merely serves to reproduce ignorance and bigotry on an ever-expanding scale? The multiparty system has produced uncontested and incontestable single-party rule. Parliamentarians do business and businessmen do politics. Civic freedoms are forever equivocal, easily crushed at a passing bureaucratic whim (ergo, Prof. Saad Eddin Ibrahim).

What is democracy? Having no intention of going the usual dull route (via ancient Greece) in search of a definition, might I suggest two basic, if distinct, ways in which the concept may be approximated. We have, first, the gamut of civil and political liberties, many of which have been codified in international legal instruments. Covering a whole range of freedoms, from free speech to free and fair elections, this is the most commonsense in which the notion of democracy is understood. There is another no less fundamental sense, however, and that concerns self-determination. The grandiloquent "government of the people by the people" is widely recognized as more rhetoric than reality. Effectively, what we are speaking about here is degrees of popular access to, and influence over, state power, which under capitalism is inherently delimited by the twin fetishes of a bourgeois economy and a bourgeois state.

This said, it is possible to contend that one sense of democracy does not automatically imply the other. Beyond liberal dogma, history (from Jacobean France through Bolshevik Russia to Peronist Argentina and Nasserist Egypt) has provided ample evidence that (the majority of the) people could have, and indeed have had, substantial access to and influence over the state under a whole range of authoritarian and highly repressive, even bloody, regimes. It is not, however, a matter of preferring one 'democracy' over the other. The ultimate winner under a repressive authoritarian system is the state bureaucracy, which inevitably sends 'the people' packing, as indeed has been amply demonstrated by the above examples of France, Russia, Argentina, and Egypt. All they're left with is the repression.

There is a further twist. To have greater and wider civil liberties but virtually no access to and influence over the state demands the proscription of the space within which such liberties may be exercised politically. And in this respect Egypt may prove to have been a trendsetter.

The modern bourgeoisie invented politics, reorganizing social life around a new *political* space. It was, however, always unhappy with its temperamental creature, which, like Frankenstein's monster, had a proclivity to turn against its master. The master would act to confine it, tame it, and, at times, strangle it, but for the greater part of some three centuries could not manage without it. Not, that is, until the end of the twentieth and the beginning of the twenty-first century came along.

From the collapse of the Soviet Union to that of the Twin Towers, from 'the winds of change' in Eastern Europe to the global "war on terror," what has been heralded is not the end of history but the end of politics. Ironically, the monster was being killed off not because it had become too fierce and dangerous but because, finally, its services could be dispensed with. The bourgeoisie no longer needs politics to rule. Welcome to the brave new world of businessmen and bureaucrats.

*Al-Ahram Weekly*, August 1, 2002

# Copts Are Not Cats

THOUSANDS OF EGYPTIAN COPTS WENT out on protest demonstrations last week.* Why is that so frightening? Peaceful demonstrations (even if they get a little out of hand, with some stone-throwing and perhaps a little rioting) are the most natural thing in the world, except, of course, in Israeli-occupied territories, where they qualify as terrorism to be stamped out by tanks, helicopter gunships, and the odd F16.

Everybody with a grievance does it, everywhere. Observe what anti-globalization protesters did to a little Swedish town a mere two weeks ago. That this is the first time in Egypt's modern history Copts have demonstrated as a group should, if anything, provoke a response of "it's about time." They have a grievance, or several; they should express it. Peaceful protest is the way to do it. Where's the fuss?

Emergency law just doesn't cut it. All but four or five of the fifty-one years I, for one, have lived as a citizen of this country have been under emergency law. What state can justify keeping its population under a

---

* "Copts are not cats" is one of my more unfortunate obscure references. I had assumed that many of my readers will have studied Aristotelian logic, as I had, in high school, including his remarkably memorable illustration of syllogisms. "All men are mortal, Socrates is a man, therefore Socrates is mortal," is a sound logical statement, but the great Greek philosopher draws our attention to another seemingly logical statement: "All cats are mortal, Socrates is mortal, therefore Socrates is a cat." Unfortunately, no one I know seemed to remember that particular high school lesson, and consequently few figured out what on earth I was referring to.

constant state of emergency for half a century? And we've been 'moving' toward democracy for the past half of that half.

There is, of course, much more to it than that. Authoritarianism is never a sufficient explanation, since it begs the question why it isn't being challenged effectively. Again and again we are forced to look at those who are supposed to take up such challenges, or, to be more specific still, those who are potentially best suited to provide direction, coherence, and strategic vision so that great challenges can be met.

It's back to Egyptian intellectuals, and once again we find ourselves besieged, even more than usual, by hysteria and hypocrisy—we are, after all, especially touchy when it comes to Copts. Take one prominent, and to my mind glaring, example: the "Copts are not a minority" refrain. Let me first make it clear that as far as I'm concerned it makes not one bit of difference to the discussion of Coptic grievances whether they are described as a minority or not. What is truly amazing is that almost everybody seems to believe it does, as Saad Eddin Ibrahim so woefully discovered. The statement, parroted repeatedly, is essentially this: "Copts are part and parcel of the fabric of the nation; [therefore] they are not a minority." Has no one noticed that there is a basic flaw of formal logic here (the 'Socrates is a cat' kind of logical flaw)? Being part and parcel of the fabric of the nation has no logical bearing on whether Copts are in fact a minority or not. One part of the statement expresses a numerical value; it's quantitative and quantifiable. The other is substantive, an expression of social, cultural, political, and ethnic cohesion.

Not to belabor the point. Whether six or ten million (speaking of quantifiable data, no one seems quite sure about this 'minor matter'), the Copts are, numerically, a minority when we are speaking about the religious affiliations of the Egyptian population. As *mulukhiya* lovers, however, they are members of a vast majority; percentages, after all, are invariably calculated with respect to a specific total. *Mulukhiya*, as it happens, does enter this equation, though not in a statistical sense, for behind the 'Coptic minority' ruckus lies the issue of ethnic identity. What our learned intellectuals and columnists really meant when they got all hot under the collar asserting that Copts are not a minority was that they are not an ethnic minority, which statement, I believe, is quite patently obvious. Why not say so, then, instead of sounding ridiculous by insisting that Socrates is, in fact, a cat? Not, I might add, that the ethnic uniformity of Egyptian Muslims and Copts says anything very significant about the 'fabric of the nation.' Fabrics, after all, could be plain or patterned. I have a decided preference for the latter kind.

The fact that one has to go on about such an obvious and insignificant point merely reveals the extent to which demagoguery and plain hysteria dominate intellectual and political debate in Egypt, leading otherwise highly intelligent and educated people to sound like utter imbeciles. How is one to discuss the legitimacy of Coptic grievances—or, for that matter, criticize many of the ways in which Coptic figures and Church officials have been formulating these grievances—when the mere act of dividing six (or is it ten?) by sixty-five and multiplying by a hundred triggers howls of, "Stop, sedition is afoot" (not to mention, "Burn the traitorous swine, hang him in a public square, lock him up and throw away the key")? To think that the State Security officers concerned have not even begun their, often highly creative, work of drawing up a charge file.

United under one God, we're all bashing the 'yellow press'—and naturally the editor of the infamous *al-Naba'*—these days. Speeches, seminars, editorial articles, feature articles, you name it, it's being deployed in ferocious battle against the 'yellow press.' So just what is 'yellow,' anyway?

Tabloid journalism is not, of course, an Egyptian invention, although in Egypt it has developed a number of unique features. What is amazing is the influence such journalism has come to exercise on our intellectual and political life in the past few years. It's taken the profession by storm. The bulk of the Egyptian press—'national,' opposition, 'independent'—has been breaking out in yellow spots. In other countries, tabloid journalism is designed for the working classes, to keep them ignorant, distracted, and ultimately compliant. It does the same here, but with the additional perk of both targeting and enlisting the intelligentsia as well. Not only do they read it, they contribute to it, vie for column space on its pages, in other words allow it, by complicity or complacency, to set the terms of intellectual and political debate in the country. And, like a cancer, it grows and grows.

There is much talk these days about the sex/religion/crime formula of the 'yellow press.' Whatever the formula, however, tabloid journalism here as elsewhere has one salient feature: the profound contempt in which it holds the readers' minds, and the truth. The 'yellow press' is the symptom of a much more serious malaise, one shared by many of its purported detractors. The first step toward a cure is for our intellectual and political debate to begin, at the very least, from a point beyond Socrates' allegedly feline nature.

*Al-Ahram Weekly*, June 28, 2001

# Tribes on the Move

FOR A LONG TIME THE PALESTINIANS liked to describe themselves as the "vanguard of the Arab nation." A fighting people, suffering extreme oppression, and with a compelling national cause tend to get somewhat self-centered. Yet, this side of half a century of Palestinian dispossession, it was yet again a Palestinian stone that was destined to disturb the stagnant waters of Arab political life. There is a new mood out there, and those who ignore it do so at their peril.

It should be clear, nevertheless, that the upheaval is only partly Palestine-focused. The Intifada did provide a backdrop to Egypt's 2000 parliamentary elections, and there is no doubt that in some instances voter behavior was directly affected by the overwhelming feelings of solidarity it triggered in the Egyptian public. In a beautifully ironic parody of the Hillary Clinton–Rick Lazio fracas over Fidel Castro–Yasser Arafat handshakes, the secretary-general of the Alexandria chapter of the ruling party (a prominent businessman) got all of three hundred votes, thanks largely to his opponents' having widely distributed a photo showing him engaged in an enthusiastic handshake with Ehud Barak.

The Intifada's most significant effect has been much less direct, however. In dramatically underlining both the cruelty of oppression and the nobility of resistance, it has inspired. People identify with both. And it so happens that parliamentary elections are taking place in Egypt. Not just any parliamentary elections—judicial supervision, extended for the first time to subsidiary polling stations, has renewed voters' confidence in the worth of their ballot.

They have gone after the National Democratic Party (NDP). And that, basically, seemed to be the extent of what the level of development of political life in the country would allow—for the time being. Punishing the ruling party has been the one identifying feature of the 2000 poll. People voted for "NDP independents" (the ruling party's overwhelming parliamentary majority will be decreased but unthreatened), the Muslim Brotherhood, and some unlikely opposition candidates. They did not, as far as possible, vote for the official ruling party ticket.

Big ruling party heads went rolling all over the country. 'Sure' opposition candidates (widely whispered to be the beneficiaries of 'electoral deals' with the NDP) failed, and unlikely candidates, whose parties had fielded for form's sake, won. The Muslim Brothers, outlawed, hounded, and battered to the very doors of the polling stations, proved that they remain the country's only real political party—a compound irony, as the Brothers, who possess no discernible political platform, are essentially an ideological, not a political, grouping.

This is all the more remarkable since the rules of the parliamentary game in Egypt remain firmly in place. Patronage relations and 'tribal' loyalties overwhelmingly determine voter behavior, and this in a highly class-stratified society where actual 'tribes' are virtually nonexistent. The bulk of candidates view parliament as a site for business, not politics, and voters concur by demanding 'services' rather than political platforms from their representatives. 'Tribalism' thus performs the vital function of providing a nonpolitical claim by constituents on their parliamentary representative and, through him, on the state. 'Tribes,' manufactured and arbitrary, are the fundamental form of popular organization and social solidarity in the country.

Who said 'civil society' was weak in Egypt?

The noncorrespondence between civil society as it really exists and its ideal form as expressed in contemporary liberal dogma was not the only area where liberal ideologues received a beating in these elections, as indeed in every other test of the liberal credo. The dismal performance of the Wafd Party (notwithstanding its youthful revival on the election's eve) should have been a shattering blow to the liberal belief system. It won't be, of course. Today's liberals are extremely reminiscent of yesterday's Stalinists (not a very difficult proposition in Egypt, as they are often the very same people). The lack of correspondence between the actually existing and the ideal, between theory and reality, is easily shrugged off as exceptionalism; reality does not correspond to the theory because, somehow, it does not correspond to the theory. Tautology is fundamental to all religions; it is, after all, a question of faith.

By all rights, the Wafd should have been, next to the NDP, the party of choice in the kind of two-party political system that best exemplifies the liberal ideal. And, let's not fool ourselves, only the Brotherhood can, in this election, rightfully complain of government intervention in the poll. In theory, the Wafd had everything going for it: over a decade of privatization, structural adjustment, and free market economic policies; a discredited ruling party in the midst of economic crisis; liberal and upper-class credentials and connections; a new 'youthful' and aggressive leadership with populist aspirations (in the one joint opposition party solidarity rally, the Wafd's new leader outbid the hardiest of Islamists and Arab nationalists by calling for 'throwing Israel into the sea'); and a fairly free poll.

As it happens, by the time the final results of the election are announced, the Wafd will most likely have fewer seats in parliament than the combined leftists, represented by the Tagammu', the Nasserists, and a handful of independents. Privatization, economic liberalization, and rising entrepreneurialism notwithstanding, the state bureaucracy remains the Egyptian bourgeoisie's 'organic representative' of choice. The bourgeoisie will compete fiercely, rebel against the bureaucracy's express will, but it will do so for greater—direct and apolitical—access to its extremely vital space.

The ruling party, with the 'independents' rejoining it in droves, will maintain its overwhelming majority. The Muslim Brothers and a few other Islamists (with a little less than 10 percent of the parliamentary seats) will be the leading, if formally unacknowledged, parliamentary opposition. There will be a few more opposition voices than in the previous parliament and, judging by their composition, they are likely to be more vocal.

Not a great difference, certainly. Debates in the forthcoming parliament promise to be more exciting than they have been for many years; the house's fundamental nature is not, however, about to change. Nevertheless, something new is afoot; change is in the air.

*Al-Ahram Weekly*, November 9, 2000

# New Eggs for Old

CAMPAIGNING FOR THE NEW PARLIAMENT is in full swing and, with judicial supervision and three weeks of polling in various parts of the country to look forward to, we are promised, if nothing much else, an interesting couple of months.

I might as well come out with my little heresy. I am not very excited about the difference 'full' judicial supervision of the voting is likely to make to the composition of the forthcoming parliament. And this is not just, or even mainly, out of fear that Justice Ministry and police meddling will sabotage judicial supervision. Nor is it really a function of the many other items on the opposition parties' list of electoral grievances, including inadequate voter registers or restrictions on freedom of campaigning. (The latter point is doubtless important in itself, as it concerns freedom of political activity in general and not just at election time. It is, however, of questionable worth as far as winning a seat in parliament is concerned.)

But before I reveal the real reason for my skepticism, I feel bound to make a passing reference to an editorial comment on the elections I read this week. The writer was responding to the opposition parties' fears and grievances regarding the fairness of the forthcoming elections. Conceding that there might have been electoral rigging in past elections, he nevertheless railed against the opposition for demanding further guarantees that no rigging will take place this time around. Why, he demanded, should they anticipate malpractice before the fact? Rather, they should wait until the elections were conducted, find out if rigging had taken place, and only then address the issue.

I am, as I have already confessed, something of a dispassionate observer with respect to this particular debate. Still, I found truly stunning the way the writer, with a few short strokes of his pen, demolished all epistemology and, along with it, the most fundamental basis of human existence. The relationship between experience, memory, and knowledge was rent asunder. Each morning was made to hold the enthralling prospect of relearning anew the taste of one's breakfast egg.

While the issue of vote rigging may provide impetus for interesting new ideas to be raised in the course of editorial commentary, however, it plays only a very minor part in the election itself, at least as regards its effect on the political composition of parliament. As it happens—and I suggest this on the basis of cumulatively learned and conceptually appropriated experience—the ruling political party does not owe its overwhelming domination of parliament to electoral malpractice, however extensive or limited, but to the erosion of politics in both parliament and parliamentary elections. With some three thousand National Democratic Party (NDP) members running as independents and the ruling party fielding a full ticket of 444 official candidates, the Arabic-language press has already dubbed the current campaign as one in which "the NDP is running against the NDP"—basically a repeat of the 1995 elections, except for the fact that even more NDP members are running against their party's official list this time around.

High-ranking state officials, I believe, would genuinely like to see greater opposition representation in the forthcoming parliament. Not much greater, perhaps, but greater all the same. One wonders, nevertheless, whether it can be done, short, that is, of extensive rigging in favor of the opposition.

The paradox to top all paradoxes, however, is that the contraction of politics in parliament, the elections, and the country as a whole has corresponded to a growing scramble over parliamentary seats, expressed both in the number of candidates contesting the elections and the fierceness of the competition. In 1995, some four thousand competed, almost double the number for the previous poll in 1990. The number rose again by a couple of hundred for this year's election. The 1995 poll was, moreover, one of the most violent in Egyptian parliamentary history, with most of the violence accounted for by NDP-versus-NDP battles.

Why should members of the same party, who presumably adhere to the same political platform, compete so widely and so intensely for a seat in parliament? Excessive zeal to advocate eloquently their party's political agenda within parliament does not, unfortunately, provide us with a convincing answer, if the images of empty benches and dozing members of the outgoing assembly are anything to go by.

The answer, in my view, lies in the fact that in this age of economic liberalization parliament is increasingly becoming a site of business rather than politics. Electoral contests have become an extension of competition in the marketplace rather than in the political sphere, and constituents have come to look to their representatives for patronage rather than political representation. And ultimately, where patronage is concerned, who can compete with the state?

*Al-Ahram Weekly*, September 28, 2000

# A Very Human Right

TODAY MARKS THE FIFTIETH ANNIVERSARY of the adoption of the Universal Declaration of Human Rights, a document which, despite its many shortcomings, records one of the great moral victories achieved by humanity in this and any other century. It is all the more remarkable in that the cutthroat states that voted for it in the United Nations General Assembly were not committed to its principles and did not have any intention of seriously observing them, not even the "right to own property." Millions of dispossessed farmers throughout the world before the declaration and after it—not to mention the little matter of a nation called Palestine—give ample testimony to the disrespect for this right capitalism actually shows outside the realm of ideology.

Ultimately, the document is a moral statement, a credo of this century, reflecting a history of human struggle against oppression, in which the defeat of fascism was then only the last of manifold chapters. And despite its shortcomings, the document has not paled with age. Rather, it is the reality we see around us, in the advanced western countries as in the rest of the world, which presents a very sorry sight when contrasted with the resolve expressed in the declaration.

How 'western' are human rights? And how is a local, nationally or culturally specific discourse on human rights developed? More important, can a human rights movement put down roots in a country such as Egypt, and how? I have tried to discuss some of these issues, in this space and elsewhere, on many previous occasions. As I write today, however, such questions seem a luxury. An influential group has apparently decided to

mark the occasion of the fiftieth anniversary of the declaration by acting to liquidate the Egyptian human rights movement. The tools of their
trade—basically a combination of brute force and vulgar journalism,
based on vicious slander, outright lies, and innuendo—are too crude to
evoke a desire for the serious debate of serious issues.

"No one shall be subjected to torture or to cruel, inhuman or degrading treatment or punishment," reads Article 5 of the declaration. Is this by
any chance a western notion, supposedly alien to our 'culture'? I have written before about the European envoy who told a Human Rights Watch
representative that "Egyptians expected to be mistreated while in police
custody." He would seem to believe that Article 5 is a western notion that
may apply in his home country but not in Egypt. But so, of course, do the
officials and 'independent' journalists for whom reports on the police raid
on the Upper Egyptian village of al-Koshh were an occasion to plunge into
a frenzied attack on the human rights movement in Egypt. Since everybody
admits that certain forms of torture and cruel, inhuman, and degrading treatment did take place in al-Koshh, there can be only one rationale
behind the accusation that only spies (in the pay of the United Kingdom
or other 'enemy' states) would object to such treatment being meted out
to Egyptian citizens. That rationale can only be that Egyptians like being
tortured, abused, and mistreated, or at least do not object to it too strongly.

I find this whole notion of 'tarnishing Egypt's image abroad' demeaning. It manages to transform us into a nation of dragomen whose only
concern is the next tourist season. But what is more 'tarnishing' to our
image anywhere, to 'expect' to be tortured and humiliated by our security
bodies or to rise up against such practices?

As it happens, Egyptians—most of whom have never read the
Universal Declaration or even heard of it—do object, very strongly, to
being tortured or subjected to any kind of "cruel, inhuman, and degrading treatment." So much so that in the 1970s, in what was then described
by officialdom as "regretful incidents," tens of thousands of people would
riot and stone and even put to the torch police stations where torture
was being conducted. Similar incidents took place as recently as this year,
most notably in the Delta town of Bilqas, though they did not take the
phenomenal form they did in the 1970s.

Article 5, I am the first to admit, does not settle the question of
whether human rights are by their very nature culturally biased or not. I
would be very happy for the moment, however, if this question at least is

settled. So long as a single person is being tortured or subjected to cruel, inhuman and degrading treatment by our security bodies, and so long as such practices take place without the most fierce denunciation from all sections of the society, then we should mark December 10 every year by hanging our heads in shame.

*Al-Ahram Weekly*, September 17, 1998

# Kiss and Kill

"WHAT COULD AMERICA DO TO help push democratization forward in Egypt?" an American friend connected to United States policymaking circles asked me recently. My usual answer to that particularly persistent question is "democratize Israel."

America's foremost ally and strategic partner is the Middle East is a self-defined Jewish state, in which 20 percent of the population are Palestinian Arabs and where 5.3 million people lord it over 5 million others, 3.7 million of whom (the Palestinians of Gaza and the West Bank) are totally disenfranchised (Palestinian self-rule remains the farce it has always been, notwithstanding all the internal bickering over who rules in an effectively empty self-rule arrangement, in which Israel holds all the strings, from money to life itself). None of it seems to provide the U.S. with a suitable model for promoting democracy in the region.

Moreover, it has been my longheld belief that Arab authoritarianism is intimately tied to Israel's continued oppression and dispossession of the Palestinians and aggression against neighboring Arab states. And this not only because it provides authoritarian Arab regimes with the excellent pretext of having to safeguard the 'internal front' or 'homeland security' against a foreign threat (a pretext with which Americans should have become quite familiar since 9/11), but even more significantly because of the extremely distorting effects this seemingly endless victimization of Palestinians and Arabs has had on the intellectual and political climate in the Arab world.

I could also have mentioned: "end the occupation of Iraq"; "let up on Iran"; "stop fanning the flames of a clash of civilizations"; "try to refrain from making statements that describe the destruction of Lebanon and murder of thousands of Lebanese civilians as 'the birth pangs of the New Middle East'"; "don't pass laws that sanction torture, obliterate due process, and make a mockery of the principle of a fair trial"; and "stop trying to undermine international humanitarian law by subverting the Geneva Conventions."

I said none of this, however. It was a friendly, laidback conversation. I was in no mood for lecturing. And, unlike many of my fellow 'intellectuals,' I make an effort to learn from experience. It would have been an exercise in futility. However polite my American interlocutor may have been, in his/her mind little wheels would have been turning to the effect that "here we go again, another Arab blaming everyone but themselves for their own failures." My awareness of that particular line of thinking is rather bolstered by the fact that, in part, I happen to share it.

So, instead, I suggested that rather than harping on about the imprisonment of al-Ghad Party's Ayman Nour, President George W. Bush should make a powerful statement defending the Muslim Brotherhood, calling for their legalization as a political party and condemning their ongoing repression. After all, the Brotherhood happens to be the largest political opposition in the country; it holds eighty-seven parliamentary seats; and it continues to suffer the greatest share of political repression. Such a statement, I pointed out, would be tantamount to dropping a whole flock of birds with a single stone.

It is only right and proper. Whether you happen to like the Brotherhood or not, there is no denying that their recognition as a legal political entity is absolutely crucial to achieving even a semblance of a democratic political process in the country. Moreover, a top-level American statement in defense of the democratic rights of the Brotherhood would go a long way toward countering the charge of double-standards with which both the authoritarian regimes and the pro-democracy opposition, in Egypt and throughout the region, hold Washington's claims of promoting democracy and human rights in the Middle East.

It would possibly help also in countering the increasingly virulent perception, from Morocco to Pakistan and beyond, that Washington's perpetual "war on terror" is in fact a war against Islam and Muslims, a new Crusade designed to undermine and subvert Muslim societies, obliterate our cultural and religious identity, and impose western-style democracy, licentiousness, and depravity on our peoples. However unfair these charges may be, a statement by President Bush in defense of the Brotherhood (with or even without benefit of a special communication from God) would be considerably more effective in changing Arab and Muslim hearts and minds than a hundred of these *iftar* banquets he's been in the habit of hosting over the past few years.

There is also the fact that since the Hamas electoral victory in the Palestinian territories early this year, most Arabs—and a considerable number of American Middle East experts as well—have come to the conclusion that the Bush administration has had a change of heart regarding its declared top-priority objective of promoting democracy in the greater Middle East. Such a perception was further reinforced when Secretary of State Condoleezza Rice visited Egypt, soon after, and met with President Hosni Mubarak. In a subsequent interview with the editors of the state-owned press, Mubarak asserted that Ms. Rice was convinced that Egypt's "gradualist approach" to political reform was the proper path to take, and that she had even told him of her belief that "a full generation" was required before democracy could be achieved in the Arab world.

True, the American administration has continued to insist that it is as committed as ever to the cause of democratization in the region, with President Bush lately issuing even stronger and increasingly more flowery statements on the matter. But, ask around. No one here really believes it, especially when they see the U.S. and its European allies starving the Palestinians for having exercised their democratic right to choose their own, albeit powerless, government.

One final, juicy bird, I suggested, tongue-in-cheek. A statement by President Bush in defense of the Muslim Brotherhood in Egypt, while only right and proper, would outstrip all the persistent efforts of domestic secularists in undermining the group's political and ideological sway.

I was reminded of all this when, last week, Ayman Nour and his party made a flurry of statements vehemently denying any involvement in a letter sent to President Bush urging him to intervene to free Nour. An official statement issued by the Ghad Party charged that the letter was a hoax perpetrated by the Egyptian Interior Ministry to "defame Nour and destroy him morally."

Some weeks earlier, President Bush singled out Minister of Industry and Foreign Trade Rachid Mohamed Rachid as a model of Egypt's young reformers on whom he pins his hopes for political and economic reform in the country. The minister hastened to make a statement denying any responsibility for Bush's compliment.

A couple of years before, the American president declared his enthusiastic support for Iran's reformers. They lost the election. In this part of the world, it seems, President Bush's kisses leave a lot to be desired.

*The Daily Star Egypt*, October 1, 2006

# Parliamentary Business

YESTERDAY, EGYPTIANS, OR RATHER SOME of them, went to the polls to choose 444 parliamentary deputies from among over four thousand contestants, including representatives of all the country's legal political parties, several illegal ones, and scores of independents. Nobody really expects any great surprises. The ruling National Democratic Party (NDP) will maintain its monopoly over parliament, comfortably clearing the two-thirds mark it deems vital for ensuring its status, and identity, as the party of government.

What will be of interest to observe in the parliament destined to lead us into the coming century/millennium is how many of the 'non-vital' third of its seats will be occupied by opposition figures, whether partisan or independent, and the relative weights of the major ideological and political currents in today's Egypt—liberal, Islamist, leftist—within the opposition mix. This is granting, of course, that parliamentary representation in Egypt is not a very accurate mirror of the relative weights of political forces outside it.

But besides the guaranteed two-thirds for the NDP, what we may be quite sure to see in the coming parliament on both ruling party and opposition benches is a sizeable number of 'deputies' who are there to do business. Parliament is supposed to be a site of politics, including politics that advocate business interests, trade union interests, and so forth. It is institutions such as the stock market, however, which are supposed to provide sites for doing business. The ten-to-one scramble over parliamentary seats in the current elections seems to involve a great deal of confusion regarding where the stock market ends and parliament begins.

It was with such phenomena in mind that, in a previous column, I disputed conventional international agency wisdom, which attributes the problems of democratization in countries like Egypt to the weakness of civil society on the one hand and the alleged omnipotence of the state on the other. I suggested that it was not the frailty of civil society but rather the feebleness of political society that lay behind the retardation of the process of democratization in Egypt.

To illustrate further, I will need to borrow from the Italian Marxist theorist Antonio Gramsci and his notion of "organic intellectuals." Briefly, Gramsci argued that in modern society classes and society groups tend to create, alongside them, groups of intellectuals—ideologues, politicians, statesmen, journalists, artists, religious figures, and so on. It is these intellectual groups that the historical process charges with the responsibility of defining the common interests and worldview of the various classes and social groups, providing them with a sense of unity, a fairly coherent social identity, and, most significantly, a strategic vision—that is, the attributes of exercising what Gramsci called a hegemonic role within society as a whole. Without these "organic intellectuals," classes and social groups exist in a state similar to Thomas Hobbes' vision of the state of nature: a war of all against all.

Now, to my mind, a salient feature of political society in Egypt today lies not so much in the absence of such "organic intellectuals" but in the fact that the lines of demarcation between them and the social groups they are supposed to represent have become extremely blurred. Political and ideological representatives of social groups simply do not seem to be focusing on their historically assigned job; they're too busy doing business for themselves. Whether in the ruling party or in the opposition, in parliament or in political bodies outside it, there are just too many 'political and ideological representatives' competing with the self-same social groups on whose behalf they are supposed to think, speak, and strategize.

A supreme, if not immediately political, example of this has always struck me: the relentless and virtually insatiable drive to privatize public space throughout the country. The few who warn and advocate remain voices crying in the wilderness, as beaches, Nile views, park space, desert space, and even sidewalks are everywhere expropriated for the personal use of private individuals.

Now, one must assume that, insofar as they are social entities, social groups have interests that go at least a little beyond the immediate interests of the individuals who compose them. As private individuals, the more privileged among us may think only of owing more, and more lavish, holiday retreats than the rest of their circle. But this is where "organic intellectuals" come in useful. Taking the long-term view, they realize that such behavior would lead to dire societal and ecological consequences, and, doing what they're supposed to do best, they address public opinion and work through parliament and other state bodies to impose a semblance of discipline on the errant and short-sighted individuals of the social groups from which they derive. One cannot expect them to do this, however, if they themselves are scrambling for their own little bit of the beach.

*Al-Ahram Weekly*, December 7, 1995

# Private Politics

BROTHER STROVE AGAINST BROTHER, FAMILIES and clans were split a sunder, the National Democratic Party (NDP) ran fiercely against the NDP, and, in one of the most heated and violent electoral battles in contemporary history, a score or more fell dead and dozens were injured. It is interesting therefore that only in a few urban centers, particularly where strong Islamist candidates were running, was the polarization along ideological and political lines. For the most part, ferocious electoral battles were waged not over politics but over business opportunities.

Three main features of the elections may illustrate this point. The ten-to-one scramble over People's Assembly seats (four thousand candidates competing for 444 seats) seemed to signal a revival of the parliamentary spirit in the country. Yet, the great bulk of these spirited candidates ran as independents, and most of them were renegade members of the ruling NDP, running against their party's official candidates. As for the country's fourteen legal political parties, as well as the outlawed Muslim Brotherhood, the total number of candidates they were able to field fell short of covering the 444 seats available. Alternative political and ideological platforms—assuming that all opposition party candidates not only had them but also campaigned around them—accounted therefore for a mere fraction, some 10 percent, of the campaigning.

The great paradox in the 1995 elections has been that the competition between politically disinterested candidates was no less heated or violent than that between political opponents, including the election's arch foes, the NDP and the Muslim Brotherhood. In fact, one of the fiercest competitions in the whole election—boasting its first incident of violence, back at the start of the campaign—was between two leading members of the ruling party. Adel Sidki, brother of the prime minister and official candidate of the NDP, was running against local party boss and multimillionaire Atia al-Fayoumi. Al-Fayoumi won in the first round.

The third pronounced feature of the election, and the subject of extensive commentary by analysts and columnists, is the enormous amounts of money spent on campaigning. While commentators have differed on the extent of violence, levels of participation, degree of fairness, and so on compared to previous elections, few would dispute the fact that these have been by far the most expensive elections ever held in Egypt. And by far the largest part of the millions spent on the campaigning came not from the political parties, including the NDP. For the most part, it seemed to come from the businessmen candidates' own pockets. Why, one may well ask, should a shrewd businessman who has little interest in politics or legislation squander some five million Egyptian pounds to win a seat in parliament? This while keeping in mind that Egypt's entrepreneur class has, in the past couple of decades, recession notwithstanding, come to expect extremely lucrative returns on investment.

General election 1995 may go down in Egypt's history as the true herald of the nation's entry into the age of liberalization. But just as liberalization of the economy is synonymous with privatization, so it seems that liberalization in the realm of politics.

Last Wednesday was above all the day of the rising class of Egyptian entrepreneurs—the favored winning horse on which the U.S. Agency for International Development, scores of international agencies, and the lonely, and largely newly converted, ideologues of neoliberalism in Egypt have long banked. It is this class, we have been told repeatedly, which will instill vigor in the economy and genuine pluralism in politics. As it turns out, the one 'liberal' idea the many money-squandering, head-bashing, ballot-box-snatching, heavy-campaigning entrepreneur candidates seem to have had in common last Wednesday was that it was parliament itself that was due for privatization. Liberalization with a twist.

Whatever the results of yesterday's second and final round of the elections, we are now certain that the coming parliament will be characterized by a very weak opposition presence: no more than 13 percent in the rather unlikely event that all opposition candidates taking part, including those of the Muslim Brotherhood, win their contested seats.

Our hopes, then, must be pinned on those who, irrespective of their politics, have made it to parliament to do politics: parliamentarians who view the house as a public domain, a state body, and not a private club where members can doze off between deals.

*Al-Ahram Weekly*, November 30, 1995

# Transition Transpired

DOES THE COMPOSITION OF THE NEW parliament tell us anything at all about the nature of the political sphere in Egypt at the end of the 1990s? I believe it does, so much so that, unlike most other disheartened commentators, I am of the view that the new parliament has already well and truly earned the historic character accidentally bestowed upon it by the Gregorian calendar, as the parliament that will lead us to the threshold of a new century, and a new millennium.

True, there is much in the new parliament that rather stretches our credulity. I am no fan of the Muslim Brotherhood or of any other Islamist political force in the country or elsewhere, but I find myself incapable of making the kind of giant leap of faith necessary for one to believe that the political support enjoyed by the Egyptian left, which for the past twenty-odd years has been in almost continuous discussion about 'the crisis of the left,' is five times stronger than both the Muslim Brotherhood and the Islamist-oriented Labor Party.

Let us grant that a more temperate electoral climate would have resulted in considerably greater Islamist parliamentary representation (in my estimate, no more than thirty to forty seats), which, while small and definitely no threat to the ruling NDP's parliamentary monopoly, is still thirty to forty times the current figure.

Notwithstanding the somewhat distortive effects of the above, the new parliament, in my view, has come adequately to reflect what is truly essential about the Egyptian political scene in the late 1990s, and in so doing seems to have settled, for the time being at least, a question that has bewildered political analysis of the Egyptian domestic scene for over a decade.

The bafflement lay in the following: Egypt embarked on a process of transition from the populist authoritarian regime of Gamal Abdel Nasser toward a more liberal style of government as early as 1975, when Anwar Sadat launched the three platforms of the left, right, and center within the then-single legal party, the Arab Socialist Union. A year later, the platforms were transferred into fully fledged legal political parties. In other Third World countries similar processes almost always led either to an entrenchment of authoritarianism, usually in different forms, or to a gradual and often swift expansion of the space of liberal democracy, ultimately leading to the transformation of the political system and the establishment of a more or less liberal democratic formula in which political power changes hands between two or more political parties.

Initially, the process in Egypt seemed to promise to move along similar lines. During the first few years, the newly founded opposition parties and their fledgling press seemed to have an impact on the political process. The mere fact that the process of democratization was crisis-ridden, with almost daily clampdowns and showdowns, seemed a sure indication that big choices were at stake, that the nation was being obliged to choose between full political liberalization or an entrenchment of authoritarianism, which in any case could not be a return to Nasserist-style populism.

With the rise of Islamism, initially fostered by Sadat's regime, an additional dimension entered the equation. Nasser's populist authoritarianism seemed destined to give way to some form of liberal democracy, but this could be just an interim phase, giving way in turn to a new form of populist authoritarianism, though of a theocratic character.

But none of these scenarios came to be. And for nearly fifteen years political analysts at home and abroad have been trying to explain why. Analysts spoke of a stalled process of political liberalization and tried to explain away the real process by enumerating various 'exceptional' circumstances. Liberal dogmatists were crestfallen that economic and political liberalization were marching out of step, but proponents continued to insist that with sufficient economic liberalization, liberal democracy in the political sphere was bound to follow. Meanwhile, Islamic revolutions were predicted at every turn.

But as the calendar kept turning over one leaf after another, bringing us closer to the end of the century, analysts found themselves having to explain away nearly a quarter of that century as somehow 'exceptional,' as 'retardation.' Indeed, the transition was fast becoming of longer duration than that which was being transposed.

The 1995 elections were by no means a historic turning point, an end to the transition. They merely underlined that a transition had already transpired, we just hadn't noticed. What analysts failed to realize was that, all their theories and models notwithstanding, the Egyptian upper middle class, the fount of authority in the country for the best part of the century, was not really interested in government through the political sphere but rather in access to the state through direct ties with the bureaucracy. Privatization, not liberalization, is the catchword.

*Al-Ahram Weekly*, December 21, 1995

# EPILOGUE

# CAME A BLACK SWAN CALLED REVOLUTION

# NDP May Get More Than
# It Bargained For

As Egyptian voters head for the polls tomorrow, the big question on the minds of election watchers both inside the country and outside it will be how 'free and fair' the election is going to be. I might as well confess to having very little interest in the answer to that particular standard question, not because it does not bear asking but rather because, in the Egyptian context, it has become extremely dull.

The question is made tedious not just by sheer repetitiveness but because the very nature of the electoral process in the country renders the answer, whatever it might be, largely insignificant.

Let's examine some of the salient features of our electoral nature. Take first the fact that the great majority of Egyptian citizens are simply not interested. I've been in the habit of conducting informal polls of friends, relatives, and colleagues to get a sense of how many of them have ever voted or, indeed, have taken the trouble to register to vote. The real figure nationwide is probably greater than the 1–2 percent I invariably get for my ad hoc polls, but I don't expect by very much. At any event, the 2005 election saw a turnout of around 25 percent according to the official figure, and 10–12 percent according to the estimates of civil rights election monitors.

This brings us to another salient feature of Egyptian elections. Most of those who do actually turn out to vote have no interest in politics at all. Indeed, Egyptian election watchers are often working under a huge delusion, which is that elections in this country are about political choice. This is an extension of yet another pervasive delusion, which is the perception of the Egyptian parliament as a political space, a site for making, conducting, and debating politics. Not true. Our parliament is more chamber of commerce than legislature, a site for conducting business rather than politics.

Our members of parliament, by and large, are either dozing or absent when public policy is being debated (Parliament Speaker and de facto National Democratic Party whip Mr. Fathi Sorour is often seen haranguing the ruling party MPs for their laxity in tones evocative of a teacher rebuking errant students, and, according to studies, a substantial percentage of members never open their mouths during their full five-year term). These same members show a great deal of vitality and forbearance, however, when thronging around Cabinet ministers to hand them little slips of paper requesting government favors of one sort or another.

Parliament in this country is first and foremost about patronage. The ruling party is, in fact, little more than a massive patronage network, while parliament is the principal, if by no means the only, instrument of operationalizing this network. Dignitaries of various sorts and sizes, from billionaire business tycoons in Armani (or Savile Row) suits to headmen in traditional (English wool) kaftans, act as intermediaries between a gigantic, heartless, inefficient, and characteristically brutal state machinery and the populace. Little wonder then that the intermediaries would demand and expect their 'cut.'

Members of the Egyptian political and intellectual elite regularly bemoan the political ignorance of the masses, but it is actually these 'ignorant' masses that possess a keen sense of how the system operates. When they complain that their MP has done nothing for them and is in it for 'himself,' they are fully aware of what they mean, which is that that particular MP has put the concerns of his own 'cut' over and above those of his intermediary role; this, a common complaint of a common, inherently systemic malaise.

It is only from this perspective that we could begin to unravel such uniquely Egyptian electoral phenomena as the frenzied scramble for parliamentary seats within that giant patronage network called the National Democratic Party (NDP), and it is only with reference to this very nature of the ruling party that we could grasp the bizarre manifestation of that party running against itself, both officially, by running more than one candidate for the same seat in 145 constituencies, and unofficially, with thousands of renegade members running as independents against the official party ticket.

It is also within such an overall perspective that we can begin to understand the tribal character that seems to dominate the elections in a country that hardly has any real tribes. Clan, or tribal, identity, however manufactured, provides a crucial vehicle for the establishment and maintaining of patronage ties. By sharing a tribal identity with your elected MP you have first claim to his or her patronage, in return for which he or she is able to draw on your electoral and other forms of support, including the beating-up of rivals. This also helps explain the seemingly incomprehensible ferocity and violence that accompanies a great many NDP-versus-NDP electoral battles. The single death that has already taken place in this electoral campaign has been in the context of a violent confrontation between the 'tribal' supporters of two competing ruling party candidates. Possibly more will occur over the coming week and until the runoff elections (a week from tomorrow) are finalized.

We need to be clear about this. The greater part of the electoral battle is about which patrons are to be picked by which collections of real and would-be clients. This is true even in the case of much of the opposition, particularly the Wafd Party, which has its own bag of local and national dignitaries, whose fortunes are possibly better this time around than in previous elections now that the public perception is that the NDP leadership is looking with fairly benevolent eyes toward its old rival.

What politics are to be watched in these elections are those constituted for all practical purposes by the challenge of the Muslim Brotherhood. There is a great deal of irony here, since the Brotherhood is much more an ideological than a political group. Be that as it may, indications are that the government is fully determined to cut the Brotherhood's share in parliament drastically down to size. The unprecedented eighty-eight seats the Brotherhood held in the outgoing parliament are to be no more.

How far is the government willing to go to achieve this, and by what means, remains to be seen. But the use of force is already justified by the 'outlawed' status of the group. Indeed, the penal code is laden with articles that would make it lawful for the government to arrest and jail for up to fifteen years every single proven member of the 'outlawed' organization. The selective use of force by the government against the Brotherhood is inscribed into the familiar 'outlawed but tolerated' designation that journalists like to pin on the group. This gives the government almost full discretion in allotting or withholding doses of 'tolerance' and repression.

Over a thousand Brotherhood members have been arrested already in the course of the campaign, and expectations are that tomorrow's polling will witness violent confrontations between group supporters and the police, especially in the once-cosmopolitan Alexandria, now the country's major base of support for the Brotherhood.

Beginning tomorrow and by the end of the week, the composition of the parliament that presumably will take us to the middle of the decade will have become known. (Parliaments, naturally, can be dissolved before the end of their term.) Indications are that the ruling party will succeed in drastically reducing the Brotherhood's share of parliamentary seats (ten to fifteen is the figure being whispered, including by Brotherhood sources).

And while this may be easy to predict, there is an interesting aspect to these elections that is much more difficult to foresee, let alone bet on. This lies in what I have come to call the NDP's experiment in 'political engineering.' Not only does the NDP leadership want to bring the Brotherhood down, but there is also very strong evidence that it would also like to see other opposition groups, particularly the Wafd Party, come up (forty to fifty seats is the figure being whispered on this front).

An overwhelming parliamentary majority for the NDP simply would not look 'nice,' either at home or abroad. It would appear like a substantial step back in the promised process of political reform launched by the government and the ruling party in 2005, mainly through constitutional amendments allowing for multicandidate presidential elections. Furthermore, whatever purpose the Brotherhood's 'scary' eighty-eight seats served is now redundant.

At the time, we might recall, George Bush Junior and his neocons had made a royal mess of the Iraq they sought to 'liberate' and 'democratize' and fell upon the idea of 'democratizing' Egypt instead. The heat was on, and whether by accident or design, a Hamas win in Palestine followed a few months later by the Brotherhood winning an unprecedented share of the Egyptian parliament was reason enough for both Washington and the European Union to review the wisdom of pushing for political reform in the Arab world, particularly among friendly countries.

Needless to say, Barack Obama—I believe wisely—has adopted a much more realistic approach to this issue, and so have the Europeans.

American pressure has always been a 'kiss of death' to the cause of democracy in our region.

And while the Brotherhood's 'bogeyman' aspect, for whatever it was worth, is no longer useful, developments within the Wafd Party have been very encouraging, from a government perspective. The new Wafd leader, al-Sayed al-Badawy, a self-made business tycoon who made his fortune in the lucrative pharmaceutical industry (especially Viagra, as rumor would have it), is widely believed to have strong ties with influential state bodies. Soon after he took over the party leadership, he bought *al-Dustur*, the most vociferously antigovernment daily newspaper in the country, led by the flamboyant editor and writer Ibrahim Eissa. Soon after buying the paper, al-Badawy fired Eissa and his editorial team, effectively ending the newspaper.

Will it work? That, in my view, is the most interesting question posed by the 2010 elections. The problem is that whatever the NDP leadership wishes might be, its own membership is quite capable of subverting it. In the 2005 elections, only about a third of the official NDP candidates won their seats, the rest of the ruling party's parliamentary majority was made up by renegade members who ran against the party ticket, only to rejoin after the elections.

So if the NDP dignitaries, in their frenzied scramble for the power and business opportunities offered by winning a parliamentary seat, are willing to defeat their own party's electoral slate, is it at all realistic to expect them to respect their leadership's wishes for another party?

If I were a betting man, I wouldn't bet on the NDP's experiment in 'political engineering' meeting with any great success. The ruling party might well find itself saddled with a parliamentary majority considerably greater than its leadership would have wished.

Ahram Online, November 27, 2010

# J'accuse

WE ARE TO JOIN IN a chorus of condemnation. Jointly, Muslims and Christians, government and opposition, church and mosque, clerics and laypeople—all of us are going to stand up and with a single voice declare unequivocal denunciation of al-Qaʻida, Islamist militants, and Muslim fanatics of every shade, hue, and color. Some of us will even go the extra mile to denounce Salafi Islam, Islamic fundamentalism as a whole, and Wahhabi Islam, which presumably is a Saudi import wholly alien to our Egyptian national culture.

And once again we're going to declare the eternal unity of 'the twin elements of the nation' and hearken back the revolution of 1919, with its hoisted banner showing the crescent embracing the cross and giving symbolic expression to that unbreakable bond.

Much of it will be sheer hypocrisy; a great deal of it will be variously nuanced so as to keep, just below the surface, the heaps of narrow-minded prejudice, flagrant double standard, and indeed bigotry that holds in its grip so many of the participants in the condemnations.

All of it will be to no avail. We've been here before, we've done exactly that, yet the massacres continue, each more horrible than the one before it, and the bigotry and intolerance spread deeper and wider into every nook and cranny of our society. It is not easy to empty Egypt of its Christians; they've been here for as long as there has been Christianity in the world. Close to a millennium and half of Muslim rule did not eradicate the nation's Christian community; rather it maintained it sufficiently strong and sufficiently vigorous to play a crucial role in shaping the national, political, and cultural identity of modern Egypt.

Yet now, two centuries after the birth of the modern Egyptian nation state, and as we embark on the second decade of the twenty-first century, the previously unheard of seems no longer beyond imagining: a Christian-free Egypt, one where the cross will have slipped out of the crescent's embrace and off the flag symbolizing our modern national identity. I hope that if and when that day comes I will have been long dead, but, dead or alive, this will be an Egypt I do not recognize and to which I have no desire to belong.

I am no Zola but I, too, can accuse. And it's not the blood-thirsty criminals of al-Qaʿida or whatever other gang of hoodlums involved in the horror of Alexandria I am concerned with. I accuse a government that seems to think that by outbidding the Islamists, it will also outflank them.

I accuse the host of parliamentarians and government officials who cannot help but take their personal bigotries along to parliament or to the multitude of government bodies, national and local, from which they exercise unchecked, brutal, yet at the same time hopelessly inept authority.

I accuse those state bodies who believe that by bolstering the Salafi trend they are undermining the Muslim Brotherhood, and who like to occasionally play to bigoted anti-Coptic sentiments, presumably as an excellent distraction from other more serious issues of government.

But most of all, I accuse the millions of supposedly moderate Muslims among us, those who've been growing more and more prejudiced, inclusive and narrow-minded with every passing year.

I accuse those among us who would rise up in fury over a decision to halt construction of a Muslim center near Ground Zero in New York, but applaud the Egyptian police when they halt the construction of a staircase in a Coptic church in the ʿUmranya district of Greater Cairo.

I've been around, and I have heard you speak, in your offices, in your clubs, at your dinner parties: "The Copts must be taught a lesson," "the Copts are growing more arrogant," "the Copts are holding secret conversions of Muslims," and in the same breath, "the Copts are preventing Christian women from converting to Islam, kidnapping them, and locking them up in monasteries."

I accuse you all, because in your bigoted blindness you cannot even see the violence to logic and sheer common sense that you commit; that you dare accuse the whole world of using a double standard against us and are at the same time wholly incapable of showing a minimum awareness of your own blatant double standard.

And finally, I accuse the liberal intellectuals, both Muslim and Christian, who, whether complicit, afraid, or simply unwilling to do or say anything that may displease 'the masses,' have stood aside, finding it sufficient to join in one futile chorus of denunciation following another even as the massacres spread wider and grow more horrifying.

A few years ago I wrote in the Arabic daily *al-Hayat*, commenting on a columnist in one of the Egyptian papers. The columnist, whose name I've since forgotten, lauded the patriotism of an Egyptian Copt who had written saying that he would rather be killed at the hands of his Muslim brethren than seek American intervention to save him.

Addressing myself to the patriotic Copt, I simply asked him the question, where does his willingness for self-sacrifice for the sake of the nation stop? Giving his own life may be quite a noble, even a laudable, endeavor, but is he also willing to give up the lives of his children, wife, mother? How many Egyptian Christians, I asked him, are you willing to sacrifice before you call upon outside intervention, a million, two, three, all of them?

We, I said then and continue to say today, are not so impoverished and lacking in imagination and resolve that we are obliged to choose between having Egyptian Copts killed, individually or en masse, or run to Uncle Sam. Is it really so difficult to conceive of ourselves as rational human beings with a minimum of backbone so as to act to determine our fate, the fate of our nation?

That, indeed, is the only option we have before us, and we had better grasp it, before it's too late.

Ahram Online, January 1, 2011

# A Uniquely Egyptian Revolution

ON JANUARY 25, EGYPTIANS SET out to recreate themselves, their polity, and the very notion of Egyptian nationhood. Dead for over thirty years, the political realm burst out from the popular uprising of the country's young women and men, fully armed, like Greek mythology had Athena spring from the head of Zeus.

It came almost surreptitiously, and, like a bolt of lightning in a clear sky, Egypt found itself in the throes of a revolution so vast, so astounding and unlike anything the country had seen in living memory; the only historical frame of reference available was the revolution of 1919 against British colonial domination. The revolution that seemed to rise out of the depths of the virtual space of Facebook, Twitter, and YouTube poured onto the streets of Cairo, Alexandria, Suez, Ismailia, Tanta, Mansura, Damanhur, Kafr al-Dawwar, Fayoum, Beni Suef, Arish, and Marsa Matruh, to name just some of the dozens of cities and towns engulfed in what some Egyptians have started calling the "Lotus Revolution."

Eight days later, on February 2, the old order fired what I am convinced will prove to be its final shot. And, as such, it was truly worthy of that order: regressive, vicious, irrational, and inept. The Middle Ages' scene of whip, stick, and sword-wielding men attacking the peaceful protesters on horse- and camelback will go down in the annals of human and not just Egyptian history, and very possibly the *Guinness Book of Records*, as among the most memorable images of a dying autocracy gone senile.

It was no laughing matter, however. Hundreds of men and women, who had been peacefully, indeed joyfully, protesting for over a week, were seriously injured. A number of them were killed.

Yet, it was on the night of February 2 that the battle for Egypt's future, and it's very soul, was fought, and won. Maybe a couple of thousand young men and women held Tahrir Square against seemingly endless hordes of trucked-in thugs hurling Molotov cocktails at everything in sight, at the demonstrators, at apartment buildings overlooking the square, and at the Egyptian Museum, Egypt's and humanity's greatest storehouse of ancient Egyptian antiquities.

On the night of February 2 and through the early morning hours of February 3, our children, my son Hossam (19), my waif-like niece Salma (whose political baptism of fire was on that same square nine years ago, receiving a police beating while protesting the United States invasion of Iraq), my adoptive nephew Mustafa (whose late father, and my beloved friend, cinema director Radwan al-Kashef, would have been tremendously proud of him today), and the hundreds of other young men and women who were with them saved both the nation's heritage and its future.

As the dawn of February 3 broke over Tahrir Square, the would-be stalwarts of stability had been pushed completely out of the square, though a couple of hundred of them continued to hurl Molotov cocktails from the safe and ineffectual distance of the top of the October 6 flyover.

The victory was achieved at a great cost and with almost unbelievable heroism. With each wave of attacks, the young men and women would mobilize—via whistles and chants, most prominent among them "save the museum"—to leap into the breach and push back the attackers, doing so under a hail of fire and stones, and occasionally gunfire.

This morning I talked with Ziad al-Eleimy, a lawyer and one of the leaders of the youth movement, who spent the whole night in the square. He told me that at least a thousand young men and women had been injured, and eight killed. The deaths were all caused by gunfire.

Eleimy also explained that in the course of that grim night's running battles, sixty-five of the attackers were captured, searched, interrogated, and then handed over to the army. Identification documents carried by the hooligans revealed that many were police officers of different ranks and others were members of the ruling National Democratic Party. Yet others said they had been hired by one of the country's top business tycoons, and a leading member of the ruling party.

The contrast between the old order, as represented by the so-called "pro-Mubarak" hooligans, and the new order being created in Tahrir Square and on the nation's streets could not have been starker. Compare February 2 with the day before, which witnessed the "million person demonstration."

On that very day, I bumped into Dana Smillie, an American professional photographer and a friend. Dana had been touring the square and the downtown area, clicking away. Exchanging congratulatory hugs, Dana told me, "I've been living in downtown Cairo for fifteen years now, and I've never felt more safe or secure as I have the past few days."

Dana's newfound sense of security was actually echoed by many. In a city where a mere week before, no woman, veiled or unveiled, Egyptian or foreign, felt safe from a whole range of sexual harassment on the street, almost everyone I have talked to, including many foreign reporters, was struck by the overnight disappearance of sexual harassment in a site where hundreds of thousands of men and women were literally crushed together.

This was just one of the many signs that a new Egypt was being created on the streets. Tuesday, the day of the "million-person demonstration" was remarkable not only for its peaceful, joyous nature but also for the self-discipline exercised by such massive crowds, who had total control of the streets.

A CNN reporter remarked that he had never seen such control exercised by so many people gathered in one place. Indeed, fair-haired and complexioned foreign correspondents could be seen everywhere in the crowd, and everywhere they were treated as welcome guests.

The next day, the so-called 'pro-Mubarak' crowds were manhandling and attacking and sexually abusing foreign journalists, photographers, and camera crews wherever they came across them.

Take also the explosion of individual creativity, with thousands of demonstrators designing and making their own placards, signs, and posters, competing not just in summing up their demands and grievances but also in expressing such ideas and sentiments in unique and innovative ways, more often than not revealing a typically Egyptian wit and sense of humor.

Meanwhile, and as the nation's almost 1.7-million-strong police force made its disappearing act, Egyptians everywhere, in poor working-class areas as in such elite districts as Zamalek and Maadi and throughout the country, formed what they called "popular committees" to defend their districts against looting, which has been widely attributed to police agents deliberately bent on creating a state of chaos in the country.

Overnight, millions of Egyptians in downtown Cairo, in the rest of the capital, and across the nation had become citizens.

Yet, old Egypt is still there, fighting desperately for survival. The outcome of the battle between the two remains to be seen, but there are already indications of the way forward.

At the moment, the protesters are engaged in the difficult process of creating a unified coalition able to speak and negotiate on their behalf. In this they face several challenges, the most significant of which is that theirs has been essentially a leaderless revolution.

Triggered by a number of youth movements, the revolution, virtually in the blink of an eye, went far beyond the scope and political and organizational capacities of both the young people who triggered it and the old people who lead the various opposition political parties. These, both religious and nonreligious, remain, essentially, creatures of the old order.

Indeed, one of the remarkable features of the past week has been the exorcism of the bogeyman of the Muslim Brotherhood, long portrayed by the regime and many inside and outside the country as a threat so imminent that it justified authoritarianism and wholesale rigging of elections.

Yet, as the diminutive, for all practical purposes nonexistent, political arena of the past thirty years gave way to a new political realm embracing millions of newly created citizens, the bogeyman proved puny, indeed. Politics is the Achilles' heel of the Brotherhood, and of the Islamist movement as a whole, for it is only in the absence of politics that ideology reigns supreme, and it is in the rarified realm of ideology (divorced from the testing ground of political practice) that Islamists of every shape and form have the absolute upper hand.

Yet, the newly created political realm is bound to infuse every single element of the long dormant Egyptian polity, not just political organizations and movements but also trade unions, social movements, and nongovernmental organizations. New political forces will evolve; some extant ones will probably fade away; the ruling National Democratic Party will most likely to disappear altogether. Those that survive will be wholly transformed.

Indeed, I would hazard that a Muslim Brotherhood that exists amid a vibrant political society will be very different from the Brotherhood we have known since the organization's revival in the mid-1970s. The Brotherhood's youth movement, in coalition with a whole range of other youth movements, is a stark indication of the Brotherhood's potential for transformation.

Still, for this process to be ensured success, a number of urgent tasks need to be done almost immediately. A consensual representative body needs to be set up with the mandate to negotiate with the army on mechanisms for a peaceful transition of power. Such a representative body will have to include representatives of the youth movements, who are due to announce the creation of their coalition later today, as well as, for what they're worth, representatives of the main political parties, including the Muslim Brotherhood.

The Egyptian army will have to play the role of powerbroker in this transition. There is no danger of this leading to military rule. Popular revolutions do not lead to military rule, coup d'états do. The army's insistence on not firing on demonstrators is already a notable indication of its ability to play this role. These negotiations, it is hoped, would produce an interim national unity government that excludes the NDP. Such a government would be charged with overseeing the constitutional, legal, and practical arrangements that would guarantee, as soon as possible, free and fair presidential and parliamentary elections.

The police force, which has run amok and is strongly implicated in a whole set of crimes, ranging from sedition to crimes against humanity and high treason, will have to be overhauled, initially perhaps under the auspices of the armed forces. Eventually, the Interior Ministry as a whole should be placed under civilian, political oversight.

Meanwhile, the streets will continue to be the decisive factor in determining the nation's future. Already today (two o'clock Cairo time), there are tens of thousands of protesters in downtown Cairo. Tomorrow, Friday, is to witness yet another call for "million person demonstrations," not only in Cairo but also across the nation.

The Egyptian revolution marches on.

Ahram Online, February 3, 2011

# "Foreign Fingers" in Tahrir

THE WOMAN BEING INTERVIEWED, or is it interrogated, on Mehwar TV had her face blurred—a privilege usually reserved for repentant prostitutes, confessing terrorists, or deep throat sources revealing information that might put them in danger.

This particular interviewee was of a different order. She was, apparently, making a voluntary confession to the effect that she had been recruited by American intelligence, which then proceeded to train her in how to overthrow the Egyptian regime. To make the nefarious machinations of American spymasters even more sinister, they were using Jewish intelligence officers to do the training.

Now, I have no doubt that intelligence services are able to provide training in sabotage, all manner of spying, terrorism, use of secret ink, taking pictures of secret documents with tiny cameras, and so forth. I cannot, however, begin to imagine how you would train a young Egyptian woman in overthrowing the Mubarak regime.

Of course, the Americans have their own experience of revolution, so quite possibly the young woman was made to read the Bill of Rights and the Declaration of Independence, or maybe instructed in different ways of dumping teabags into the Nile.

I had dismissed Mehwar TV's 'revelations' as yet another example of the effect of the hallucinogenic substances that the managers and staffs of Egyptian television have obviously started imbibing, or injecting, since

January 25. How else could one explain their cameras being constantly turned to an empty stretch of the road, even as hundreds of thousands are standing a mere half an inch turn of the camera lens away?

Or what about the constant hectoring, interminable blathering, by reporters, by anchors, by guests, by countless numbers of callers, all wailing and gnashing their teeth over the havoc and chaos the Tahrir protesters are wreaking on the country, wholly ignoring the fact that a 1.7-million police force had up and disappeared in the blink of an eye, leaving homes, properties, and 82 million citizens easy prey to criminal gangs of murderers and looters and thugs; gangs, moreover, which a substantial body of evidence shows were actually being run by members of that disappeared police force, in close cooperation with the oligarchs of the ruling party.

How do we explain their tear-jerking elegies about the state and the Mubarak regime and equally mournful eulogies about the stability that the insidious agents of chaos in Tahrir had thrown out the national window, and their forgetting that the state they bemoan had shirked the first duty of all states, which is to protect the lives and property of their citizens?

Neither could Egyptian television, drugged and hyped up, apparently popping both uppers and downers in quick succession, see who was actually attacking whom. It totally escaped its unremittingly chattering anchors, talk show hosts, and armies of voluble, if inarticulate guests, to note the glaring fact that for the duration of Tuesday's million person protest not a single incident of violence took place, not a single shop was broken into, not a single piece of movable or stationary property was harmed.

Nor did they seem to note that it was only when their—oh so patriotic—throngs came onto the street the next day, driven by their passionate concern for our beloved Egypt and for President Hosni Mubarak, who has given so much for us (these are almost direct quotes, by the way), that only then did we see Molotov cocktails being thrown and the killing and wounding of hundreds of citizens of this so beloved nation of ours.

Be that as it may, the confessions of the Jewish-trained American agent of revolution were comic. In my Facebook status I wrote "Egypt media is proving as senile as their regime handlers," my terminology somewhat influenced by the occasion. A friend commented, "Yes, I saw it . . . some light relief in these trying times."

It was only on the next day that the joke turned sour. First came the attacks on foreign journalists. Next came the bizarre interview with the vice president—bizarre because the interviewer kept insisting on cuing the interviewee, which service the latter really didn't seem to need at all. Indeed, Omar Suleiman, who spoke so rarely over the past several years of public exposure that few Egyptians could identify the sound of his voice, seemed to be making up for lost time.

In the course of the interview, Suleiman kept hinting at dark conspiracies by unnamed foreign powers, though the hints seemed on occasion to come pretty close to the U.S. and Israel (ironically, both of which love the man, let alone that Israel is until today practically the only country in the world that is fighting tooth and nail to keep President Mubarak in power).

The interviewer, who is a top Egyptian TV manager, kept jumping on these hints like the answer to a prayer, adding his own little bits of spy savvy, making references to foreigners having been spotted in Tahrir, to which 'revelation' I can give full testimony, especially as the foreigners in question were not lurking about but rather hanging on top of whatever relatively elevated surface they could find and wielding great big video cameras, even as their equally fair-skinned colleagues were pushing through the crowds with mean black microphones pointed at all and sundry.

I don't expect much from the whirling dervishes of Egyptian TV, but I truly hope that the vice president will come to realize just how dangerous such nonsense can be.

As I was going out of the Ahram building yesterday afternoon, I came across a throng of easily recognizable thugs of the citizen-bashing, Molotov cocktail-throwing variety. They had laid siege to some car, which I couldn't see from the crowds. I approached and asked one of the bystanders what was going on. "They've caught a Libyan car, with two Israelis inside," he told me in all seriousness. The absurdity would have been hilariously funny had it not been for the unknown fate of the two alleged Israelis with Qadhafi connections.

Foreigners, meanwhile, have been attacked by similar mobs throughout Cairo, and possibly outside it. And not just foreigners; beware all you fair-skinned Egyptians.

This morning I found out that Hazem Zohny, an immensely talented journalist and a colleague at Ahram Online, was attacked by a mob while taking pictures of a fire that broke out in a mall in the Cairo suburb of Sheikh Zayed, very possibly by the self-same hoodlums who had torched the place. Hazem, who thankfully is recovering well from the attack, is fair skinned.

The overzealous students of Mr. Goebbels running our TV networks are not to be taken seriously, for they know not what they do. But is the vice president willing to pay the price of crushing the revolution by transforming Egypt into some kind of foreigner-free Taliban enclave?

I certainly hope not.

Ahram Online, February 4, 2011

# Egyptians Have Chosen, Time for the State to Accept Their Choice

THE CHOICES FACING EGYPT ARE not between dialogue and coup d'état, as the vice president said yesterday, but between a rickety authoritarianism and a full vibrant democracy.

It totally escapes me what the vice president was talking about when he issued the dire warning that Egypt faces two choices, either "dialogue" or "coup d'état." Trying to make sense of this most ominous statement, one is first of all struck by what coup d'état is supposed to mean in the context of our current reality. There are two senses in which General Suleiman's use of the term may be taken, a 'nice' one and a 'grim' one, though neither appears to render the statement awfully comprehensible. In the nicer sense, the vice president is telling us that if the army, which is starkly the single power running the country these days, responds to the revolution's demands and asks Hosni Mubarak to step down, this would be tantamount to a coup, which—reading between the lines—would lead to military rule.

The argument, if that's what it is, fails to convince. A popular revolution has been sweeping the country for the past two weeks, and all indications are that it is gaining momentum rather than losing steam. For the state to bow to the people's will, as expressed on streets throughout the country, is not a coup d'état, nor can it under any legal or moral standard be deemed as such.

We're not reinventing the wheel here: it happened in Tunisia a few weeks ago; it swept through Eastern Europe in the late 1980s; indeed, it's been happening across the globe from Latin and Central America to South and East

Asia. In fact, it has been our long-benighted Arab region that seemed to be the exception, standing immune to waves upon waves of democratization making themselves felt everywhere else.

It so happens also that the army, here as in most of the above examples, has been the state body able to step forward and play the role of powerbroker and guarantor of the transition to democracy.

Neither is the implied threat of military rule very credible. Popular revolutions, I wrote before, do not create military governments, military coups and counterrevolutions do.

This brings us to the other, darker possible interpretation of the vice president's warning: a counterrevolution. Certainly, that remains a possibility, but I'm sure the vice president is fully aware that it is becoming more remote with every passing day.

The thing is, we've already had one counterrevolution and it has failed miserably, though at a horrible cost. We now have a pretty clear idea of how that counterrevolution was conducted and the identity of some of those who directed it.

We now know, and I am sure the vice president and the prime minister are equally aware if not more cognizant of the facts that an alliance of National Democratic Party officials and oligarchs, the Interior Ministry, and Egyptian state television pursued a deliberate 'scorched earth' strategy aimed at sowing fear and panic among the Egyptian people and the international community to show that without the Mubarak regime Egypt would fall into inescapable chaos and destruction.

So that we do not forget, the cynical criminality of this strategy involved the killing of some three hundred peacefully protesting citizens and the wounding of thousands, the torching of public buildings, the attempted looting, torching, and destruction of the Egyptian Museum, the overnight disappearance of the whole internal security apparatus, the synchronized opening of prison gates around the country, and the loosing of criminal gangs of police agents alongside police and oligarch-run networks of thugs and diverse criminal elements to attack private citizens and public and private property, and to murder, torch, and loot. This, by the way, is the same 'coalition' that was responsible for the wholesale rigging of the 2010 and other elections.

The counterrevolution's last card lay in the madness of the 'foreign fingers' in the Egyptian uprising. The police agents and their thuggish friends were sent to infiltrate the 'popular committees,' spread misinformation and hysteria about alleged Israeli, American, Iranian, Hamas, Hizbullah, and all sorts of other foreign conspiracies to foment revolution in the country. Foreigners, including a great many 'foreign-looking' Egyptians, were exposed to brutal attacks everywhere. The very people who were bemoaning the loss of foreign investment and tourism were willing to ensure that no one elsewhere in the world will even nod our way, possibly for a great many years.

By yesterday, and as Egypt witnessed its largest popular demonstrations ever, involving millions across the country, the counterrevolution looked dead and buried.

This is not to say that a revival of the counterrevolution is impossible. Neither can we as yet totally discount the possibility of a different kind of counterrevolution, for instance, in having the army at last shoot at the people. Both scenarios are unlikely, however. For its part, the army's commitment not to resort to violence against the people is now stronger than ever. We've even had the vice president saying that President Mubarak, rather late in the day, has ordered all security forces to refrain from harming the protesters in any way.

It is not beyond the bounds of possibility that the axis of evil, mentioned above, will once again resume its activities. After all, we are yet to see any of those responsible for crimes ranging from murder to high treason arrested or prosecuted, despite repeated promises.

The network remains intact, but there is every indication that it's done its worst, it has been defeated, physically, as well as exposed. With the police agents and their thugs out of the picture, the hundreds of thousands in Tahrir Square continue to amaze the nation and world by the peaceful and outstandingly self-disciplined nature of their ongoing revolution.

The vice president is right, however, in saying that Egypt today faces two choices. He still needs to become aware of what these really are, however, for these two choices are none other than to maintain the old authoritarian order, cosmetically pluralized, or to effect a radical transition to a fully democratic system of government.

Cosmetically treated authoritarianism we've had for the past thirty years. Indeed, that's what we have had more or less of since the late President Anwar Sadat launched his experiment in controlled pluralism way back in 1976. And, if a full-scale revolution is any indication, we've had enough.

Yes, Mr. Vice President, we are faced with two choices. The people have chosen; it's time that you accepted their choice.

Ahram Online, February 11, 2011

# Good Morning Revolution: A To Do List

BEFORE TRYING TO TAKE ALL, or even just bits, of it in, and keeping for the moment tight control over the need to express the sheer joy of it all, I believe we should urgently debate the most immediate tasks ahead. Here are some suggestions:

1. Don't fight ghosts: The army is not about to seize political power, nor is there a threat of military rule. I understand the concern, but do not sympathize with the phobia. We should stop letting the ghosts of our past interfere with how we conceive of our present and determine our future. Popular revolutions, I have written more than once over the past couple of weeks, do not result in military rule, coup d'états and counterrevolutions do. So let's by all means not waste precious energy on fighting windmills. It's civil, not military government that lies ahead. The point is to ensure that it will be one that is situated within a fully democratic political system.

2. End the state of emergency: By the time this is posted, the state of emergency might have been lifted already. In any case, this is a top demand of the revolution, as well as a pledge of the military. There is absolutely no excuse for keeping the state of emergency a single minute longer. "Until the current circumstances are over" does not hold water. Egypt's revolution will go down in history as the most peaceful, nonviolent, and self-disciplined revolution the world has ever known. The violence is now clearly exposed as the product of the defunct regime. The state of emergency must be lifted TODAY.

3. Release political prisoners: All political prisoners must be released immediately, including all prisoners held without detention or trial under the provisions of the infamous emergency law. The argument that this will involve the release of possibly hundreds of militant Islamists, some of whom may have been involved in terrorist acts, is groundless. We have every right to expect the Egyptian revolution to be an example to the world, including to Barack Obama's America itself. If they're not held in strict accordance with due process, they should be released. A genuine democracy knows no exceptional circumstances, and a genuinely democratic society is able to deal with the consequences.

4. Prosecute police and National Democratic Party (NDP) crimes and overhaul the domestic security apparatus: Over the past two weeks we have seen what the internal security apparatus, allied to NDP top officials and oligarchs and jointly running a huge network of criminal gangs, is capable of. Over the past thirty years, under the protection of a continuing state of emergency and the pretext of fighting terrorism, the domestic security apparatus has been brutalized and corrupted to such an extent that it is effectively a giant lawless militia, handing out torture and murder at will. We must not forget that the revolution was, in large part, triggered by the behavior of this apparatus and has from the very start identified it as among its top targets, next only to the removal of the man who was responsible for its creation and operation. Moreover, during the past two weeks, this apparatus went rogue. We need not go back over the evidence, it is widely known, and I've expounded on it in previous articles. Suffice it to say that the blood of over three hundred martyrs continues to cry out for retribution. Nor is a democracy of any kind even remotely possible in the presence of such a security apparatus. The so-called fact-finding committee formed by former vice president Omar Suleiman to investigate the matter is a patently ridiculous attempt at a coverup. All those responsible for the scorched earth strategy of murder and mayhem (whether in the police apparatus or among NDP officials and oligarchs) launched by the defunct regime over the past weeks must be arrested immediately, and a thorough investigation and prosecution process initiated by civil prosecution authorities under army protection and guarantees. The whole domestic security apparatus should be put under combined military/civilian oversight (including representatives of the human rights movement) in order to begin a full overhaul.

5. A provisional government: A provisional, national unity government of technocrats and widely respected public and political figures will need

to be established as soon as possible to take charge of running the country and laying the groundwork for the transition to a full democracy. There is a near consensus on what this government should look like, and even on several of the names that should be included in it. This process, however, needs to be closely monitored and intervened in by the various bodies set up by the revolution, particularly the youth movements. Radical changes of government open up a great many appetites, and as wondrous as our revolution has been, it has not transformed us into a nation of angels. We must expect a lot of grabbing and grappling on all levels of the state in the coming weeks and months, and we need to both take it in our stride and try to create as many guarantees as possible that the process will be as clean, transparent, and accountable as possible. Needless to say, the provisional government should be all-inclusive, a rainbow coalition not only of the various ideological and political trends in the pro-democracy movement but also of the nation's various sectors, most notably women and Copts.

6. A provisional constitution and bill of rights: One of the most urgent tasks of the revolution will be to enact a provisional constitution and, I suggest as well, a bill of rights. Needless to say, the measures adopted by the defunct regime to amend the constitution have been rendered null and void. The army, respected legal, political, and public figures, and representatives of the revolution need to agree on a provisional constituent assembly, fairly small in number so as to be effective and yet large enough to be all-inclusive, that will enact what should be a concise provisional constitution, and, I might add, a bill of rights setting down the democratic and human rights principles that have been at the very core of the Egyptian revolution.

7. Clean up legislation: At the same time, the Herculean process of cleaning up the Augean stables of authoritarianism needs to be started as soon as possible. Again, bodies set up in accordance with the criteria mentioned above should begin operating as soon as possible to oversee such things as the clearing up of the legal code of the massive array of authoritarian, antidemocratic legislation and drawing up new provisional legislation that would reflect the aims of the revolution and those set out in the provisional constitution and bill of rights. This will include, to name the most notable examples, new electoral legislation, new legislation governing local government on all levels, clearing the penal code of antidemocratic legislation (some of which goes back to British colonial rule), and providing for the free exercise of political rights and freedom of

expression, including the right to organize politically, the right to establish trade unions and nongovernmental organizations, and so on.

8. A National Salvation Front: There have been a great many ideas and initiatives aimed at setting up representative bodies and organizational structures for the revolution. It is my conviction that the coming months will witness a tremendous political revival that will change and transform the whole political map of the country in ways we cannot even begin to predict now. As I wrote before, extant political forces will be transformed, new ones will come on the stage, and not a few will simply fall into oblivion. No crystal ball is needed, however, in the case of the NDP: it's dead already (I just hope the Muslim Brotherhood will resist the temptation of allowing the expected hordes of repentant NDP bosses into its ranks). However, ideas such as the Front of National Salvation floated by the youth movements might be the very thing to create new organizational structures able to reflect the unique features of the revolution as well as provide much-needed instruments of oversight to render the above processes as transparent and accountable as possible.

9. A youth party: One of the most interesting aspects of the youth revolution has been the crystallizing of a novel ideological and political discourse, which seems to have evolved on its own, away from the traditionally warring ideological and political factions of the country. This is a wholly new entrant on the nation's political stage, most likely evolved in cyber space, and I fully admit it has taken old guys such as myself completely by surprise. It is an Egyptian nationalist discourse, almost intrinsically liberal, showing a deep commitment to fundamental human rights, but spreading out to include secular, religious, leftist, and Islamist leanings, all in happy coexistence and continuous dialogue. I see no reason why this new discourse should not find organizational expression. The idea of creating a new political party, the January 25 Revolution, has been floated in the past couple of days. I fully support this initiative and can only hope that the revolution's youth will not allow the old geezers to sabotage or usurp a refreshing new entrant on the Egyptian political stage that is most uniquely theirs.

10. Independent trade union: Finally, the Egyptian labor movement is yet another crucial entrant on the nation's political stage. Over the past couple of days, it helped tip the balance in favor of the revolution. A call has been made already to create a new Federation of Egyptian Trade Unions, as a long overdue alternative to the government-owned and run,

Soviet-style dinosaur of the same name, which has been no more than a headstone set up on the grave of basic trade union freedoms and rights, crushed by police force. The post-revolutionary stage in Egyptian history promises to bring Egyptian labor back onto the political stage, off which it was pushed some sixty years ago. This is a new actor, crucial to guaranteeing that the fruits of economic development will be distributed as equitably as possible and giving a social dimension to the political system, making it the truly vibrant and representative democracy we have long aspired to and which during the past eighteen days we proved to ourselves and to the whole world we truly deserve.

A final note: We need to guard against the urge to rush into elections. The urgent tasks noted above, and many more, are absolutely crucial to guaranteeing that truly democratic elections can be conducted. A new order is being born, but the old order is still rattling its chains. Let's first exorcise the ghosts from our national home, only then can we furnish it at our leisure.

Ahram Online, February 12, 2011

# Military Minds and
# That Crucial Extra Mile

THE MIND OF THE EGYPTIAN military seems to have undergone a second dramatic shift over the past few days, the first having been the decision to overthrow Hosni Mubarak. That first shift came fast on the heels of a last-ditch effort to save the old regime by the former president and his then vice president, Omar Suleiman, in two consecutive television addresses on the evening of Thursday, February 10.

We still don't know what precisely happened between Thursday evening, when Mubarak made his fateful last address, propped up shortly after by an ominous, threatening address by Suleiman, and 6:00 p.m. Friday, when an obviously shattered Suleiman announced that Mubarak had stepped down. We can be certain, however, that the millions who descended on Tahrir Square and poured onto streets across the country triggered a decisive shift within the ruling power structure, within which the military had become a predominant actor. Neither could there be any doubt in our minds that Mubarak did not in fact resign but was overthrown.

The second dramatic shift in the minds of the military was subtler, though on close inspection it becomes practically self-evident. Friday night, hundreds of military police launched a vicious attack on the protesters who had decided to resume their sit-in in Tahrir Square, on the grounds that most of the revolution's demands had yet to be met. For the first time since they were ordered onto the streets nearly a month ago, the military found itself risking the hard-earned goodwill of the people. A shift did take place, however, sometime between the attack on Friday night and the next day, when the army issued a profuse and, for the military, remarkably uncharacteristic apology for the previous night's attack, immediately released all those who had been arrested in the course of the attack, and pledged never to attack Egyptian civilians again.

And though the army blamed the Friday night attack on low-ranking officers who were acting on their own initiative, only the hopelessly gullible could give any credence to this excuse, though most have been happy to turn over that particular leaf. Since the apology, it's been a week of one concession after another. First, there was a four-hour meeting between the military council and seventeen representatives of the Coalition of Youth Movements, in which promises are made that the military will respond to the revolutionary demands, and that Ahmed Shafiq's Cabinet will be dismissed "before the elections."

Then came the most outstanding development since Mubarak's overthrow: the announcement by the prosecutor general that he had ordered the freezing of the Mubarak family fortune, not only in Egypt but also abroad, and that Interpol had been contacted to take measures to ensure this is done. This was tantamount to a declared intention to prosecute Mubarak and his family for corruption—a full shift from the previous posture of 'honoring' the former president. It was also the most potent evidence yet that a seismic shift had indeed taken place in the minds of the military or, more precisely, in the balance of forces within the Supreme Council. For it was widely known that Mubarak's stepping down had been accompanied by a promise of immunity for him and his family granted by the military.

All this climaxed in the prime minister's resignation on Thursday and the appointment immediately after of Essam Sharaf, who, though a minister under Mubarak, had been for several years a vocal critic of the regime and had joined the protesters in Tahrir Square in the days preceding Mubarak's removal from office. Sharaf's was one of two names the youth coalition had suggested for the post in their meeting with the military earlier in the week.

Yet, Egypt continues to live in the shadow of counterrevolution. Some of the most crucial of the revolution's demands remain unfulfilled, while the makeshift character of concessions creates an anomalous situation that could well threaten not just the achievements of the revolution but also the very stability and political future of the nation.

Take for a start the fact that until today, even as one case of corruption, profiteering, and plunder of state resources follows another, we have yet to see a single coherent case directed against the officials and oligarchs responsible for the mayhem, wholesale murder, and destruction created by the attempted counterrevolution. There is now incontrovertible, even if as yet largely circumstantial, evidence that the "scorched earth" policy pursued by an alliance of top National Democratic Party officials, the domestic security apparatus, and ruling party oligarchs had been a previously conceived contingency plan that was put into effect as soon as the powers that be realized that the traditional security apparatus could not roll back the people's revolutionary upsurge.

The mind boggles at the sheer unscrupulousness, cynicism, indeed the depravity of Egypt's failed counterrevolution. Muammar Qadhafi has madness as an excuse, but here we had a cool-headed, carefully laid out plan involving a junta made of hundreds, possibly thousands of government and security officials, having the perverse objective of setting the nation ablaze, destroying not just its present but also its past and future.

There is absolutely no way that the military is not by now fully cognizant of the lengths Mubarak, his oligarchs, and his security bodies were willing to go to in order to keep him in office, nor yet of the persons responsible. An abundance of factual evidence, confiscated identity cards, and confessions by culprits is available to all, let alone to an armed forces command that saw it all happen before its very eyes, and in fact acted to bring a stop to it. Indeed, the mere fact that the attacks, first against the protesters, then against public and private property, and finally against foreigners, were each brought to a halt virtually overnight is in and of itself ample proof that they were planned and that a higher authority (which could not have been other than the military) intervened to have them stopped, most likely with dire warning of harsh retribution.

Certainly, we have here a Pandora's box of crimes ranging from high treason to terrorism, arson, and murder. The military's hesitation in bringing the sordid details under public scrutiny is probably motivated by considerations that include concern over the extent of popular outrage, worry over the country's image overseas, and such. It will not wash. Continuing procrastination in this matter will only confirm the already widespread feeling that there is an attempt at a coverup. Too many people have lost their lives; too many have been seriously injured; the whole country was made to live in terror for nearly a month; and the Egyptian

Museum, the greatest storehouse of ancient Egyptian antiquities in the world, was looted and nearly torched. None of it is forgivable. All of it cries out for retribution.

But no less important is the fact that the bulk of the insidious forces that orchestrated and implemented that destructive campaign are still in place, and are still up to their dirty tricks. The conspicuous and wholly unjustified absence of any real policing in the country, even traffic police, accompanied by rather farcical attempts at staging demonstrations calling for the "return of the police," are just a couple of indicators among many that the counterrevolution is lying in wait for a comeback.

Neither can the military explain or begin to justify the fact that not a single measure has yet been taken against the Interior Ministry, the major culprit in the abovementioned crimes, whose top officials stand accused at the very least of criminal dereliction of duty. Not a single step has been taken to bring ministry officials to account or even to bring what has clearly become a rogue body of the state to heel, subject to military/civilian oversight.

The core criminal body at the heart of the Ministry of Interior is, of course, State Security Intelligence. I would be pleasantly surprised if there is a single officer of that service whose hands are not drenched with the blood of torture victims, and worse. Yet, the head of the service is removed from his post, only to be replaced by one of his deputies.

A great deal still needs to be done before the Egyptian revolution is realized, as it insists that it should be, and as it has earned the right to be. Only a fully democratic Egypt is acceptable; anything short of that goal will simply not do.

During the past week, the military has taken great strides toward the people. It's time it also traversed that crucial extra mile, for only then will the Egyptian revolution have met with success, and only then can we begin properly to undertake that at once most challenging and most satisfying of jobs, the job of rebuilding our nation.

Ahram Online, March 3, 2011